Explorations in the Digital History of Ideas

What would the history of ideas look like if we were able to read the entire archive of printed material of a historical period? Would our 'great men (usually)' story of how ideas are formed and change over time begin to look very different? This book explores these questions through case studies on ideas such as 'liberty', 'republicanism' or 'government' using digital humanities approaches to large-scale text datasets. It sets out the methodologies and tools created by the Cambridge Concept Lab as exemplifications of how new digital methods can open up the history of ideas to heretofore unseen avenues of inquiry and evidence. By applying text mining techniques to intellectual history or the history of concepts, this book explains how computational approaches to text mining can substantially increase the power of our understanding of ideas in history.

Peter de Bolla is Professor of Cultural History and Aesthetics at the University of Cambridge. His publications include *The Architecture of Concepts: The Historical Formation of Human Rights* (2013), which won the Robert Lowry Patten Award in 2015. He is the author or editor of nine books, including *The Discourse of the Sublime: Readings in History, Aesthetics and the Subject* (1989), *Art Matters* (2001) and *The Education of the Eye: Painting, Landscape and Architecture in Eighteenth Century Britain* (2003). He directed the Cambridge Concept Lab between 2013 and 2017, a £1.5 m funded project on the structure of concepts. He is an International Honorary Member of the American Academy of Arts and Sciences.

Explorations in the Digital History of Ideas

New Methods and Computational Approaches

Edited by

Peter de Bolla

University of Cambridge

CAMBRIDGE
UNIVERSITY PRESS

Shaftesbury Road, Cambridge CB2 8EA, United Kingdom

One Liberty Plaza, 20th Floor, New York, NY 10006, USA

477 Williamstown Road, Port Melbourne, VIC 3207, Australia

314–321, 3rd Floor, Plot 3, Splendor Forum, Jasola District Centre, New Delhi – 110025, India

103 Penang Road, #05–06/07, Visioncrest Commercial, Singapore 238467

Cambridge University Press is part of Cambridge University Press & Assessment, a department of the University of Cambridge.

We share the University's mission to contribute to society through the pursuit of education, learning and research at the highest international levels of excellence.

www.cambridge.org
Information on this title: www.cambridge.org/9781009263580

DOI: 10.1017/9781009263610

First published 2024

A catalogue record for this publication is available from the British Library.

A Cataloging-in-Publication data record for this book is available from the Library of Congress.

ISBN 978-1-009-26358-0 Hardback

Additional resources for this publication at www.cambridge.org/deBolla

Contents

Additional appendix resources at www.cambridge.org/deBolla

Figures

Tables

Contributors

MARK ALGEE-HEWITT is an associate professor of Digital Humanities and English at Stanford University.

PETER DE BOLLA is professor of Cultural History and Aesthetics at the University of Cambridge.

RYAN HEUSER is a research software engineer in Princeton's Center for Digital Humanities.

EWAN JONES is an associate professor for English at the University of Cambridge.

PAUL NULTY is a lecturer in the Department of Computer Science and Information Systems at Birkbeck, University of London.

GABRIEL RECCHIA is a cognitive scientist at Modulo Research Ltd, Cambridge.

JOHN REGAN is a lecturer in Literature and the Digital and the Creative Industries at Royal Holloway, University of London.

NATALIE ROXBURGH is a lecturer in English at the University of Hamburg.

CLAIRE WILKINSON is an assistant professor in Eighteenth Century English at Robinson College in the University of Cambridge.

Acknowledgements

Academic work in the Digital Humanities is fundamentally collaborative, and this in part contributes to its potential game-changing power. Not all collaborations, of course, are happy, but in this case it gives me great pleasure to acknowledge the individuals who have in the main been co-creators of the work here presented. The deep origins of the project lie in a Mellon Foundation seminar/workshop that I convened with Cliff Siskin at Cambridge, where we were hosted by the Centre for Research in Social Sciences and Humanities in 2012. We called that workshop 'The Experimental Concept Lab' and I thank all the participants in those meetings for their creative input and their willingness to withhold scepticism, at least for a while. Two of the members of that group, Ewan Jones and John Regan, would follow me into the next phase of the project. This was facilitated by the generous grant from the Foundation for the Future to Cambridge University for establishing work in the Digital Humanities. I was lucky enough to win a substantial portion of the grant, which enabled me to found the Cambridge Concept Lab, which I directed from 2014 to 2018. I thank the Foundation and its director, Andrew Thompson for his support and belief in the potential transformative power of collaborative work using computational methods in the humanities. As I also thank the then Director of CRASSH, Simon Goldhill, who also provided invaluable support and encouragement.

The Cambridge Concept Lab comprised four then post-docs, with myself as Director, and our project was to ascertain if it might be possible to discern what we thought of as 'digital signatures' for concepts. All of our work was intensely collaborative, and all four of my collaborators were equal partners in our endeavours. I thank them here – Ewan Jones, John Regan, Paul Nulty and Gabriel Recchia – for the amazingly generous spirit of their contributions. In many ways the four years of the project were some of the most intense, creative and productive moments of my research career. They were also (for the most part) fun.

A parallel Lab operated in the United State, under the direction of Cliff Siskin, and although it was not fortunate, as we in Cambridge were, to be funded by an external grant, and therefore operated on a very different timetable supported only by good-will and interest in the project, it nevertheless provided a different axis to the work we did. I thank the participants in that Lab: Mark Algee-Hewitt, Bill Blake, Ryan Heuser, Yohei Igarashi, and Bill Warner, as I also thank its Director, Cliff Siskin, for all of their contributions to what was fundamentally a speculative project.

The Cambridge and American labs eventually took slightly different directions, but not before we had jointly presented our work on two occasions on the West Coast of the United States. The Stanford Literary Lab was our host for two days in May, 2016 and I thank the members of that Lab, and its then Director, Franco Moretti, for the invitation and interrogation we were pleased to be subjected to. We then moved south to the University of Santa Barbara, where Alan Liu hosted us, and I also thank him for his incredibly generous support for the team and the project. Bill Warner was also extremely generous while we were in Santa Barbara, and I thank him on behalf of the entire team.

As the funding for the project began to reach its terminus the Lab's thoughts turned to issues of legacy. The most pressing task in this respect was the establishment of a digital repository for the tools we had created. We were fortunate to have locally in Cambridge some very forward-looking and helpful colleagues in the University Library, and in particular I thank Huw Jones for his practical and organisational skills. The Lab's tools are now available through the Library portal at https://concept-lab.lib.cam.ac.uk/. The second issue we turned to was the development of a new area of inquiry, represented by the chapters in this book, which we thought of as the Digital History of Ideas, and we began to collect our thoughts and resources so as to bring this notion to the wider academic community. Some time later, following some early published papers, I proposed to my erstwhile collaborators that we might attempt to launch a new initiative in the history of ideas, one which explored the affordances of computational methodologies. The book you have in your hands is the result. I am pleased to note that my initial inquiry with a publisher, Cambridge University Press, and the editor of its Intellectual History list, Liz Friend-Smith was a very productive one. Liz immediately saw the potential for the project, as did the two anonymous reviewers, whom I also thank. I am also very happy to thank the production team working for the Press, Geethanjali Rangaraj and Alexander Mcleod, who oversaw the final stages of publication with extraordinary care, great skill and punctilious observation of the schedule.

My final thanks are both more conceptual and personal. Without the willingness to suspend ego, disbelief, aggressive investments in personal advancement, truly collaborative work cannot even get started. All of the contributors to this volume left these undesirables at the door and it has not only been a pleasure working with them, it has also been conceptually formative – perhaps, dare one say, the instantiation of the notion that concepts are, to the very core, emergent forms.

Cavalaire-sur-Mer, July, 2023

Part I

Computational Methodologies for the History of Ideas

1 Introduction

Peter de Bolla

This book explores the ways in which computational techniques for text mining can contribute to the history of ideas. Traditional approaches to intellectual history are based on the careful, close scrutiny of texts and contexts, reading at a human scale in order to construct lines of transmission and genealogies of ideas. These approaches have served us well: the history of political thought, for example, has established deeply researched canons of texts and writers that are widely accepted as being in dialogue with each other. Over the last twenty years, however, the migration of analogue archives to digital corpora has opened up the possibility of reading at scale, creating the conditions for inspecting the transmission of ideas across hundreds of thousands of texts. Most of these texts have been deemed too obscure or insignificant for sustained close attention, and they remain at the outer margins of our standard histories of ideas. But when they are aggregated in large-scale datasets that capture a culture's ways of thinking, they open up the possibility of reconfiguring the history of ideas, expanding traditional accounts of ideas as personal property exchanged between independent minds so as to include within such accounts the dispersal and transmission of ideas across an entire culture. Moreover, heretofore the history of ideas has been modelled on a linear transmission, in which one thinker engages in dialogue with another or one text provides the foundation for its successors. Today, using computational techniques, we have the potential to create different models that can track the emergence and transmission of ideas in networks and clusters of concepts that are constellated in many dimensions thereby replacing a single linear thread of transmission with far more complex interwoven lines of connection. The use of such techniques opens up far more granular accounts of how transmission is often 'lumpy' in which long periods of stability are punctured by intense moments of change. Such models, based on computational methods of interrogating archives – now rendered as datasets – that often derive information from texts that are orthogonal to the canons of great texts and thinkers, have the capacity to substantially augment our traditional histories of ideas as we move from the individual to the social or cultural in general, tracking the movement of ideas across the largest 'bandwidth' we can assemble in order to understand how such ideas operate as cultural entities.

Over the last ten or so years, digital humanities (DH) approaches to historical research have become more common as researchers take advantage of earlier waves of digitisation of archives. Projects that have turned to DH methods include, among others, the University of Stanford's Mapping the Republic of Letters, an ambitious collaboration between a number of international partners, including the University of Oxford's Cultures of Knowledge project; Groupe d'Alembert, hosted by the Centre National de la Recherche Scientifique; and organisations in both Holland and Italy, which set out to map the correspondence networks within which scientists, *salonnières* and travellers operated during the Enlightenment. At the University of North Texas, Andrew J. Torget set up the Texas Slavery Project, which explores the expansion of slavery between 1837 and 1845 in the territories that would eventually become the state of Texas. Although not solely focused on historical projects, the Helsinki Centre for Digital Humanities, hosted by the University of Helsinki, has undertaken a number of research initiatives that bear upon historical inquiry.

In common with many early adopters of digital methods, these projects and others draw upon statistical and computational methods first developed in the social sciences for mapping the movement and circulation of varying forms of information. Alongside many other projects in the field of historical research, they use geospatial information system techniques for creating layered representations of these flows. Some universities, especially in the United States, were early to the party – notable here is the University of Virginia, which developed methods in the digital exploration of humanities scholarship and trained many of the first generation of DH scholars – but in the more recent past centres and projects dedicated to digital methods have become commonplace in many national and international scholarly contexts.

In spite of this welcome flourishing of the field of DH across the disciplines, this book is the first to focus explicitly on the history of ideas in its narrow guise as the inquiry into the history of political thought. Although a number of collections of essays have been exemplary in introducing various methods and techniques for studying ideas in a general sense – here one might look to Chloe Edmundson and Dan Edelstein, *Networks of Enlightenment: Digital Approaches to the Republic of Letters*, or to Simon Burrows and Glenn Roe, *Digitizing Enlightenment: Digital Humanities and the Transformation of Eighteenth-Century Studies* – none have yet set out to explore the ways in which DH approaches and methods might contribute to the long tradition of scholarship that is closely associated with the monograph series published by Cambridge University Press and entitled *Ideas in Context*, that was initiated by Richard Rorty, Jerome B. Schneewind and Quentin Skinner over thirty-five years ago. The monographs published in this series have, of course, been varied in their topics and their authors more or less affiliated with what has become known as the Cambridge School in the history of ideas, an approach to intellectual history that has been at the core of the discipline – even if it has found critics and advocates of alternative approaches – for over forty years. In common with many robust and well-developed scholarly interventions into a disciplinary field, the Cambridge School has had its vicissitudes – indeed some scholars claim that there never was such a school. The present book does not seek to contribute to what at times, inevitably, may seem to be merely academic turf wars in the discipline of intellectual history. Instead, it takes as a given the utility of studying ideas 'in context' and asks what might happen when that context can be scaled up using digital resources, both databases and computational methods and statistical techniques. Given that it is just one volume, the explorations presented here can only be exemplary – essentially shining a light on just a few topics or areas of research within the larger terrain of the history of ideas. And given the restriction of space it was decided to softly limit the historical reach of the case studies that feature in Part II of the volume to the long eighteenth century. The purpose here is to simultaneously enquire into the particular features of this period as in some sense ripe for digital methods and into specific case studies built upon those methods. In part this was also motivated by the fact that another tradition in the history of ideas, which is associated with the German scholar Reinhart Koselleck and known as *Begriffsgeschichte* (or conceptual history), is grounded in the hypothesis that the period we direct our attention to here has a very distinctive outline in which, it is claimed, the character, shape or form of concepts in general began to shift into something that we might recognise as the structural composition of concepts in modernity. This argument is explored most carefully by Ryan Heuser in Chapter 12, the last chapter of the book, but we see all of the case studies as operating with this hypothesis in the background. The aim, then, is to create a layer of coherence across the chapters that would have been much attenuated if the aperture onto the history of ideas had been wider, that is if our historical sweep had been more capacious.

The methodology and tools that are used in most of the case studies in Part II of this book were developed by the Cambridge Concept Lab, which I directed from 2014 to 2018. The Lab set out to test a number of hypotheses regarding the structure and compositionality of concepts and, using computational techniques, built a suite of tools that enabled us to discern the computational 'signatures' of discrete concepts. Chapter 2 sets out in detail how the Lab proceeded, and introduces the various methods and measures we developed. Once we were confident that we had created a robust method for generating such signatures we began to work on a number of case studies that tracked conceptual forms over time. The Lab experimented with a number of datasets, including small-scale resources such as the North American News Text Corpus, but we directed most of our attention to the very large text database Eighteenth Century Collections Online, whose affordances and problems are also outlined in Chapter 2. This book enhances that work and assembles twelve chapters split across two parts, authored both collaboratively (as all of the work of the Concept Lab was) in slightly changing formations or teams, as well as some sole-authored contributions. The first part is methodological and is intended to introduce DH methods, in general, to researchers in the field of intellectual history, and to provide detailed explanations of the specific techniques used in most of the chapters in Part II. In Chapter 2 readers will be introduced to the field we call Distributional Concept Analysis and to the ways in which it might contribute to more traditional histories of ideas. Chapter 3, a sole-authored chapter by Paul Nulty, provides a detailed account of some of the tasks researchers are confronted with when designing DH projects. This chapter explains a number of the decisions that are fundamental to the construction of a specific, targeted project that seeks to enquire into the history of conceptual forms and ideas and is intended to provide an explanation of why, in designing the tools in the Concept Lab, we took the decisions we did. It should be noted, however, that this window onto the technical aspects of designing a DH project is also intended to be exemplary, not prescriptive, for future projects in the digital history of ideas.

Part II collects nine cases studies on topics such as the idea of government in the long eighteenth century, the idea of liberty in roughly the same time period, and the conceptual foundations of the modern idea of economic growth. The design of the book is intended to address both researchers in the history of ideas who might have very little experience working with digital methods and those who may have more familiarity, as we point forward from the chapters in Part I to those in Part II, where particular computational techniques are taken up. And, conversely, in Part II we refer back to chapters in Part I that provide the technical material for understanding how the methodology adopted has been formulated. Thus, armed with the methodological apparatus set out in the first part of the book, readers from both camps will be able to follow the arguments in the second. It is also important to note that the selection of the topics or ideas taken in each case study has been determined in two ways – once again seeking to provide exemplifications of how more traditional approaches to the history of ideas might begin to work computationally. The first approach is to identify a 'hard case' – as lawyers call them – in the history of ideas in the long anglophone eighteenth century, such as the idea of liberty, the topic of Chapter 4. This approach works, as it were, from the analogue to the digital, and it is important to register the reason for taking it: we mean to test the findings of our digital methodologies against the substantial literature within the traditional history of ideas. The second approach works the other way around: in accord with what we deem to be best practice in DH work based on massive datasets, we did not frame a question or topic before we had inspected the dataset and the information derived from it in the form of relative values of distributional probability function (*dpf*, explained in Chapter 2); rather, we let the data drive the formulation of the questions. This is an important aspect of work using such techniques and approaches: it fully takes account of the transformation of the analogue text base into a digital format that both creates new information and at the same time provides different access to the data, the most obvious of which is the scale at which one can read the archive. In this second approach, then, we mean to test the arguments put forward by the traditional history of ideas against the findings derived from the interrogation of digitised textual materials. Here one might compare Chapters 5 and 9, which take the second approach, with Chapters 4 and 6, which take the first.

It will be noted that the chapters in the second part of the book intersect with long-standing arguments about and characterisations of these candidate ideas in hopes that they will speak with immediacy to researchers in the field. Chapter 4, for example, takes its point of departure from Isaiah Berlin's famous account of liberty and asks whether his notion of a divergence between positive liberty – 'freedom to' – and negative – 'freedom from' – maps onto a digitally constructed view of the anglophone late seventeenth and eighteenth centuries. And in its last section it places its findings alongside one of the most powerful accounts of liberty in the Cambridge School tradition of the history of ideas that has been consistently explored by Quentin Skinner over the last forty or so years. Similarly, Chapter 6 on republicanism engages with the various arguments intellectual historians have proposed concerning the ideological bases for the American Revolution, and using digital methods concludes that the idea of republicanism could not have been one of the foundation stones for the construction of the first modern republic in what became

the United States of America. Here the connections and links to traditional ways of thinking about 'ideas in context' are used in order to test
and interrogate the new digital methods employed in the creation of
contexts that would be impossible to construct without computational
methods. While the underlying mode of inquiry, seeking to recover the
precise contexts in which ideas circulated and were minted in the past,
remains the same, the main purpose is to explore whether or not the
computational construction of context at a massive increase in scale
provides us with new evidence and new avenues of inquiry, thereby
complementing and extending traditional intellectual history as we
develop a new digital history of ideas.

Some of the case studies take a very narrow focus, such as
Chapter 8, by John Regan, on the idea of commercial society as it
was used by the late Istvan Hont in his posthumously published
Carlyle Lectures, or Chapter 7, which seeks to explain how the components of the contemporary idea of economic growth can be traced
back to Adam Smith in ways that unsettle the standard picture of
Smith's modelling of political economy. Similarly, Chapter 9 unsettles
a very long-standing characterisation of the period from around the
mid-eighteenth century to the mid-nineteenth as an 'age of sensibility'
by uncovering the conceptual networks that coalesced around the idea
of irritability. Its authors, Ewan Jones and Natalie Roxburgh, note in
conclusion that perhaps the time has come to refer to an 'age of
irritability'. Chapter 10, on the South Sea Bubble, explores the ways
in which that event has become a kind of place-holder for the idea of
unstable financial markets – a bubble that was inevitably going to
burst – and demonstrates how at the time it was conceptualised very
differently. Here Claire Wilkinson notes that a kind of back formation
seems to have operated, and it has coloured the history of both the
event and the idea of speculative bubbles for generations of historians,
both economic and cultural.

Chapter 11 introduces some novel methods of data mining that use
a set of techniques developed in the field of word embeddings. Although
the methods used here are different, rather interestingly the computational objects produced resemble in some ways those produced by the
Concept Lab methods. Here the idea of revolution in the sense of mechanical movement and in the sense of political upheaval is tracked across
the eighteenth century as Mark Algee-Hewitt presents an account of the
ways in which ideas evolve over time. Chapter 12, the final chapter, takes
up the challenge of thinking about conceptual history over the long *durée*,
as Ryan Heuser engages with the work produced within the school known
as *Begriffsgeschichte*. He speculates that the period of time taken as a

focus for most of our case studies was itself crucial with respect to the entanglements of concepts – their varying rates of change and alteration in structure and form – as he asks if digital methods can make some headway into a question that Reinhart Koselleck thought to be intransigent, namely whether the rate of change in social and political concepts distinctively increased in the period he called the *Sattelzeit* – roughly, 1770–1830.

Although the book as a whole does not set out to promote a single line of argument – indeed the intention is to present interlocking but independent examples of the ways in which a small selection of DH methods might reinvigorate and contribute to more traditional histories of ideas – there are, nevertheless, some common themes and preoccupations. Each of the case studies, for example, explore in their own ways the utility of modelling concepts and ideas as distinct but overlapping modes of thinking or cognition. And, in their different ways, they all seek to illustrate and interrogate the methodologies proposed by this book, which use computational and statistical techniques for establishing a more fine-grained account of the linguistic contexts in which concepts scale up into ideas. This can also be understood in a number of other ways, as, for example, the movement from concreteness to abstraction (as Chapter 7 remarks with respect to 'improvement'), or from the local to the general (as, for example, the singular local event of the crash of the speculative market in South Sea stock became the idea of speculative markets and their tendency to 'burst' in general). The same type of transformation is mapped in Chapter 5, in which we explore how the concept of government, used as a way of thinking about a *type or form* of government, 'scales up' as it came to be used as a way of thinking about government in general as a kind of universal category intended to make the hard distinction between order (government) and chaos (anarchy, despotism). And in Chapter 11 the intriguing hypothesis emerges that the political idea of revolution was created by the same forces of conceptual upscaling as the term transformed from its technical, mechanical sense into an abstract idea whose precise components (the necessary and sufficient conditions for something to be conceived as a political revolution) remained unarticulated.

This is to note that each case study identifies a curious phenomenon in conceptual and ideational behaviour whereby the scale at which one might think is significantly increased, or to put that another way, the utility of thinking in general categories coupled with the discovery of what might be called epistemic fundamentals becomes very apparent. Our case studies, then, track a kind of transformation in epistemology, noting that within the period to which we direct most consistent attention – say from the mid-eighteenth century into the early decades of the nineteenth – it became both possible and desirable to think on a new scale, to ground human knowledge in what were thought to be the irreducible elements of human understanding. To some extent this might be considered to be a very rehearsed story of the aims and ambitions of Enlightenment inquiry, or a confirmation of Koselleck's notion of the *Sattelzeit*, but if it does indeed correspond to those long-standing historicisations of the European project in knowledge – which we know under the clumsy rubric of 'the Enlightenment' – we mean to make our argument at a level of granularity that only becomes possible using digital methods.

Thus, one might note the following similar patterns across the chapters: John Regan notes that the idea of commercial society was scaled up from its early formulation as a *segment* of the social in which commercial activity took place, to a characterisation of society in general: modern societies in the age of expansion were reconceived as through and through commercial. In Chapter 9 a similar alteration in scale is outlined by Ewan Jones and Natalie Roxburgh in which something that was understood to occur to an individual body – irritable nerves – was scaled up to aid understanding of a general category, the human. In Chapter 7 we outline the ways in which our modern idea of economic growth has its deep ideational roots in the entanglements of 'growth' and 'improvement', which led Adam Smith to experiment with the notion that 'growth' might become autotelic, that is in and for itself, as distinct from its application to something. In Chapter 11 Mark Algee-Hewitt shows how the concept of revolution looked both ways across the century, towards the specifics of mechanical forces and to the ideational explosions that were associated with political upheaval. Here the time frame becomes extremely interesting as we begin to note differences in the temporal envelopes of what we might think of as the event-time of conceptual and ideational change. Some of the transformations we explore across the book have very impacted or explosive event horizons: the publication of Whytt's essay on the involuntary motion of animals marked a decisive intervention into the conceptualisation of the human. Others are more like slow burns, such as 'culture', as outlined by Ryan Heuser in Chapter 11, or 'liberty', as tracked by Paul Nulty in Chapter 3. In these cases, a set of affordances lie deep within a concept's architecture, surfacing and resurfacing over time before eventually settling into one or another stable form, or coming to be replaced by a new configuration and articulation better suited to the contexts in which it is to be used.

These observations of themes and continuities across the book are intended to provoke and encourage further exploration. There are numerous ways in which such suggestive lines of inquiry might be extended and subjected to rigorous evaluation. That is for future work, which we hope will become fully conversant with and contribute to a digital history of ideas that has the potential to transform the discipline of intellectual history.

2 Distributional Concept Analysis and the Digital History of Ideas

Peter de Bolla, Ewan Jones, Paul Nulty, Gabriel Recchia and John Regan

In this chapter we introduce the computational tools and their theoretical justification that were developed by the Cambridge Concept Lab between 2014 and 2018.[1] Many of the chapters in Part II, which present case studies, make use of these tools extensively. Although the research agenda of the Lab was directed at a general investigation of the ontology of conceptual forms, the dataset we investigated most comprehensively, Eighteenth Century Collections Online (ECCO) (commented upon in Section 2.2.3), is derived from a diachronic archive that enables one to track historical change within it year by year across the eighteenth century. Thus, the Lab's inquiry into conceptual forms, which we named 'distributional concept analysis', was continuously informed by diachronically sensitive information, thereby providing a background to our analyses that pushed us towards an investigation of the history of these forms, tracking their evolution over the time frame of the dataset. Our initial task, however, was to test a number of hypotheses about conceptuality, which led to the creation of computational tools that could create 'digital signatures' for individual conceptual forms, explained in Section 2.1.2, and we used these tools on a variety of datasets, essentially hardwiring into their design the capacity for use with different inputs or digitised text databases. The Lab's central focus for the first three years was to establish 'proof of concept' with respect to the methodology, only moving into more specialised case studies in its last year. The work presented in this volume builds further on this as it seeks to make an exemplary intervention into the field of intellectual history.

The Concept Lab was founded on a number of axioms and observations derived from a very salutary fact: there continues to be very little

---

[1] The members of the Lab were Peter de Bolla, Ewan Jones, Paul Nulty, Gabriel Recchia and John Regan.

12

agreement or overlap between the ways in which different disciplinary fields understand the nature of concepts, that is to say in what their ontology consists in, where the word ontology is being used to refer to what 'kind of thing' an entity is, including the kinds of relationships that it enters into with other entities.

Reviewing the extensive literature in just one discipline that takes concepts or conceptuality to be at its core, cognitive science, it becomes immediately clear that no consensus pertains as to what the central object of study, concepts, might be.[2] And once one moves across a range of disciplines, from philosophy to software engineering, intellectual history to linguistics, the inconsistencies in use of the term concept are immediately apparent. Indeed, under one rubric developed within the philosophical sub-discipline of aesthetics, the concept of 'concept' may fall into that class of concepts that are deemed to be 'fuzzy', that is without clear or consistent outlines and hence susceptible to many, varied and inconsistent uses.[3] Given the ubiquity and promiscuity of the term it seems likely that any attempt to apply consistency in its uses will fail, and here, as elsewhere in the publications that came out of the Cambridge Concept Lab, we do not seek to impose one. We do, however, propose to explore the affordances of taking a particular restricted approach that applies a consistent set of axioms to the investigation of the objects in view. These objects include both 'concepts' and 'ideas', and we model their ontologies in Sections 2.1.1 and 2.1.2.

2.1   Setting the Agenda

The first axiom that governed the research agenda of the Lab is the following: concepts are not only what some cognitive scientists call 'mental entities' held by cognitive agents as they engage in cognitive processing but also 'cultural entities' held by many agents collectively, that is held by a 'culture'. Our aim was not to make a kind of 'cultural turn' in the study of concepts; rather, we made the gambit that if one could inspect all the uses to which words were put, that is inspect the totality of a 'culture's' language use in a kind of recovery of all the speech acts that occur or occurred at a particular time, it would be possible to observe the shape or contour of each concept at this most general level. The point is not to invoke issues of cultural difference and practice; rather, it is one of scale.

---

[2] For a succinct overview, see Stephen Laurence and Eric Margolis, 'Concepts and Cognitive Science', in *Concepts: Core Readings*, ed. Eric Margolis and Stephen Lawrence (Cambridge, MA: MIT Press, 1999), 3–81; especially 5–6.

[3] Such concepts are also known as 'open'; see Morris Weitz, *Theories of Concepts* (London: Routledge, 1988).

The term culture here is merely a place-holder for the generality of language and conceptual use. This, as shall become clear in Section 2.1.2 in our characterisation of a different field of inquiry, the history of ideas, is intended to complement rather than replace the study of how individual agents used words in the past, and hence what they intended those words to mean – that is to complement the focus and methodology of the Cambridge School in the history of ideas by scaling up the data and interrogating them using computational methods.

This observation immediately raises a possible confusion or elision in the foregoing, that is the relationship between words and something that might either be expressed in those words, namely ideas, or somehow taken to underly their uses, namely the concepts that sit in the background of communicative acts or, in a more mentalistic model, that create mental worlds or cognitive maps. In Section 2.1.2 we set out how we see these three things – words, ideas and concepts – as being compacted and propose a way of extracting them from each other and from a digitalised dataset of language use, thereby exploiting the distinctions between the terms in ways that become instrumental in tracking diachronic movements in their histories, and thus proposing an intervention in the history of ideas. We begin, however, with the axiom employed by the Lab that was intended to keep in clear focus the distinction between words and concepts, that is they have different ontologies. Part of the research agenda for the Lab was to construct robust 'signatures' for concepts that could be computationally grounded from the evidence of word occurrence behaviours in massive lexical datasets. These signatures were composed of metrics (explained in Section 2.2.1) devised to enable us to dig deep into the structures and patterns of lexical co-occurrence, thereby revealing or discovering the unique forms – shapes or functions – of specific concepts. We also took it as axiomatic that these signatures were not only diachronically operational; they were also contextually sensitive, where context itself could be atomised into multiple lexical localities: context in this sense is determined by what some cognitive scientists call 'compositionality', that is the capacity for lexis to be combined and recombined in high order magnitudes of possible linguistic coherence. Thus, we set out to map the contexts in which every lexical item in the dataset might co-occur with every other lexical item by developing counts for one-to-one co-association across the entire dataset.[4] Context here, then, is co-association. And having done this we

---

[4] Note we deliberately use the term co-association in contrast to co-occurrence, the term used in computational linguistics, in order to highlight the fact that our method develops data on both co-occurrence where two terms are held in a semantically and grammatically

then began to inspect the ways in which these one-to-one co-associations are linked in combinatorial networks or chains, thereby building an ontology of ideas and concepts based on the observable data of lexical co-association. We think of our baseline data, therefore, not as words or lexis, nor their frequencies of use, but as a statistical extrapolation of the likelihood of one word appearing in close proximity to another word in a dataset derived from linguistic use. As it is these contextual relationships or associations that are the object of study – the concepts and ideas we are seeking to map and whose architectures we seek to explore – we use the term word-concept in order to make a distinction between the word as word and the entity created through statistical analysis whose label is a word. In the specific case histories of Part II of this book that address the development and evolution of ideas across the Anglophone eighteenth century, this dataset is composed of printed text, and we outline its features in Section 2.2.3.

The thinking behind this model of conceptual forms was ambitious but also fundamentally intuitive: if one could inspect every utterance in a language, what patterns would emerge with respect to each word's likelihood of being in the company of every other word? Put this way we mean to signal that our modelling of conceptual signatures was very close to what is known as 'neo-Firthian' approaches to semantics and their application in more recent artificial intelligence research, in which the so-called distributional hypothesis is used as a basis for constructing computational methods for discerning the meaning of terms. But our focus of interest was not meaning as such, or indeed meaning at all if meaning is understood to be an extension of a lexical item, or in another, older, model its reference. This is because we held fast to our axiom that words do not precisely share the same ontology as concepts. Although concepts, like words, have uses and thus, according to one account of language, meanings, we were trying to dampen down the semantic signal so as to be able to observe what we hypothesised as non-meaning properties of conceptual forms.[5] This led us to the investigation of concepts in terms of what we characterised as their functions.

This hypothesis also moved us towards a different schematisation for conceptuality in which we began to see the lower levels of cognitive processing – what underpins the flow of language and its higher-level articulations of sense and meaning – in terms of an information system

---

meaningful way and on much looser ties in which terms may be said to be co-associated over very wide spans. See Section 2.2.1.

[5] It is important to note that computational linguists do not use the term 'semantic' in as restrictive a sense as we do here, where the term essentially operates as a placeholder for 'dictionary definition of specific words in a natural language'.

that operates according to protocols governing the movements and flow of that information. In such a model it is not the meaning of a concept that like a synapse fires when it appears or is used; rather, it is a particular operational modality that is turned on or off. We tested this hypothesis by inspecting the behaviours of the signatures we had created, which led to a classification of these functional modalities. Work on this classification is ongoing.[6]

2.1.1 Modelling Concepts

The work of the Cambridge Concept Lab was primarily aimed at the development of greater transparency with regard to the ontology of conceptual forms, essentially focused on providing insight into the kinds of concepts that would seem to have some measure of complexity. Here we made a distinction between how the term concept is often used as a synonym for word, which leads inexorably to the strong welding together of concept and meaning (whereby, say the concept of tree is the meaning of the word tree), and the modelling of concepts as effectively 'theories'.[7] This is to note that at base we were not concerned with developing a theory or account of language as such and therefore in understanding how cognition in general might operate (say, through the

---

[6] For an interim report on this, see Peter de Bolla, Ewan Jones, Paul Nulty, Gabriel Recchia and John Regan, 'Distributional Concept Analysis: A Computational Model for Mapping the History of Concepts', *Contributions to the History of Concepts*, 14.1 (2019), 66–92, from which parts of the present chapter have been extracted.

[7] There is a substantial literature on the ontology of concepts within cognitive science that has established what is commonly referred to as the 'classical theory' in which concepts are in effect the definitions of the words that instantiate them. This theory was first contested by 'neoclassical theories' and then by 'prototype theories', 'exemplar theories' and more exotic hybrids. None of these revisions significantly weaken the supposition held in common with the 'classical theory' that concepts have extension and that the means for identifying both the constituent parts and ontological character of conceptual forms is a type of 'analysis' by which either (1) the propositions said to convey or stand for the real-world extension of the concept in question are interrogated, or (2) the content of the real-world extension of the concept is modelled in some other way, for example as the set of all objects that a cognitive agent has mentally labelled with a particular word. This is to note that so-called analyses of concepts – be they prototypical, neoclassical or otherwise – are essentially inquiries into the uses of meanings of the words that are supposed to capture the *content* of the putative concept. Even those studies of categorisation that seek to refine the model of prototypicality resort at base to a semantic inquiry. See E. Margolis and S. Laurence, eds., *Concepts: Core Readings* (Cambridge, MA: MIT Press, 1999); Gregory Murphy, *The Big Book of Concepts* (Cambridge, MA: MIT Press, 2002); Dennis Earl, 'Concepts and Properties', *Metaphysica*, 7.1 (2006), 67–85; S. Armstrong, L. Gleitman and H. Gleitman, 'What Some Concepts Might Not Be', *Cognition*, 13 (1983), 263–308; E. Rosch, 'Principles of Categorization', in *Cognition and Categorization*, ed. E. Rosch and B. Lloyd (New York: Lawrence Erlbaum Associates, 1978), 27–48.

mentalistic representation of the extensions of any and every lexical item), and we ended up directing our attention to a subset of terms in a language, to what some linguists would see as abstract concepts.[8] In a more prosaic formulation, we came to think of concepts – that is those that are represented in words that either are commonly identified as abstractions, such as the political concept of liberty, or uses of words that are more generally considered to be concretions (here, once metaphor is operationalised this includes all nouns in the language) when such uses lean towards abstraction – as something like a road map: concepts provide the protocols for moving from one place to another, or they provide the scaffolding that enables one to understand whatever is the object of attention and thought.[9]

We began, however, by taking an agnostic approach to conceptual types as we set about the inspection of the data provided by our tools without regard to a putative distinction between types. At first, we wanted to test the hypothesis that we could create computational signatures for concepts in general. As we gathered very large data dumps from the tool that enabled the construction of the signatures (which we call the 'shared lexis tool', explained in Section 2.2), we began to get a feel for how these data might support our aim in identifying the behaviours of conceptual forms that were not strongly determined by their narrowly semantic component. In other words, we began to be more confident that our initiating axiom, that words and concepts do not have identical ontologies, could lead to the discovery of a more properly conceptual realm, something that operates as it were in the background of human cognition. A simple way of characterising how this might make intuitive sense is to note that when one enters into a conversation about, say, democracy, it is not evident or even necessary that each participant in the conversation be able to access in its plenitude a definition of the word democracy. Indeed, it may be that many if not most acts of communication function as emergent environments in which one-to-one correspondence between a term and its definition is held in suspension as the process of understanding what is being said and heard unfolds in real time. Here the model that many linguists, behavioural scientists, philosophers of cognition and neuroscientists are currently exploring in which cognition is said to be

---

[8] The standard distinction made by linguists is between 'object concepts' or 'concrete objects' – plants, animals and so on – and 'abstract concepts' – love, dignity. See Edward E. Smith and Douglas L. Medin, *Categories and Concepts* (Cambridge, MA: Harvard University Press, 1981); N. Khokhlova, 'Understanding of Abstract Nouns in Linguistic Disciplines', *Procedia-Social and Behavioral Sciences*, 136 (2014), 8–11.

[9] This representation of concepts was based on a putative typology of conceptual forms developed in Peter de Bolla, *The Architecture of Concepts: The Historical Formation of Human Rights* (New York: Fordham University Press, 2013), 31–9.

both based on complex predictions based within partial and changing information flows, and distributed across many agents in a cognitive environment seems to be very germane to how our modelling of concepts developed.[10]

As we gathered data on candidate word-concepts, that is on the behaviours of selected lexical items inputted to the search query function of the shared lexis tool, we began to refine the ontology. Our first line of inquiry was to inspect the co-association patterns of candidate terms at a range of distances or windows – that is the number of words from the search query (which we call the focal term, explained in this section) to its co-associated or 'bound' term – in order to ascertain if certain terms, say those whose extension or referent is a political abstraction, might attract more or less lexical co-association where the measure is the number of terms in a co-association list that have been cut off 'above the bend in the curve' (explained in Section 2.2.2). We thought of this attraction as a kind of binding force that operates according to different strengths and with various outcomes. Some terms, we discovered, are strongly linked or bound together, according to our measure, with a small number of other terms, while others have a weaker binding to hundreds of other terms. And these patterns are sensitive to the distance or range between the focal term and its co-associate. Why should this be so? One hypothesis is that the semantic vector embedded in the term is likely to determine the strength of binding and thus the length of a co-association list: one can think of this as a consequence of the range of contexts in which a term might be used. Such patterns of lexical distribution are certainly sensitive to meaning, but when we began to inspect the lists of co-associated lexis that our tool produced at different distances of window sizes, essentially aggregating binding across distances in order to discern the lexis that persists across sample distances – effectively mapping the company a term keeps at varying window sizes – we became confident that we were beginning to pick up on something else: a conceptual component that is embedded in a functional analysis of how the concept operates in an information system. A number of the chapters in Part II explore the ways in which the discernment of this persistent lexical company can throw light on how ideas evolve and mutate over the time frame of a diachronic dataset, and thus contribute to more standard histories of ideas.[11]

Once again, we can model this conceptual ontology intuitively: the persistent lexical company, that is the list of terms that are most likely to

---

[10] See, for example, Andy Clark, *Supersizing the Mind: Embodiment, Action, and Cognitive Extension* (Oxford: Oxford University Press, 2010); Andy Clark, *Surfing Uncertainty: Prediction, Action and the Embodied Mind* (Oxford: Oxford University Press, 2016).

[11] See Chapters 4, 6 and 10.

co-associate with a candidate word-concept created by extracting the common terms in the aggregated lists generated at varying window sizes, is essentially a list of those words in whose company the focal term most frequently finds itself, taking into account both strong and weak, even absent syntactic or grammatical binding (see Section 2.2.2). This bound lexis is likely to include synonyms for the focal term as the commonly applied convention of elegant variation operates in which marked and very noticeable repetition of the same word in a small segment of language, say across a few contiguous sentences, is said to diminish the 'elegance' of the utterance and hence the preferred use of synonyms. But it is also likely to include antonyms as, say, an argument sets out the differences and distinctions between the focal term and its opposites. But as the immediate environs in terms of the length of a segment of coherent language stretches away from close up to the focal term, say within 5 words, to far away, say 100 words, the terms in the binding list are likely to find the basis for the company they keep in something other than syntactic or grammatical coherence (see Section 2.2). Again, if we think of this intuitively, a word-concept that is common to our ways of thinking about car maintenance, for example, is likely to find company with many terms that are applied in this domain: carburettor is likely to find itself in company with camshaft. One can think of this as a topic or a discursive environment, or to evoke a more cognitive metaphor, one can think of this common bound lexis as a set of protocols or algorithms running in the background as one processes the information stream that is an ongoing and increasingly large dataset of linguistic use – a discourse in motion. We found, however, that many of the examples of persistent lexical company we found were not exclusively composed of terms that can persuasively be said to comprise a topic or discourse, and this pushed us towards the formulation of a different hypothesis for their structuration. We began to think of this persistent company as comprised of not only words that are topically related to each other but also of lexis carrying a signal that either attracted or repelled other words – call it a conceptual relation that was overlaid upon the topical relation. In many of the chapters in Part II, we explore the affordances of modelling concepts in this way, as we direct attention to the diachronic evolution and establishment of ideas, to which we now turn.

2.1.2 Modelling Ideas

As we began to work with the computational signatures we derived from the shared lexis tool in diachronically sensitive ways, mapping how these signatures altered and evolved over the time frame of the dataset, it became clear that our initial modelling of the word-concept category could be refined and applied to what we most commonly think of as ideas, where such a term does not refer merely to a single dictionary definition – a one-to-one homology between the label for an idea, say justice and its dictionary definition – but to something broader. We saw this as being informed by both our initial rejection of a model of concepts used by some cognitive scientists in which concepts are considered to be simply the meaning of the labels that convey them, and our efforts to understand the increasingly complex signatures generated by our tools.[12] We began to see that these complex signatures, the entities we had initially thought of as concepts, were also articulated or networked in larger constellations that might be better considered as the units of thinking we commonly refer to as ideas. This is to note that, although we do think of ideas as compacted or condensed within a single word, we also frequently have recourse to a number of words when calling them to mind. Under this rubric, ideas are similar to or contain statements that might be hinged to other statements, and in a technical sense they are arguments, that is a sequence of statements that comprise a process of reasoning. Once again, the overlap between how we model concepts and ideas becomes apparent as the arguments we may take ideas to be are essentially ontologically similar to the theories that on one account of concepts, concepts are said to be (the 'theory-theory' model of concepts). Thus, if one were to take the example of 'commercial society', which is the focus of the case study in Chapter 8, it is perhaps uncontroversial to claim that this phrase conveys or contains both a concept and an idea.

When we turn to the discipline of the history of ideas, however, it is noteworthy that notwithstanding the fact that we can, and often do, use the terms idea and concept interchangeably, the two most distinctive approaches to the history of ideas over the last quarter century have preferred one of them over the other: the Cambridge School of intellectual history or the history of ideas selects the former, while the tradition of conceptual history associated with Reinhart Koselleck and his collaborators selects the latter. In some measure this preference has little bite, since both the Cambridge School and *Begriffsgeschichte* are focused on the

---

[12] This view is succinctly put by Ray Jackendorff: 'The expression *concept* is used to mean essentially 'a mental representation that can serve as the meaning of a linguistic expression'; see 'What Is a Concept, That a Person May Grasp It?', in *Concepts: Core Readings*, ed. Eric Margolis and Stephen Lawrence (Cambridge, MA: MIT Press, 1999), 309. The fiercest critic of this model within cognitive science is Jerry Fodor who, along with Zenon Pylyshyn, argues that 'like so much else of what they taught you in grade school, the theory that concepts are definitions most likely isn't true'. See Jerry A. Fodor and Zenon W. Pylyshyn, *Minds without Meanings: An Essay on the Content of Concepts* (Cambridge, MA: MIT Press, 2014), 33; as also Fodor's earlier broadside, Jerry A. Fodor, *Concepts: Where Cognitive Science Went Wrong* (Oxford: Oxford University Press, 1998).

extension of words into reference and meaning, even if the approaches to how one might ascertain meaning are different. In the case of the Cambridge School, as is very well known, the emphasis is on the accurate recovery of the contexts of an utterance so as to assess and exhume the meanings that must have been intended by historical actors at the time of their utterances. Although Koselleck maintained that words are not identical to concepts, the project of conceptual history as formulated by *Begriffsgeschichte* tracks the changing uses of words over time, and hence their changing meanings as a way of getting under, as it were, the corresponding history of conceptual change.[13] Notwithstanding these similarities – although Quentin Skinner, perhaps the scholar most closely and consistently associated with the Cambridge School, has remarked in print on his late coming to the work of Koselleck and his colleagues and in the course of these remarks has tried to find or see similarities in approach and objectives – it remains the case that the two traditions of inquiry into the history of ideas have gone their separate, if overlapping ways.[14] We contend that they can be made to speak to each other more fruitfully if one were to model the relations between word, idea and concept in a more elastic and complex way than either tradition does. That is, we propose that a history of concepts, characterised in the ways presented here, can be used as a means or technique for parsing the history of ideas, making the latter more granular and sensitive to the cultural deployments of concepts that create the larger-scale contexts within which ideas take shape and find their cohesion. These larger contexts are, for sure, social, political, national and so forth – precisely the locations for the discourses interrogated by intellectual historians of the Cambridge School – but our hypothesis is that one can find patterns of use and structuration at the most general level of language behaviour, within, say, the aggregated linguistic culture-at-large, that allow one to see the conditions of possibility for local instantiations of concepts-ideas. Taking such a global view dampens the specificity of approaches that insist on the narrow context of socially and historically contingent acts of speech or writing, but it correspondingly enhances our attempts at understanding the resources for thinking provided by a culture and its language at the largest scale – call it the community of accreted use over deep time, Saussure's *langue* in infinite extension.

---

[13] For a good account of this, see Hans Erick Bodeker, 'Concept – Meaning – Discourse', in *History of Concepts: Comparative Perspectives*, ed. Iain Hampsher-Monk, Karl Tilmans and Frank van Vree (Amsterdam: Amsterdam University Press, 1998).

[14] See Quentin Skinner, 'Retrospect: Studying Rhetoric and Conceptual Change', in *Visions of Politics*, 3 vols. (Cambridge: Cambridge University Press, 2001), I, 179–80; and for an intimate history of the misconnections between *Begriffsgeschichte* and the Cambridge School, see Jan Ifversen, 'The Birth of International Conceptual History', *Contributions to the History of Concepts*, 16.1 (2021), 1–14.

This way of modelling ideas is intended to help negotiate an intransigent problem in any account of concepts or ideas, that is their representation or instantiation in words. Unless one were to suppose an exact correlation between brain activity as it can be observed and measured using contemporary technologies and the ideas or concepts humans employ in cognitive processing, this problem will continue to be unfixable: in order to focus the object of study (concept or idea), we are forced to use the words we take to be the instantiations of such ideas or concepts. This is to note that in all of the case studies in Part II, when we are trying to parse a conceptual architecture or trace its diachronic evolution, we are bound to concatenate concept or idea with the word. But the model we propose for distinguishing concepts from ideas, the former being a lower level or less complex articulation of the latter, is intended to provide a heuristic for discerning the lineaments or building blocks of specific ideas and, using the computational approaches outlined here, for constructing their more focused histories through recourse to a dataset that is structured diachronically.

In considering ideas as occupying a higher or more combinatorial level of articulation than concepts, we do not mean to suggest that concepts are always articulated at a lower level. Rather, we set out to explore the affordances of supposing that such a distinction can be made to hold in a digital framework for developing a history of ideas. If we suppose ideas, for example, to find their home in discourse – strings of lexis that can be considered as arguments or statements – we can also, correspondingly, suppose concepts to find their home in networks or clusters of one-to-one or one-to-many relations with other concepts – call them maps or pathways rather than statements or arguments. We think of this as a technique for investigating the data produced by our tools and not as a description or theory of either concepts or ideas. It is no accident that this way of modelling ideas, as being discursively composed, sits quite comfortably with the manner in which one of the founding scholars of the Cambridge School, John G. A. Pocock, sees the history of ideas, namely as undertaking an investigation of discourse as an historical form.[15] This is because we deliberately set out to model the overall space – concept–word–idea – as susceptible of being seen from many viewpoints, so that, for example, like a glove being turned inside out, our object of study might take a particular shape or form when seen from the side, as it were, of conceptuality and

---

[15] See John G. A Pocock, 'The Reconstruction of Discourse: Towards the Historiography of Political Thought', in his collection of essays *Political Thought and History* (Cambridge: Cambridge University Press, 2009), 67–86; also see Melvin Richter, *The History of Political and Social Concepts: A Critical Introduction* (Oxford: Oxford University Press, 1995), 128–9.

another when seen from the side of ideation. Similarly, discourse, or coherent statements and arguments, might be inverted so as to see their molecular structure, as it were, in the concepts that compose them. But it needs to be underscored that in both cases we are observing the behaviour of words.

This leads us to note that one of the criticisms levelled at the methodology we propose deems that the fact that the shared lexis tool (explained in Section 2.2) operates through the aperture of a single focal term – the search query that initiates the generation of a *dpf* with a ranked list of co-associated terms – essentially hampers our attempts to find the signatures of concepts: we are simply observing patterns in the co-occurrences of words in our dataset. We demur, however, on two counts. The first derives from our modelling, which is to note that we take words to be simply the material instantiation of concepts; hence, any attempt to understand the latter must operate through the former – as we have already noted, there is simply no other way to gain access to putative concepts. The second, explained in Section 2.2, is that our analyses of conceptual behaviour are built upon the metrics created in the shared lexis tool and not upon the raw counts of lexical co-association that underly these metrics. And these metrics are used to create computational entities – the complex interleaving of ranked *dpf* lists explained in Sections 2.2.4 and 2.2.5 and in Chapter 3, which outlines the method used for visualising these entities – which are the objects of our inquiry.

2.2   The Shared Lexis Tool

In this section we outline the process by which we designed the shared lexis tool, and we set out our arguments for the choices we made in our design. We begin with a brief account of the background to these decisions. Recent work in cognitive science and neuroscience have used conceptual models derived from statistical corpus analysis to verify the robustness of psychophysical and neuroimaging experiments.[16] Working from the other direction, computational linguists have used corpus statistics to replicate conceptual models identified by psychological experiment and neuroimaging.[17] In addition, many natural language processing

[16] See T. M. Mitchell, S. V. Shinkareva, A. Carlson et al., 'Predicting Human Brain Activity Associated with the Meanings of Nouns', *Science*, 320 (2008), 1191–5; and T. Yarkoni, R. A. Poldrack. T. E. Nichols, D. C. Van Essen and T. D. Wager, 'Large-Scale Automated Synthesis of Human Functional Neuroimaging Data', *Nature Methods*, 8.8 (2011), 665–70.

[17] See Collin Kelly, Barry Devereux and Anna Korhonen, 'Acquiring Human-like Feature-Based Conceptual Representations from Corpora', in *Proceedings of the NAACL HLT 2010 First Workshop on Computational Neurolinguistics* (Stroudsburg, PA: Association for Computational Linguistics, 2010), 61–9; and Franciso Pereira, Matthew Botvinick and

tasks believed to require conceptual or 'common-sense' knowledge – for example machine translation, analogy solving, question–answering and natural language inference systems – have been tackled with some success by researchers using distributional semantic models derived from large text corpora.

Irrespective of theoretical motivations, the computational implementations of these methods have much in common. Word, phrase or document meanings are approximated by deciding on a word-distance window within which to count word co-occurrences or compare the paradigmatic context, and counts of word or context co-occurrence are tabulated into a vector. The vectors can be compared directly to measure word associations or combined into a matrix to measure the similarity of documents.

One of the most widely applied document-based methods today is a generative probabilistic model of the relationship between words and documents known as topic modelling.[18] Topic modelling discovers groups of associated words by modelling a process in which documents are generated by selecting from subsets of words with varying probabilities. The resulting clusters of associated words are intended to capture topics in the corpus, and to allow comparison of documents by topic and measurement of diachronic change in topic emphasis. The method has been widely applied outside of computer science, for example to measure political attention and literary style.[19]

Applications that focus on measuring word rather than document association often use paradigmatic similarity of contexts shorter than document length.[20] The meaning of a word in such models is represented as a point embedded in a high-dimensional space defined by the contexts in which its occurrences are counted. The context may be a short window of words around the target word or defined by a grammatical relation

---

Greg Detre, 'Using Wikipedia to Learn Semantic Feature Representations of Concrete Concepts in Neuroimaging Experiments', *Artificial Intelligence*, 194 (2013), 240–52.

[18] See David M. Blei, Andrew Y. Ng and Michael I. Jordan, 'Latent Dirichlet Allocation', *Journal of Machine Learning Research*, 3 (2003), 993–1022.

[19] See K. M. Quinn, B. L. Monroe, M. Colaresi, M. H. Crespin and D. R. Radev, 'How to Analyze Political Attention with Minimal Assumptions and Costs', *American Journal of Political Science*, 54.1 (2001), 209–28; and J. M. Hughes, N. J. Foti, D. C. Krakauer and D. N. Rockmore, 'Quantitative Patterns of Stylistic Influence in the Evolution of Literature', *Proceedings of the National Academy of Sciences*, 109.20 (2012), 7682–6.

[20] Weaver first suggested this kind of similarity as a method for word translation in Warren Weaver, 'Translation', *Machine Translation of Languages*, 14 (1975), 15–23. And for an overview of word-context models, see Will Lowe, 'Towards a Theory of Semantic Space', in *Proceedings of the Twenty-Third Annual Conference of the Cognitive Science Society*, ed. Johanna D. Moore and Keith Stenning (Mahwah, NJ: Lawrence Erlbaum Associates, 2001), 576–81.

discovered by automatic syntactic parsing of the text.[21] Since the number of possible contexts may be many times the size of the vocabulary, dimension-reduction methods such as singular value decomposition are often used to reduce the complexity of the model, with the drawback that the resulting dimensions are no longer directly interpretable. Word-context models with dimensionality reduction result in a 'word vector', usually of the order of a few hundred dimensions – these are commonly referred to as 'word embedding' models (see Chapter 3). An efficient and widely used implementation of this kind of model is the word2vec package, which uses a neural network trained to predict word contexts, and encodes the meaning of the word in its parameters rather than explicitly counting word contexts.[22]

Some work in computational linguistics describes types of word co-occurrence in terms of Saussure's syntagmatic and paradigmatic relations: words that tend to occur close to one another in a passage of text have a syntagmatic relation, while words that tend to have similar contexts – one word may be easily substituted for the other – have a paradigmatic relation. These different kinds of contextual similarity reveal different conceptual relations: syntagmatic similarity captures meronymy, phrasal association and general conceptual association, while paradigmatic similarity captures synonymy, antonymy and hyponymy.

An advantage of syntagmatic counts is that the type of semantic association required can be precisely defined. For example, the hypernym relation between animal and dog is easily inferred by their paradigmatic distribution – dog can be used in most contexts where animal is acceptable, but the converse does not hold. The relation between dog and bark is more clearly instantiated in syntagmatic co-occurrence patterns. The two terms often occur in the same region of text, but one is rarely substitutable for the other. Recently, researchers have used specific

---

[21] See Kevin K. Lund and Curt Burgess, 'Producing High-Dimensional Semantic Spaces from Lexical Co-occurrence', *Behavior Research Methods, Instruments, & Computers*, 28.2 (1996), 203–8; Dekang Lin, 'Automatic Retrieval and Clustering of Similar Words', in *ACL '98/COLING '98: Proceedings of the 36th Annual Meeting of the Association for Computational Linguistics and 17th International Conference on Computational Linguistics*, II (Stroudsburg, PA: Association for Computational Linguistics, 1998), 768–74; Omer Levy and Yoav Goldberg, 'Dependency-Based Word Embeddings', in *Proceedings of the 52nd Annual Meeting of the Association for Computational Linguistics*, ed. Kalina Bontcheva and Jingbo Zhu, II (Stroudsburg, PA: Association for Computational Linguistics, 2014), 302–8.
[22] See David E. Rumelhart, Geoffrey E. Hinton and Ronald J. Williams, 'Efficient Estimation of Word Representations in Vector Space' (2013), arXiv: 1301.3781; D. R. G. H. R. Williams and G. E. Hinto, 'Learning Representations by Back-Propagating Errors', *Nature*, 323 (1986), 533–6.

co-occurrence patterns to learn precise kinds of semantic relation.[23] For example, a meronymy relation between word X and word Y may be determined by computational analysis of counts for phrases like '*Xs consisting of Y*' in a large corpus, whereas syntagmatic patterns for arbitrary semantic relations can be learned from example seed pairs.[24] Descriptions of distributional semantic methods focus on measuring and evaluating word similarity, but although it is not always explicitly stated, the possibility that these models encode information that could be considered conceptual rather than simply lexical is recognised in the literature.

As we reviewed these techniques, we settled on the decision to focus our primary measure on *lexical co-association* and developed code that can search through massive historical datasets of language use in order to first identify effectively the co-associations between all terms in the corpus exceeding our frequency threshold. Our code then uses a statistical measure to ascertain the likelihood of one term co-associating with another over a notional baseline of a random distribution of the terms within the dataset. This allows us to construct a metric, *dpf* (commented upon in Section 2.2.1), which gives us an indication of the strength of probable co-association between every term.[25] This measure can be plotted above a baseline that is calculated by assuming that the target term could in theory be found in proximity to every other term were that term to be randomly distributed within a string of lexis. It is important to note that our measure is not sensitive to grammar or syntax, which allows us to inspect co-association at large spans or distances between terms. Thus, our tool enables us to inspect spans from close up (five words either before or post the target term) to far away (100 words either before or post). The purpose of doing this is to capture information on lexical behaviour through the discovery of patterns of co-association between terms so as to construct a 'conceptual signature', a unique identification for any concept based upon data derived from distributions in lexical use. Most linguistically slanted research that utilises similar techniques based on neo-Firthian distributional semantics is interested in the features of

[23] See Marti A. Hearst, 'Automatic Acquisition of Hyponyms from Large Text Corpora', in *COLING '92: Proceedings of the 14th Conference on Computational Linguistics*, II (Stroudsburg, PA: Association for Computational Linguistics, 1992), 539–45.

[24] See Roxana Girju, Adriana Badulescu and Dan Moldovan, 'Automatic Discovery of Part–Whole Relations', *Computational Linguistics*, 32.1 (2006), 83–135.

[25] We use the term co-association to emphasise that we would like to measure a reciprocal (or symmetric) association: the association score for (A, B) ought to be the same as for (B, A) in type and degree.

a language that enable or construct coherence.[26] And in work of this kind aimed at understanding conceptual relations, statistical regularities in grammatical structure are a key component. Our approach differs in that it does not use this method and does not try to detect relations like meronymy and hypernymy; rather, we detect a general association relation from supra-sentential co-occurrences.[27] Thus the co-association data we capture help us identify the widest lexical terrain within which a target term operates without regard to immediate syntactic placement or grammatical aspect. When we inspect both close up and increasingly distant behaviour of two co-associated terms, we can begin to assess the strength of 'binding' that occurs between any two terms. In this way we can move from strictly semantic or syntactic binding – as in phrases that are common in the English language – to a different kind of binding that we think of as more narrowly conceptual. We conjecture that this conceptual binding sheds light on the construction and articulation of ideas, effectively identifying the components out of which they are made as set out in Section 2.1. In effect, it provides a more granular picture of the lexical terrain within which ideas circulate and are given shape, structure and form.

2.2.1   Creating a Metric for Shared Lexis

In constructing a metric that would allow us to inspect the behaviour of concepts, we considered a number of computational-linguistic techniques and approaches, mindful of the fact that for our purposes we had three important desiderata: *transparency, sensitivity to frequency* and *sensitivity to distance*.

(1) *Transparency*: an ideal measure of association should not be a 'black box'. If such a measure identifies two terms in a corpus as having a strong association to each other, it should be possible to understand why. In particular, it should be possible to identify specific documents or uses of these terms in the corpus that helped lead the model to this conclusion.

---

[26] See J. Sinclair, S. Jones, R. Daley and R. Krishnamurthy, *English Collocational Studies: The OSTI Report* (London: Continuum, 2004); M. Hoey, M. Mahlberg, M. Stubbs and W. Teubert, *Text, Discourse and Corpora: Theory and Analysis* (London: Continuum, 2007); and for a review of the field, see Tony McEnery and Andrew Hardie, *Corpus Linguistics: Method, Theory and Practice* (Cambridge: Cambridge University Press, 2012).

[27] See John R. Firth, 'The Technique of Semantics', *Transactions of the Philological Society*, 34.1 (1935), 36–73; John Sinclair, *Corpus, Concordance, Collocation* (Oxford: Oxford University Press, 1991); and for a good overview of historical semantics, see Christian Kay and Katheryn L. Allan, *English Historical Semantics* (Edinburgh: Edinburgh University Press, 2015).

(2) *Sensitivity to frequency and data sparsity*: a word (e.g. democracy) will likely co-occur more frequently with words that are very frequent in the corpus as a whole (was, of) than with less frequent terms (government, aristocracy), even though democracy and government are more strongly related semantically. An ideal measure of association should therefore take frequency into account. However, it should do so in a way that also considers *data sparsity*. That is to say, no matter how large one's corpus is, it will always contain a large number of terms whose counts are relatively infrequent and less statistically reliable as a result. This difference in statistical reliability should somehow be accounted for as well.

(3) *Sensitivity to distance*: because we wish to capture associations that lie outside purely linguistic operations, it is important that our measure be able to distinguish how strongly associated two terms are at one distance (e.g. 100 words away) compared with another (e.g. 5 words away).

The standard procedures for deciding whether two terms x and y 'co-occur' are (a) whether y appears in a window of text that extends some specific number of words to the left and/or right of x, or (b) whether x and y appear in the same document. The most common way to implement (a) is for the window of text to begin at x and extend outward in both directions. As such, a classic window of 100 words will include all words that appear just 1, 2, 3 ... words away, which is not desirable if we wish to exclude words that primarily only appear with x in adjectival phrases, idiomatic expressions and other relations that have more to do with syntax than conceptual relatedness. Because we are interested in long-range relationships and the ways in which associations vary with distance, we use the term co-association rather than co-occurrence, as the latter frequently implies that the two terms appear in the same phrase or collocation.

We came to the conclusion that such standard procedures do not meet all of the desiderata described above. Neural networks, topic models and word embedding models all produce famously non-transparent mathematical representations, although there has been some research aimed at improving their interpretability.[28] If we were to be able to make strong

---

[28] See M. Setnes, R. Babuska and H. B. Verbruggen, 'Rule-Based Modeling: Precision and Transparency', Part C (Applications and Reviews), *IEEE Transactions on Systems, Man, and Cybernetics*, 28.1 (1998), 165–9; J. D. Olden and D. A. Jackson, 'Illuminating the "Black Box": A Randomization Approach for Understanding Variable Contributions in Artificial Neural Networks', *Ecological Modelling*, 154.1 (2002), 135–50; Hongyin Luo, Zhiyuan Liu, Huanbo Luan and Maosong Sun, 'Online Learning of Interpretable Word Embedding', in *Proceedings of the 2015 Conference on Empirical Methods in Natural*

claims about *conceptual* associations and to trace those claims back to specific occurrences of relevant terms in the original text, we needed a more transparent methodology.

Simple measures of co-occurrence are much more transparent. For example, *pointwise mutual information* (PMI) is frequently used either on its own as a measure of lexical association or as a starting point for the construction of more complex measures.[29] As shown in Eq. (2.1), PMI is given as

$$I(x,y) = \log_2 \frac{P(x,y)}{P(x)P(y)} \tag{2.1}$$

where $P(x)$ and $P(y)$ can each be approximated as the frequency of x and y (respectively) divided by the total number of terms in the corpus, and $P(x,y)$ as the number of times that x and y co-occur divided by the total number of terms in the corpus.[30] Thus $P(x, y)/P(x)P(y)$ has an intuitive interpretation: it simply expresses the ratio between the number of times x and y co-occur, divided by the number of times one would expect them to appear if their appearances throughout the corpus were randomly distributed. A ratio of two would indicate that one is twice as likely to see x and y together than one would expect to if these words were randomly and uniformly distributed throughout the corpus; that is if we assume that x and y were to retain the same corpus-wide frequencies, but their positions relative to other words in the corpus were completely random. What qualifies as a co-occurrence is up to the user of the measure and the most popular choice is appearance in the same window or document.

A feature of PMI is that it is highly transparent – two words will rank as highly associated if and only if they appear together in the same contexts more frequently than would be expected by chance, and the contexts in which they appear together in the corpus can be directly inspected (e.g. by searching the corpus for documents/windows that contain both). However, it has other problems with respect to the work that we wish a measure of co-association to do. Although PMI is sensitive to the global frequency with which words appear in a corpus, it is insensitive to data

Language Processing (Stroudsburg, PA: Association for Computational Linguistics, 2015), 1687–92.

[29] See Kenneth W. Church and Patrick Hanks, 'Word Association Norms, Mutual Information, and Lexicography', *Computational Linguistics*, 16.1 (1990), 22–9; Jeffrey Pennington, Richard Socher and Christopher Manning, 'GloVe: Global Vectors for Word Representation', in *Proceedings of the 2014 Conference on Empirical Methods in Natural Language Processing*, ed. Alessandro Moschitti, Bo Pang and Walter Daelemans (Stroudsburg, PA: Association for Computational Linguistics, 2014), 1532–43.

[30] See Chris Manning and Hinrich Schütze, *Foundations of Statistical Natural Language Processing* (Cambridge, MA: MIT Press, 1999).

sparsity – the fact that the most infrequent words in the corpus also provide the least reliable information. If x and y each appear 100 times in a corpus, and co-occur with each other on 99 of those instances, this should be treated as more important than if x and y only appear once in a corpus and happen to co-occur in that singular instance. However, PMI does not penalise rare, statistically unreliable events in any way. As a result, if one were to rank the words in a corpus that co-occurred with some fixed term x according to their PMI with x, one would find an inverse relationship between rank and frequency: the higher the rank on the list, the lower the frequency. A common band-aid is to impose a minimum frequency or co-occurrence count – an approach that mitigates the problem but does not remove it.[31] In sum, most simple measures of co-occurrence tend to be transparent but not sensitive to both frequency and data sparsity, while the reverse is true for 'state-of-the-art' approaches such as topic models and neural networks.

Although most practitioners define co-occurrence in terms of appearance in the same window or document, this is more a matter of convention than necessity. Window-based measures can be readily adapted to distance-based measures: one can specify that in order to count as a co-association with x, a word y must appear some distance d words away from x, plus or minus a word or two. This is the approach we took because we wished to capture data on patterns of lexical distribution that move from close up where semantic or syntactic coherence is strongest to far away where it is weakest. By taking this wider view, we sought to discover relations of binding that go beyond or underpin strictly local semantic ties. Thus, we used what could be called a 'sliding window', as it involves a window of a fixed size that, rather than being centred on x itself, is centred on a word d words away.

In our deliberations regarding the basis for constructing an ideal measure for our purposes, we explored combining the transparency of PMI with the ability of more complex methods, such as word embeddings (see Chapter 3), to exhibit sensitivity to lexical frequency and data sparsity. One possible method was suggested by Levy, Goldberg and Dagan, who reported an intriguing connection between PMI and one of the most popular word-embedding models, word2vec SGNS (skip-grams with negative sampling). They note that one of the features of word2vec corresponds to a 'smoothed' version of PMI in which 'all context counts are raised to the power of α', and they apply this modification, along with many others, to a relatively simple and transparent model of lexical

---

[31] See Manning and Schütze, *Statistical Natural Language Processing*.

association.[32] They report that among all modifications applied, this was one of the most effective in increasing performance on a range of benchmark tasks, measuring their performance at $\alpha = 0.75$. They did not hypothesise why this value worked well, except to point out that similar work had found success with this value.

A plausible reason for the success of this value is that it may hit the sweet spot in the trade-off between frequency and data sparsity, which are naturally in opposition. An alpha of 1 corresponds to standard, unsmoothed PMI, which ignores data sparsity and gives too much weight to the specious evidence provided by highly infrequent words. However, an alpha of 0 ignores a word's corpus-wide frequency, causing all words to appear most associated with highly frequent words like the, and, of. We therefore adopted a simple variant of PMI which drops the logarithm and introduces a smoothing exponent in the denominator, because we were primarily interested in the rank order of terms as they are co-associated with a focal term X. Since the logarithm does not affect this rank ordering it can be dropped without loss of generality. Doing so highlights the fact that the measure we constructed is essentially a small modification to the measure sometimes referred to simply as 'observed over expected': the number of times two words are observed in conjunction, divided by the number of times one would expect to see them together by chance. This measure, which we refer to as a *dpf* since it expresses the extent to which a term is predicted to be distributed across the dataset, is shown in Eq. (2.2):

$$dpf(x,y) = \frac{P(x,y)}{\left(P(x)P(y) \right)^{\alpha}} \tag{2.2}$$

The measure cannot actually be calculated without a means of estimating $P(x, y)$, $P(x)$ and $P(y)$. The standard approach is to consider $P(x)$ to represent the probability that an arbitrarily chosen context window in the corpus would contain $P(x)$; given a context window of width w and a corpus with N tokens, $count(x)$ of which are the term X, this is approximated by $w \times count(x)/N$. The number of tokens in the corpus is approximately equivalent to the number of context windows in the corpus, provided that the corpus is large and the context window size is small. $P(y)$ follows the same logic. For $P(x, y)$, recall that we estimate $count(x, y)$ by counting 'co-associations' – cases in which y appears some particular distance d away from x.

[32] Omer Levy, Yoav Goldberg and Ido Dagan, 'Improving Distributional Similarity with Lessons Learned from Word Embeddings', *Transactions of the Association for Computational Linguistics*, 3 (2015), 211–25.

Note that the decision as to whether to raise the entire probability $w \times count(x)/N$ to the power of α, or only the counts as in the previously mentioned work of Levy et al., is somewhat arbitrary. However, it hardly matters with respect to *dpf* calculations computed on the same corpus; because N and w are always the same, the only difference that it makes whether one uses $(w \times count(x)/N)^{\alpha}$ or $w \times (count(x))^{\alpha}/N$ is that the final score ends up being scaled by a constant factor. In practice, the network visualisations in this book use the former formulation, while the tables use the latter (unless otherwise specified). The precise equation (see Eq. (2.3)) used to generate the numbers in the tables throughout this book therefore differs from the more elegant formulation of *dpf* in Eq. (2.2) by a constant factor (for a given corpus and window size), despite the unwieldy form it takes when hashed out in terms of counts and window sizes:

$$dpf_{estimated}(x,y) = \frac{\frac{w(count(x,y))}{N}}{\left(\frac{w(count(x))^{\alpha})}{N}\right) \times \left(\frac{w(count(y))^{\alpha})}{N}\right)} \tag{2.3}$$

When we calculated the value of α that minimised the inverse correlation between rank and frequency described above, we found the optimal value for our corpus to be 0.78, very close to 0.75. Higher values corresponded to a negative correlation between rank and frequency, while lower values corresponded to a positive correlation. In other words, with an appropriate value of alpha, *dpf* is sensitive to data sparsity as well as frequency, and retains the simplicity and transparency of PMI. Subsequent references in this book to the *dpf* between two words therefore refer to Eq. (2.3) with an alpha of 0.78, unless otherwise specified.

This measure meets all three of our fundamental desiderata. The next sections describe how this measure is employed to build a 'profile' of a lexical co-association with respect to a particular time period and distance, and how these profiles can be used in the investigation of conceptual forms.

2.2.2   Constructing a Profile of Lexical Co-associations

Computing *dpf* scores between all possible pairs of words in a corpus (between a focal and bound term) yields an enormous range of values. Thousands of pairs appear high to the eye – but how high is high? In this kind of environment, mainstays of parametric statistics, such as the use of

Table 2.1 *The top twelve terms having the highest* dpf *values with despotism at a distance of 50 among all documents in ECCO published from 1780 to 1800 (73,104 documents; 3.8 billion tokens; 19,474 instances of despotism).*

Bound token	*dpf*	*N* (total)	*N* (with focal)
despotism	14978.4	19474	192
despotic	3928.8	19295	50
monarchy	3572.3	64119	116
arbitrary	3012.2	65964	100
discontinuance	2947.1	5959	15
governments	2726.7	50944	74
aristocracy	2557.7	11001	21
decaying	2548.0	4825	11
statesmen	2389.1	6492	13
revolution	2291.6	145492	141
repelling	2236.0	6378	12
tyranny	2222.7	80269	86

p-values to determine statistical significance, are not appropriate.[33] How should we decide whether a co-association between two terms is strong enough to merit our attention?

The approach we selected is similar to the common technique of determining which components of a factor analysis to preserve by looking for the 'elbow' or 'bend in the curve' in a scree plot.[34] Consider, in Table 2.1, the list created when one computes the *dpf* between a particular term of interest (the 'focal term') and a large number of other terms.

If these *dpf* values are plotted against their rank on the list, one typically obtains a smooth curve that is well fit by a power function. By fitting a power function to this curve and solving for where the derivative is equal to -1, the *dpf* at which the 'bend in the curve' occurs can be identified. This value serves as a threshold that separates the 'short head' of the curve from the 'long tail'.

---

[33] See Anders Søgaard, Anders Johannsen, Barbara Plank, Dirk Hovy and Hector Martínez Alonso, 'What's in a P-Value in NLP?', in *Proceedings of the Eighteenth Conference on Computational Natural Language Learning*, ed. Hwee Tou Ng, Siew Mei Wu, Ted Briscoe et al. (Stroudsburg, PA: Association for Computational Linguistics, 2014), 1–10.

[34] See Donald A. Jackson, 'Stopping Rules in Principal Components Analysis: A Comparison of Heuristical and Statistical Approaches', *Ecology*, 74.8 (1993), 2204–14.

Our measure *dpf* is similar to PMI, word2vec and many other measures commonly employed by computational linguists to quantify lexical association, in that the specific identities or lengths of the documents in which the lexical co-associations occur do not figure in the calculation. Like most computational linguists, we see this as an advantage rather than a disadvantage: the measure is sensitive to the number of co-associations and not to the number of documents or contexts in which co-associations appear (which would require semi-arbitrary decisions to be made about what counts as a 'document' or 'context'). At first glance, this may seem like a counter-intuitive approach. If sewing has a high *dpf* to needle at a distance of 100 words away, such a strong connection might be considered to be simply a feature of a tightly constructed lexical terrain around the concept of needlework. And, given that our method does not control for document-level effects of word distributions, our calculation of the *dpf* may appear to be skewed (since, say, a manual on needlework might have dozens of uses of these two words). Our aim, however, is to capture the strength of binding between terms across the full dataset: if the index to that binding is substantially based on very few documents (say only those manuals on needlework), the point remains that *conceptually* this activity is culturally understood through the usage of the identified strongly co-associated lexis. It is also important to note that we make no claim as to the specific importance of a distance or span: we investigate *dpf*s at large distances not to suggest that there is anything deeply meaningful about a peak in *dpf* at some specific distance, but rather firstly to distinguish between co-associations that are more likely to be conceptual versus those that are more likely to be driven by syntax or the syntax-semantics interface; and secondly because quantifying a co-association strength at a specific distance serves as a useful building block for more informative investigations. For example, it allows us to quantify the reliability with which two words tend to appear together at a great variety of distances, or to identify cases in which a word X is much more likely to precede word Y than the reverse for non-syntactic reasons.[35]

2.2.3   The ECCO Dataset

The Cambridge Concept Lab built tools that are capable of operating with any text-based dataset, suitably configured.[36] As we experimented with different metrics and techniques for data mining, we used our

---

[35] See de Bolla, Jones, Nulty, Recchia and Regan, 'Distributional Concept Analysis'.
[36] A manual for use can be found at 'Tools and Resources', The Concept Lab, https://concept-lab.lib.cam.ac.uk/.

developing tools on a range of such datasets, including newspaper archives as well as large-scale digital archives of texts. We ended up concentrating our research, however, on ECCO.[37] Once we had access to the hard disk (called a target disk mode) supplied by the rights holder to the dataset – at that time the company Thomson Gale – we were able to access the XML files of the metadata and the optical character recognition (OCR) text using a bespoke code that we created, enabling us to calculate the *dpf* for all terms in the dataset. In this section we outline some general issues with respect to this dataset.

The terabyte hard drive we worked with (the target disk mode) comprises some 180,000 titles, 200,000 volumes and more than 33 million pages of text. It is the world's largest digital archive of books from the eighteenth century, containing 'every significant English-language and foreign-language title printed in the United Kingdom between the years 1701 and 1800'.[38] The entire corpus has been scanned and OCR has been applied to the texts, resulting in a 'machine-readable' version of each that can be subjected to computational analyses. A limitation of this resource is the high degree of error in the recognised text. The Early Modern OCR Project, a project aiming to build a bespoke process for applying OCR to early modern texts in such a way as to achieve high levels of accuracy, ultimately was only able to achieve 86 percent accuracy, and even the most up-to-date version of the OCR-based ECCO texts offered by Gale Cengage have been estimated at only 89 percent accuracy.[39] Because OCR errors are far more likely to result in non-words than they are to transform words to other valid words, digital searches for particular terms (e.g. freedom) will underestimate the frequencies of these words. Our analyses primarily *compare* frequencies and associations of particular terms (in Chapter 5 we work with the terms freedom and liberty) and phrases (again in Chapter 5 the example is 'freedom to' compared with 'freedom for'), so it is proportions that are important rather than absolute frequencies. As there is no reason a priori to believe that one of these words or phrases will be vastly more subject to OCR error than the other,

[37] For a detailed account of the creation of this dataset, see Stephen H. Gregg, *Old Books and Digital Publishing: Eighteenth Century Collections Online* (Cambridge: Cambridge University Press, 2020).

[38] Eighteenth Century Collections Online, Gale, accessed 6 July 2018, www.gale.com/pri mary-sources/eighteenth-century-collections-online.

[39] Laura C. Mandell, Matthew Christy and Elizabeth Grumbach. *EMOP Mellon Final Report*, Initiative for Digital Humanities, Media, and Culture, Texas A&M University, 30 September 2015, accessed 6 July 2018, http://emop.tamu.edu/news; Laura C. Mandell, Clemens Neudecker, Apostolos Antonacopoulos et al., 'Navigating the Storm: IMPACT, eMOP, and Agile Steering Standards', *Digital Scholarship in the Humanities*, 32.1 (2017), 189–94.

we have confidence that the OCR error is not having a disproportionate impact on our conclusions, but it must be kept in mind as a source of noise.[40] Our use of a frequency threshold to exclude very low-frequency types also serves to limit the number of garbled tokens that enter into our analyses.[41]

We also configured the tools to work with a dataset of seventeenth century materials, Early English Books Online (EEBO), which consists of over 125,000 books published in English, primarily between the years of 1600 and 1700, drawn from Pollard & Redgrave's Short-Title Catalogue (1475–1640), Wing's Short-Title Catalogue (1641–1700), Thomason Tracts (1640–1661) and the Early English Books Tract Supplement (16th and 17th centuries).[42] In contrast to ECCO, for which results of the application of OCR to the scanned images are licensed to universities with a subscription to the resource, this is not the case for EEBO. The Early Modern OCR Project – the only research group of which we are aware that has attempted to apply OCR to the full EEBO corpus – ultimately achieved word accuracy levels of 68 percent and produced files that can be searched online at www.18thconnect.org. A researcher who makes manual corrections using this online interface is permitted to download the specific files that he or she has corrected. However, the Early Modern OCR Project's license ultimately did not allow them to make a machine-readable version of the whole of EEBO available to the wider research community in a format suitable for text and data mining. For this reason, our analyses on EEBO are necessarily restricted to the manually transcribed texts of EEBO-Text Creation Partnership (TCP). The dataset EEBO-TCP continually grows in size as new texts are transcribed and added to the dataset. At the time we obtained access to the corpus, it contained 52,915 texts in total, over 90 percent of which fell between the years 1600 and 1700, and these digitally accessible texts were also included in the analyses we present in Chapter 5.

Two further notes of explanation with respect to our use of the dataset ECCO may be helpful. It is often remarked that books printed during this period have a complex relation to the notion of the 'original' edition or to

---

[40] We have also applied a bespoke 'clean up' method in order to improve accuracy. A full explanation of this method can be found at https://concept-lab.lib.cam.ac.uk/ocranalysis .pdf.

[41] For practicality we excluded terms with a frequency of less than 13,567 in the corpus as a whole. This preserved over 95 percent of the linguistic tokens in the ECCO corpus while keeping calculations manageable. This cut-off was chosen by ranking terms by frequency and retaining the top 25,000 terms. In the case of the ECCO dataset this produced over 594 million data points.

[42] See 'Collections', Historical Texts, https://historicaltexts.jisc.ac.uk/collections%23eebo.

reprints.[43] For this reason counts of the uses of words that are based on the entire content of the dataset need to be tempered with respect to the vagaries of eighteenth century 'publication'. Furthermore, as has become clear following the detailed analysis of the dataset by Mikko Tolonen et al., the shape of the data with respect to reprints across the time frame is 'lumpy'.[44] It has also been remarked that the headline claim made by Gale, that ECCO essentially contains the vast majority of printed texts in the period, is not completely accurate. As Stephen Gregg, among others, points out, this dataset, like all datasets, is a construction.[45] This means that many decisions were made regarding the criteria for inclusion in the database: should it include variant editions of a work; what, indeed, qualifies as a 'variant' edition; how many 'marginal' authors (women, persons of colour) should be included. In the case of twenty-eight designated 'major authors', it was decided to include all variant editions. These authors were all male and white. Furthermore, the dataset is substantially slanted to long-form texts, thereby editing out the very significant production of short-form print in the period (single sheets of print that were the most common media for ballads and other forms of writing and communication an earlier generation of scholars designated as 'ephemera'). These decisions are said by some commentators on the dataset to be biases, which in one sense they are. But calling them thus runs the risk of implying that it is possible to construct an unbiased dataset, which is a fallacy: data, as the digital humanities scholar Johanna Drucker has noted, are always 'capta', constructions. It would be better to call these 'selection decisions' and to ensure that they are transparent to users of the dataset.

Noting that all data have bias should not, however, divert us from noting that the selection decisions made in the construction of ECCO do indeed have consequences. For some scholars these consequences are decisive with respect to the interpretations of the data derived from the dataset: in the current scholarly environment it has become routine to note that the failure to include texts by women or people of colour necessarily means that uses of the dataset must reproduce and perpetuate discrimination against those excluded. We agree with those who note that exposure of the silent ideologies of scholarship that underpin the selection of data in the construction of the dataset on which we base much of the

---

[43] On the book trade in the period, see James Raven, *The Business of Books: Booksellers and the English Book Trade, 1450–1850* (New Haven, CT: Yale University Press, 2007); James Raven, *Judging New Wealth: Popular Publishing and Responses to Commerce in England, 1750–1800* (Oxford: Oxford University Press, 1992).

[44] See Mikko Tolonen, Eetu Mäkelä, Ali Ijaz and Leo Lahti, 'Corpus Linguistics and Eighteenth Century Collections Online', *Research in Corpus Linguistics*, 9.1 (2021), 19–34.

[45] See Gregg, *Old Books and Digital Publishing*.

work here presented is long overdue. Not only this, we also agree with those who point out that the period we base most of our work on, the anglophone long eighteenth century, itself promoted certain values in its construction and preservation of the printed record – values that it is not unreasonable to characterise as inhospitable to women professionals, especially writers, and persons of colour who were viewed – for much of the century – by the culture of the time as unproblematically indentured people (and in terms of the construction of the polis non-persons).[46] It should also be said that although there are notable exceptions, the printed record of the period as represented in and by ECCO is also only sparsely sensitive to texts produced by largely self-taught persons (i.e. outside the formal structures of education at the time) who would most likely have been included in what the period determined as the category of labouring people (and only later deemed to be members of the working class).

If these are the silences that need to be heard, we should also note the weighting in the dataset towards 'official' British culture, whereby inclusion of texts published in Ireland and Scotland, for example, far outweighs those published in the colonies (a decision that was made with respect to what to leave out from the English Short Title Catalogue (ESTC), which is the primary source for the dataset).[47] Furthermore, the number of documents included as the century lengthens increases, thereby hard baking into the dataset the 'rise of print' thesis.[48] In relation to the chronological arguments we make in the chapters in Part II, the normalisation that our calculation of dpf employs controls for this lumpiness in the representativeness of the dataset with respect to the global archive, which is to note that our calculations of the binding of terms over the time frame of the dataset takes account of relative sparsity/density. For this reason, we believe that our claims with respect to the historical evolution or composition of concepts and ideas are securely founded. But our code does not control for other features of this lumpiness, such as the changing weights within the dataset for inclusion/exclusion of different textual genres.[49]

---

[46] See Chapter 4 for a discussion of this in relation to slavery.

[47] For further information on the construction of the eighteenth-century short title catalogue, see Gregg, *Old Books and Digital Publishing*, 12–13. It should be noted that the second generation of the ECCO dataset went some way to rectifying this, adding many texts first published in colonial America.

[48] We note here the long-standing account of the 'rise of print culture' and its causes. See William St Clair, *The Reading Nation in the Romantic Period* (Cambridge: Cambridge University Press, 2004); and also Raven, *Business of Books*.

[49] This is addressed briefly in Chapter 12. Some work is ongoing with regard to this, and we expect to present some observations at a later date.

But should these omissions and silences prevent *any* interrogation of the dataset? The issue for us is the *kind* of questions one seeks to find answers to. If, for example, one was interested in recovering the relative popularity of novels published in the period, the dirty data (its exclusions and repetitions) will have determining effects: if one takes re-editions of a text, for example, as an index to popularity, the decision to include variant editions of only twenty-eight 'major' white male authors will simply reproduce the 'bias' in the construction of the dataset. Arguments and interpretations of this kind are bound to be inaccurate. Similarly, if one was attempting to characterise the period's sensitivity to the injustice of colonialism, the fact that the dataset excludes printed materials that an earlier scholarly tradition deemed to be unimportant – ephemera – will determine the arguments and interpretations offered. Once again these are likely to be misleading with respect to the lived experience of the period. Here we believe that attention needs to be directed at how the dataset is interrogated, the uses to which such interrogation is put and the claims entered that result from such interrogations. With respect to the last of these, it should be apparent that any claim made based on the ECCO dataset must be provisional – which is to say such claims await their verification or ratification of their salience when future datasets become available that are based on different selection criteria.

With respect to how the dataset is interrogated in the work presented in this book, we set out to phrase corpus-level queries that can be explored using statistical techniques. Such a methodology cannot get around the constructedness of the dataset, but it can explore the extent to which such a massive increase in scale might be able to contribute to both the history of ideas in general (i.e. an exemplification of a methodology in the first instance) and to the more specific history of ideas in the period loosely considered to be the Enlightenment. We see both as equally significant, even when we take into account the fact that the dataset of most of the chapters in Part II is compromised by the selection criteria outlined earlier in this section. Indeed, we believe that one – albeit unintended – consequence of working with ECCO as it is currently composed is that it provides us with an opportunity to undertake further work that will probe in more exacting ways the extent to which increasing the sample size and type (i.e. including marginal voices and more varied textual forms) might alter the patterns of distribution – and hence the conceptual signatures – we here present. This is to say that it is not immediately evident, for example, that the shapes and contours of the concepts we examine in Chapters 4 through 9 would significantly change as the metric we use, as outlined earlier in this section, controls for lexical sparsity/frequency. To put the same point in a more prosaic form, one might consider the hypothesis that women, for example, in the anglophone long eighteenth century were unlikely to have operated with a significantly different concept of democracy to the one we discern in our case study, perhaps in part because women for the entire length of the historical period we examine were excluded from the publicly accredited conception of the political sphere. Such a hypothesis suggests that the inclusion of texts by women in the dataset would likely reinforce our assessment of the sexism of the age, and its deep reach into the conceptual apparatus available to all persons at the time. Whether or not this is the case is for future work to determine. And the same point can be made with respect to Chapter 4, which uncovers the complex ideas of liberty and freedom as they operated in the period effectively blind to the ways in which the official, male and white discourses of politics constructed the idea of slavery so as to hide or erase the practice of widely acknowledged chattel slavery (see Chapter 4, Section 3).

Some scholars have taken the view that given the OCR issue and the construction decisions made when ECCO was produced, it is better to use the more accurate but massively reduced-in-size dataset ECCO-TCP. That dataset, of course, was also subject to selection decisions: in this case the database has a very high proportion of novels. As noted above, we made the decision to use the full ECCO in many of our case studies in full knowledge of its constructiveness, and we did so because the kind of data analytics we wanted to carry out are enhanced by scale. Thus, we recognise that there are trade-offs in respect to the decision to use the full ECCO dataset as opposed to the more textually accurate ECCO-TCP. Such trade-offs are implicit in the initial decision to move from human-scale reading, with its inbuilt selection criteria and accuracy level, to machine scale. And the issue of scale kicks in again when considering full ECCO against the small selection of it in ECCO-TCP. Moreover, when using this subset of the corpus, the selection process has been effectively 'squared' as another set of criteria operate in the construction of the smaller but more textually accurate hand-corrected dataset. Reading at scale, at the largest scale currently available, knowing that the dataset is about 50 percent smaller than the ESTC on which it is based, and that it contains OCR noise, is still an improvement over hyper-selective human-scale reading of a massive archive if one is intending to make general statements about trends, traditions, histories in the period as a whole. Although it is not frequently acknowledged, traditional humanities research that aspires to present accurate accounts of large-scale trends, movements or histories based on human-scale reading is necessarily hampered by its highly selective use of 'representative' extracts, quotations and intuitions about the shape and content of the full archive.[50] While machine-scale analytics are also skewed by selectivity and construction decisions, they provide a more secure underpinning for general statements about the archive.

2.2.4   *Constructing Co-association Profiles from ECCO*

Once we were confident that the tools we were constructing were able to open up the architecture of concepts to inspection, we began to work on a number of case studies that were focused on diachronic desiderata. How, for example, was the concept of liberty configured over time, and did its configuration map seamlessly onto the structure of the concept freedom?[51] Our focus had also become firmly centred on ECCO because it not only provided us with access to a massive dataset (massive, that is, for historians and humanities scholars more generally), but also because its chronological segmentation allows one to track diachronic change (in this case year by year, or decade by decade or any other year spread across the eighteenth century). The tools we had built provided the basic data on, effectively, the co-associations between each and every term in the corpus.[52] And we represented this data via a metric (*dpf*) that ranked scores for every pair of bound terms in the dataset. With respect to the shape of the dataset indicated earlier in this section, it is important to note that the metrics we employ do not merely count the number of times that pairs of terms co-associate in different time frames, but also account for the overall frequencies of those terms within those time frames. Combined with the fact that we are attending to how co-association strength changes over time in relative (not absolute) terms, our metrics were designed to control for the fact that fewer documents are available for some time frames within the dataset than for others.[53]

---

[50] For a good and balanced account of this issue, see Andrew Piper, *Can We Be Wrong? The Problem of Textual Evidence in a Time of Data* (Cambridge: Cambridge University Press, 2020).

[51] This case study is presented in Part II, Chapter 5.

[52] For practicality we excluded terms with a frequency of less than 13,567 in the corpus as a whole. This preserved over 95 percent of the linguistic tokens in the ECCO corpus while keeping calculations manageable. This cut-off was chosen by ranking terms by frequency and retaining the top 25,000 terms. In the case of the ECCO dataset, this produced over 594 million data points.

[53] For purposes of computing the metrics described in Section 2.2.1, the 'dataset' corresponds to the subset of the corpus in the time slice under investigation. Suppose some term A co-associates most with term B, less with term C, and still less with term D from 1701 to 1730. If the underlying distribution is identical for some other time frame – say 1770–1800 – this relative ordering will typically remain consistent (in expectation) even if the number of documents sampled from that time frame is much larger. Conversely, if a different pattern is observed in the latter time frame – say, term D shoots up to the top of A's list – then the causes of this may merit further investigation.

Let us recall that we say that lexical terms are bound when they are considerably more likely than in random distribution to co-associate, and for this to be so, the strength of their co-association must be higher than the threshold described in Section 2.2.2. As we have already noted, the most obvious cause of such binding at proximity, say within five words, must be grammar or idiom. Black co-associates with white because there is a common English phrase 'black and white'. But when we find strenuous binding (high levels of *dpf* and large numbers of bound terms above the threshold) at much larger range, say 100 terms apart, the co-association can only be partially explained in this way.

Here, as an example of the kinds of analytic work that will feature in the case studies, we present a comparison of two co-association profiles, one for the term aristocracy and the other for liberty. In each case we have restricted the time frame to 1760–1800, and in each case we have made a comparison between the profile at a distance of 10 and of 100 terms apart. Table 2.2 shows the shape we find for aristocracy.

Note that the list of 650 bound terms at distance ten has been ranked according to the *dpf* value with the highest appearing at the top of the list, and for immediate purposes we have curtailed the list after ten terms. Here one can see that a *dpf* value is always going to be higher at closer distance, but the decrease of that value over distance varies considerably term by term. The total number of terms that appear on this ranked list at

Table 2.2 *The top ten terms having the highest* dpf *values with focal token aristocracy at distances of 10 and 100 among all documents in ECCO published from 1760 to 1800 (118,166 documents; 6.3 billion tokens; 13,532 instances of aristocracy).*

Distance 10 (top 10 of 650 total)				Distance 100 (top 10 of 473 total)			
Bound token	*dpf*	N (total)	N (with focal)	Bound token	*dpf*	N (total)	N (with focal)
democracy	64840	18497	366	aristocracy	44309	13532	196
aristocracy	37979	13532	168	democracy	13995	18497	79
monarchy	14205	100405	300	impeded	5603	12984	24
monarchical	11518	14234	53	monarchy	4593	100405	97
despotism	7858	24368	55	republics	4046	20766	25
plebeians	6900	10476	25	independents	3964	8321	12
republics	6474	20766	40	governments	3725	75519	63
republic	6352	167540	200	monarchical	3477	14234	16
nobles	6347	121945	156	nobles	3418	121945	84
patricians	6268	12461	26	legislators	3272	16629	17

distance 10 – 650 – is relatively high (see Figure 2.3, which indicates that the average number is just less than 475). Thus, we can say that aristocracy has strong binding since both the values of the *dpf* scores for each bound term (see following example) and the total number of terms to which it is bound (over the threshold) is high. We can compare this profile with that for liberty (see Table 2.3).

Here one can see that the highest bound *dpf* value for this term at a distance of 10 terms is ten times lower than for aristocracy (6,457 compared with 64,840). And the number of terms that appear on its ranked list of bound terms – 222 at distance 10 and 114 at distance 100 – is around about one third as many. In this case we say that, comparatively, liberty has weak binding, where the criterion for strength is the number of co-associates and the value of *dpf*. This can be understood conversely as an index to the coherence and consistency of the concept or to the intensity of its focalisation. This immediately raises a question about the correlation between word frequency and strength of binding, addressed below in our corpus-level analyses.

These profiles can be inspected across the time frame of the dataset and in slices that can be as fine grained as year by year. If one takes an earlier forty-year slice, 1710–50, the profile for aristocracy is remarkably stable across distance: 586 bound terms at a distance of 10 terms apart and 598

Table 2.3 *The top ten terms having the highest* dpf *values with focal token* liberty *at distances of 10 and 100 among all documents in ECCO published from 1760 to 1800 (118,166 documents; 6.3 billion tokens; 1,006,661 instances of* liberty*).*

Distance 10 (top 10 of 222 total)				Distance 100 (top 10 of 114 total)			
Bound token	*dpf*	*N* (total)	*N* (with focal)	Bound token	*dpf*	*N* (total)	*N* (with focal)
liberty	6457	1006661	23736	liberty	4913	1006661	18060
slavery	5137	81379	2655	freedom	2029	304737	2937
licentiousness	4813	19069	802	slavery	1904	81379	984
bondage	4042	61827	1686	despotism	1809	24368	365
despotism	3886	24368	784	the	1732	342936734	601339
freedom	3755	304737	5435	rights	1653	382943	2859
servitude	3278	36319	903	of	1644	217896928	400764
tyranny	3173	128449	2341	government	1641	1213708	6983
restraint	2888	45292	945	despotic	1620	30363	388
tyrants	2769	63198	1175	constitution	1602	427234	3019

at a distance of 100. Furthermore, the *dpf* values are considerably higher: the top score is for the term democracy and is 106,703 at distance 10. This can be compared with the profile of liberty: at distance 10, 128 terms are on its binding list, and at distance 100 terms this falls to 45. And the *dpf* values are correspondingly low: the top bound-term at distance 10 is liberty itself with a score of 4,439.

The Lab created profiles for thousands of terms in the dataset ECCO in order to ascertain if patterns might emerge that would help us understand the architectures of concepts more clearly. In the case studies presented in Part II, we demonstrate ways in which such profiles can complement traditional histories of ideas through what we think of as an 'emergent digital history of ideas', for which we provide some context in Section 2.3. Here we set out some corpus-level interrogations of the dataset in order to create benchmarks against which the more detailed dives into the data in our case studies can be set. The first graph, Figure 2.1, indicates the overall shape of the corpus in terms of number of tokens, and it can be seen that the size of the corpus in each year increases steadily from 50 million tokens to 150 million tokens between 1700 and 1780. The size each year accelerates for the final twenty years of the century, with approximately 200 million tokens per year by 1800.

Throughout the book we present data for individual terms in relation to their bound terms, and one benchmark that will be invaluable is the

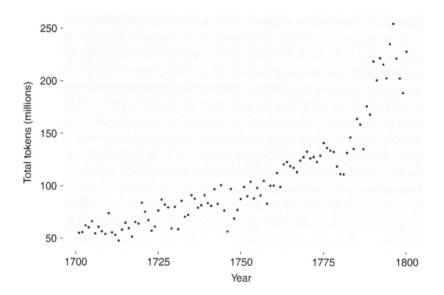

Figure 2.1 Number of tokens per year. Source: ECCO.

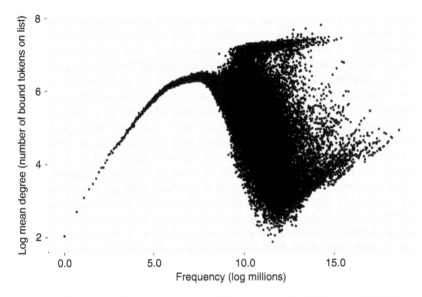

Figure 2.2 Correlation of word frequency with *dpf.* Source: ECCO.

relation of word frequency to the number of co-associated bound terms. Figure 2.2 provides the corpus-level analysis of the effect of frequency on lexical binding.

Figure 2.2 plots the mean degrees of all terms above our frequency threshold, aggregated across multiple distances and time slices – that is the average number of terms on the *dpf* list for all combinations of four distances (10, 40, 70, 100) and ten decades (1701–10, 1711–20, etc.) that share a common frequency. These mean degrees are plotted against the frequencies of the terms in the corresponding time slices. This shows that at very low frequencies there is a strong association between word frequency and degree. However, for words that have overall frequencies in the tens of thousands, there is no strong relationship between frequency and degree. The overall correlation between frequency and degree is weak (Pearson correlation = −0.063).

The next benchmark, Figure 2.3, indicates the corpus-level degree to which a word is bound to co-associates as a function of window size or distance. It can be seen that, on average, the number of items on a word's list is just less than 475 when the context window is at distance 10 from the target word. The average degree is within a fairly narrow range across the four distances tested (10, 40, 70, 100), but there is a slight decline at longer distance.

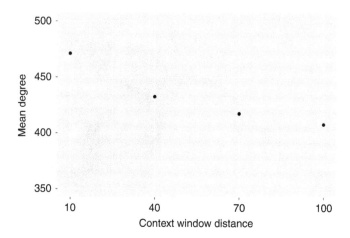

Figure 2.3 Average (i.e. mean) number of terms on the *dpf* list after the bend in the curve is correlated with window size. Source: ECCO.

Averaging does not show the distribution or dispersion of degree for all tokens at a particular distance. To examine this, Figure 2.4 shows box and density plots for the degree of all tokens at each distance, indicating the median and the interquartile range. This confirms that for most tokens the degree is concentrated within a range of 250–750.

Does the corpus indicate that our measurements of *dpf* are driven by warps in the distribution of documents over time? Figure 2.5 indicates that the average number of co-associates for any term (mean degree) varies little over the century, although it does rise very slightly in the middle of the century.

A focal term's 'neighbours' are those terms that are bound to it, those terms that appear on its *dpf* list. How likely are any given term's neighbours to be connected to each other, and how does that vary by term frequency, context-window size and time? The standard measure for this is the *local clustering coefficient*.[54] This is calculated for a given term as the number of connections between its neighbours, divided by the number of connections that are theoretically possible if the network were fully connected. In network terminology, we have 'directed edges' – term X can appear on term *y*'s *dpf* list without

---

[54] Duncan J. Watts and Steven Strogatz, 'Collective Dynamics of "Small-World" Networks', *Nature*, 393 (1998), 440–2.

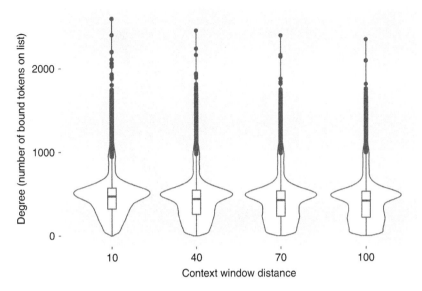

Figure 2.4 'Violin' plot showing density, median and interquartile range of degree for all tokens at each distance. Source: ECCO.

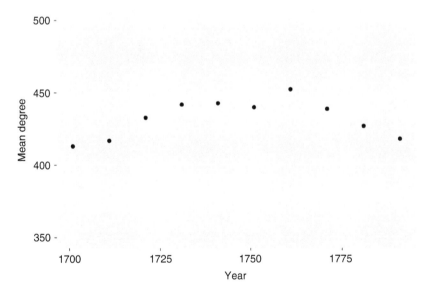

Figure 2.5 Average number of terms on *dpf* correlated with year. Source: ECCO.

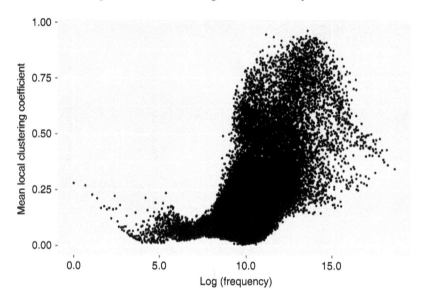

Figure 2.6 Relationship between clustering coefficients and term frequency. Source: ECCO.

the reverse being true – and we therefore use Watts and Strogatz's formula for computing local clustering coefficients for directed graphs. Figure 2.6 illustrates the relationship between clustering and (natural) log frequency.

In Figure 2.2, we saw that the strong relationship between frequency and degree came apart for words whose frequency within a particular time slice exceeded 8 million. Here, we see that the relationship between clustering coefficient and frequency starts to come apart at far lower frequencies – namely when the natural log of the frequency is ~7 (frequencies around ~1,000). This suggests that even for many terms that are strongly correlated with mean degree (e.g. those with Ns less than 8 million), the clustering coefficients indexing broader patterns of connection are less influenced by frequency. Figure 2.7, however, illustrates that as distance increases, clustering coefficients increase, which is likely to be a consequence of the lower length of the *dpf* lists at the larger distances noted in Figure 2.3.

Similarly, because word frequency is correlated with time, and time is correlated with degree, it is not surprising to see a relationship between clustering coefficients and time, as shown by Figure 2.8.

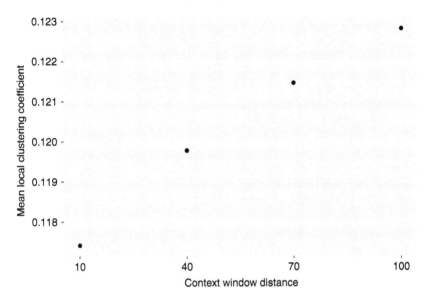

Figure 2.7 Relationship between clustering coefficients and distance. Source: ECCO.

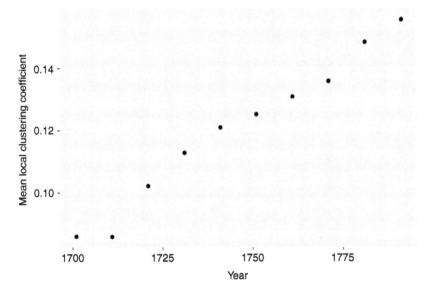

Figure 2.8 Relationship between clustering coefficients and time. Source: ECCO.

2.2.5   *Persistent Lexis and the Construction of 'Conceptual Cores'*

The shared lexis tool enables one to discern the company a term keeps at spans from 5 words to 100 words away. This presents us with an opportunity to experiment with different ranges of distance counts in order to dig deeper into what we consider to be the conceptual rather than the purely semantic ties that bind terms in a co-association pattern or distribution. If, as Firth maintained, the meaning of a term is determined by the 'company it keeps', what can we discover if we extend the range of that company, from close to distant? And then ascertain what bound lexis persists across different distances. In Chapter 4 we construct this measure by taking the distances at three markers (10, 50 and 100) in order to compare the profiles for two candidate terms, liberty and republican, as we explore the slow entanglement of these concepts in the evolution of the modern idea of liberty. In Chapter 7 we take this measure further in our discernment of what we take to be the 'core' of a conceptual form. Here we take each *dpf* list at increasing sizes of ten, that is at distance 10, 20, 30 and so on, up to 100 and aggregate the common bound-lexis to all ten lists. The resulting list of terms – those that are bound at all distances – represents what is most strenuously in the company of the candidate concept.

2.2.6   *Vector Subtraction and Pearson Correlation*

As we have seen above, the shared lexis tool creates binding lists for any search query at any distance 5, 10, 20, . . . 100 and for every year or date range in the ECCO dataset. The lists of bound lexis are cut off 'above the bend in the curve' (see Section 2.2.2) and each co-association is given a score (*dpf*) that we take to measure the force of its binding. We can calculate the mean score of binding for any list as also the total number of terms on the list, and these calculations constitute a computational *vector*. It now becomes possible to inspect the differences and similarities between two or more such vectors, by performing a range of calculations upon them. These enable us to see how the same term's binding profile changes across time or at different lexical windows, or to inspect the salient similarities or differences between two or more different terms.

The tool also enables us to make vector comparisons by using simple maths: addition, multiplication, subtraction and division. Each reveals different statistical trends. Vector *addition* enables the user to note where two (or more) terms have a high combined *dpf*. Vector *multiplication* is similar but demonstrates more clearly where two (or more) terms *both* have a high *dpf*. (If terms A and B each bind term C with a *dpf* of 7, multiplication will generate a value (49) much higher than if the respective bindings were 1 and 14; whereas with addition, the latter would have a higher value.) Vector *subtraction* allows us to perceive a significant discrepancy between two *dpf* values. Vector *division* similarly reveals disparities but gives a clearer indication of their relative value. (If term A and term B bind term C with a *dpf* of 14 and 7, respectively, subtraction will yield 7, and division will yield 2; if term D and term E bind term F with a *dpf* of 28 and 21, subtraction will still yield 7, but division will yield a much lower value of 1.333.)

In Chapters 6 and 9 we explore ways in which vector subtraction can help us understand the profiles of candidate concepts as historical forms. In Chapter 6 we use this subtraction to discern the changing composition of the concept across the eighteenth century. In Chapter 9 something similar is applied to the concept irritability, and its profile is also compared through vector subtraction with those of other concepts (habit and system).

We have also explored ways in which statistical methods designed to make high-dimensional spaces more intelligible can help us discern large-scale patterns in lexical co-association. One such method, using a Pearson correlation, is employed in Chapters 5 and 6. Here we briefly outline the basis for using such a method. Let us begin by considering what it means to represent a word as a point in a high-dimensional space. To express the location of a point in a three-dimensional space requires three numbers, commonly denoted x, y and z. Although we cannot visualise mathematical spaces exceeding three dimensions, it is nevertheless the case that a list of 1,000 numbers can be conceived of as a point in a 1,000-dimensional space, and we can calculate the 'distance' between these points using mathematics analogous to that used to calculate the distance between two points in the physical world. If 1,000 numbers are generated for two words in such a way that these numbers will be similar if the words appear in similar lexical contexts, then we can quantify how 'close' or 'far' their lexical contexts are away from each other. In this context, the standard Pearson correlation frequently used in statistics can be regarded as a measure of the 'closeness' of two words' lexical contexts.[55] Thus, in Chapters 5 and 6 we have computed Pearson correlations between lexical vectors constructed from the indicated *dpf* lists, which (remember) include an element – the value or score – representing the force of binding between the focal term and all its listed co-associates. If one turns to Chapter 5, Section 2, we can see an example at work. In this case the 22nd, 23rd and

---

[55] See, for example, Douglass L. Rohde, Laura M. Gonnerman and David C. Plaut, 'An Improved Model of Semantic Similarity Based on Lexical Co-occurrence', *Communications of the ACM*, 8 (2006), 627–63.

24th elements of the vector for government contain the values for *dpf* (government, abbess), *dpf*(government, abbey) and *dpf*(government, abbot), respectively; likewise, the 22nd, 23rd and 24th elements of the vector for tyranny contain the values for *dpf*(tyranny, abbess), *dpf*(tyranny, abbey) and *dpf*(tyranny, abbot). When we correlate these lists using the Pearson correlation, we are able to discern in more granular detail the extent to which the candidate concepts (here government and tyranny) share a high-dimensional space. As will be seen throughout our case studies, the purpose for doing this is to capture computationally the emergence of ideas from a conceptual substrate represented by the high-dimensional co-association patterns we have discovered.

2.3   Text Mining and the Emergent Digital History of Ideas

The aim of the current volume is to present some explorative work in the digital history of ideas. Although this kind of work has yet to become widespread, as it develops it will need to be contextualised with other projects that have begun to use text mining techniques based on computational methods in fields adjacent to the history of ideas. In the case studies that follow in Part II, we demonstrate the utility of these exemplary methods for reading at scale. As has already been noted, the findings we present are intended to complement and not replace traditional modes of reading the archive upon which the history of ideas has been built over the last half century. In some cases, we seek to confirm the conclusions and arguments within this tradition of scholarship; in others we seek to revise them. The potential benefit of this new way of reading the archive is the production of a kind of counterweight to the history of ideas that locates such ideas in 'persons', actors who engaged in social and political activities in the past, of which speech was one such action or deed. Our exemplary case studies work from the evidence of culture-wide uses of language to be found in historic textual datasets – which we take to contain the traces of the ways in which ideas in the past were articulated – effectively mapping the various constructions and contestations of ideas at the most general level of the printed archive. We acknowledge that this exploration of the digital history of ideas uses a selective and partial dataset, but we also contend that, at the current time, it provides the most extensive computationally interrogatable access to the print culture of the anglophone long eighteenth century.

This approach can be compared to a number of other projects that use the same or similar techniques, mostly focused on a slightly different area of inquiry, semantic change. The Linguistic DNA project, based in Sheffield, for example, also uses methods developed in corpus and computational linguistics. This project focuses on the early modern period, using a transcribed subset of EEBO (EEBO-TCP) in combination with a thesaurus categorisation of word senses from the period to examine the change over time of raw word association frequencies and PMI scores between pairs of terms of interest.[56] A different project based in Amsterdam, Texcavator, allows users to explore the development of sentiment around issues in newspaper text, presenting results in the form of histograms of word clouds and word and sentiment dictionary frequencies, alongside document metadata.[57] And a project based in Brussels has created a method for multidimensional scaling of distributional semantic change, in order to analyse a change in meaning in positive evaluative adjectives in American English from 1860 to 2000, using PMI weighted co-occurrence scores derived from ten word windows around the term of interest.[58] Lastly, there is also a project based in Helsinki that aims to analyse publication trends in the field of history in early modern Britain and North America in 1470–1800, based on ESTC data.[59] The major difference between the work we present here and these other projects is our intended aim to contribute a new methodology for the history of ideas.

[56] See Susan Fitzmaurice, Justyna A. Robinson, Marc Alexander et al., 'Linguistic DNA: Investigating Conceptual Change in Early Modern English Discourse', *Studia Neophilologica*, 89. S1 (2017), 21–38.

[57] See Joris van Eijnatten, Toine Pieters and Jaap Verheul, 'Using Texcavator to Map Public Discourse', *Tijdschrift voor Tijdschriftstudies*, 35 (2014), 59–65.

[58] See Kris Heylen, Thomas Wielfaert and Dirk Speelman, 'Tracking Change in Word Meaning; A Dynamic Visualization of Diachronic Distributional Semantic Models', DGfS 2013 Workshop on the Visualization of Linguistic Patterns, University of Konstanz, Germany, www.yumpu.com/en/document/view/17822745/tracking-change-in-word-meaning-a-dynamic-visualization-of-.

[59] See Mikko Tolonen, Leo Lahti and Niko Ilomäki, 'A Quantitative Study of History in the English Short-Title Catalogue (ESTC), 1470–1800', *Liber Quarterly*, 25.2 (2015), 87–116.

3 Operationalising Conceptual Structure

Paul Nulty

3.1 Introduction

When discussing the structure of political and social concepts, writers in the humanities and social sciences often make use of metaphors that suggest structured and networked representations. Perhaps responding to these metaphors, or perhaps simply because of the striking nature of the images that can be produced, researchers in DH have begun to produce network diagrams in order to illustrate the connections among concepts. Since at least the work of Walter B. Gallie on essentially contested concepts, writers have often described concepts as having a 'common core' shared among multiple 'conceptions' – possible versions of concepts that may be held at different times or in different cultures, sharing a core meaning but differing in their 'periphery' or their 'topography'.[1] Working in the same area of political theory, Michael Freeden allows that particular descriptions are not only normative but 'empirically ascertainable and describable'.[2]

John Gray, again examining the notion of essential contestability, gives perhaps the most visually descriptive and explicitly structural example:

> there are concepts, identifiable by their users by appeal to a common core of meaning, whose history is marked by persistent and apparently intractable dispute as to the criteria of their correct application. . . . Contenders in any such definitional dispute will typically be found to disagree about the correct criteria of a whole range of contextually related concepts, where these disagreements are not haphazard or random, but will tend to be mutually supportive or interlocking. Each use of a contested concept of this kind typically rests upon, presupposes, or endorses a definite use of a whole constellation of satellite concepts, so that definitional disputes in relation to such concepts are indicative of conflicts between divergent patterns of thought – which are often, if not typically, partly constitutive of rival ways of life. . . . [This research] seeks to uncover and bring to

---

[1] John Rawls, *A Theory of Justice* (Cambridge, MA: Harvard University Press, 1971), 5.
[2] Michael Freeden, 'Political Concepts and Ideological Morphology', *Journal of Political Philosophy*, 2.2 (1994), 140–64.

light the skeletons of rival patterns of thought whose existence is intimated by protracted definitional disputes over single concepts.[3]

Given this tendency towards picturing or visualising concepts and their relations to each other using networked structures, it would seem appropriate to engage with modes and methods of visualisation that are available to us using computational and mathematical forms of modelling.[4] In this chapter I outline some of the steps that are necessary in building models for representing concepts using some of these methods. In particular I draw attention to some of the crucial choices one faces in this task that determine not only how the resulting visualisations look but also, and more importantly, what these visualisations reveal or allow us to inspect. Furthermore, as shall become clear, the very foundation of the data that feed into the visualisation algorithms is itself subject to choice. This is to note that there is more than one way of measuring word association, the underlying metric used in most of the case studies in this book, and indeed the very basis for capturing 'association' between words is itself far from self-evident.

These considerations apply both to the instrumental task of drawing a conceptual network on a screen or a page in order to inspect it, and also to the deeper question of what properties conceptual networks might actually have if we believe that concepts are in some sense truly or intrinsically networks in their cognitive or cultural manifestation. This chapter addresses the choices we make when representing concepts structurally and argues that the method of measuring their associations should not be left to statisticians or network scientists but rather be interrogated by historians of ideas as they pursue specific research questions. I proceed by presenting examples of various choices of word association measures, and show how the distribution of association scores and the degree and weight thresholds employed to create edges in network graphs help us to understand the structure of particular groups of nodes. These methodological choices are themselves motivated

---

[3] John N. Gray, 'On the Contestability of Social and Political Concepts', *Political Theory*, 5.3 (1977), 331–48.

[4] Another example of this perspective, with a particular resonance for the method of distributional semantics, is found in Foucault's *Archaeology of Knowledge*: 'one does not attach the constants of discourse to the ideal structures of the concept, but one describes the conceptual network on the basis of the intrinsic regularities of discourse; one does not subject the multiplicity of statements to the coherence of concepts, and this coherence to the silent recollection of a meta-historical ideality; one establishes the inverse series: one replaces the pure aims of non-contradiction in a complex network of conceptual compatibility and incompatibility; and one relates this complexity to the rules that characterize a particular discursive practice'. Michel Foucault, *The Archaeology of Knowledge* (New York: Pantheon, 1972), 69.

according to the specific theory or model of cultural and cognitive knowledge that one might subscribe to.

In what follows I demonstrate the utility of a method by which one
iteratively moves through a precise set of computational steps in order to
establish both a robust metric of word association and a representation
of conceptual structure. This is intended as an example of the general
practice of operationalisation in DH, and it aligns with the working
practices of the Cambridge Concept Lab in its promotion of a functional
analysis of concepts. What is meant by 'operationalisation' can be gleaned
from the sixth pamphlet published by the Stanford Literary Lab in which
Franco Moretti begins by quoting a passage from Percy W. Bridgman's
Logic of Modern Physics (1927) where the 'operational point of view' is
put forward, using as an example the concept of length:

> What do we mean by the length of an object? To find the length of an object we
> have to perform certain physical operations. The concept of length is therefore
> fixed when the operations by which length is fixed are fixed: that is, the concept of
> length involves as much and nothing more than the set of operations by which
> length is determined. In general, we mean by any concept nothing more than a set
> of operations; the concept is synonymous with the corresponding set of
> operations ... the proper definition of a concept is not in terms of its properties
> but in terms of actual operations.[5]

Paraphrasing Bridgman, but using the concept of word association
instead of length, we might ask: what do we mean by the association
between words? The concept of word association involves as much and
nothing more than the set of operations by which word association is
determined. According to this definition of conceptuality, the proper
definition of word association is in terms of the actual operations that
we perform to calculate it. This is to note that word association is
a measurement. In the following I outline a selection of available methods
that I consider to be accessible to researchers who do not have deep
statistical training. Such methods embrace a range of word association
measures and network visualisation techniques. The chapter is intended
to be exemplary, as it is often remarked in DH that more productive
collaborations between humanists and computer scientists can be fos-
tered by increasing each other's understanding of their respective fields,
that is for humanists to have greater understanding of digital methods and
for computer scientists to have fuller appreciation of historical context
and theory. But when seen in the light of operationalising concepts,

---

[5] Franco Moretti, '"Operationalizing": or, The Function of Measurement in Modern
Literary Theory', Stanford Literary Lab Pamphlet 6 (2014), 1, where he is quoting
Percy W. Bridgman, The Logic of Modern Physics, III (New York: Macmillan, 1927), 5–6.

mutual intelligibility is not just desirable but essential, because the humanist and the scientist are engaged in the same task.[6]

3.2 Measuring Word Association

As outlined in Chapter 2, we set out to map conceptual structures by measuring how words associate with each other based on counts of their co-occurrences in context in large bodies of text.[7] This is familiar ground in corpus linguistics, and the same principles, with somewhat more opaque and intricate methods, are widely applied in natural language processing.

The precise details of these methods are often not fully laid out in work in the humanities that relies on them, perhaps because they are thought to be too technical, or perhaps because particular methodological choices are thought to be best left to the statistical or computational experts who build the tools. However, in many cases, the decisions that must be taken when algorithmically operationalising qualitative concepts such as association, similarity or relatedness depend on prior judgements about what such notions are taken to capture. When looking for a formula to capture the notion of word association from a table of word co-occurrence counts, one cannot simply ask the statistician or corpus linguist to supply it without also specifying how the notions of association, similarity or relatedness are themselves to be operationalised. Of course, some abstraction is appropriate – if every single detail of the underlying algorithm were necessary, the map becomes the territory and generalisation is no longer possible – but I hope to show here that many details of the implementation are in fact part of the normal work of humanists engaged in the study of the history of concepts and ideas. Having said this, the issue is made more complicated by the vast and ever-expanding volume of research in corpus linguistics, computational linguistics and cognitive psychology that sets out methods for measuring word association, in which each discipline and sub-discipline has subtly different goals and intellectual genealogies.

3.3 Different Conceptions of Association

Currently, perhaps the most widely used methods for calculating word associations from corpus statistics are word vectors or word embeddings. In this approach, a vector of relatively low dimension (several hundred

---

[6] I have so far spoken of operationalising word associations, while the title of this chapter refers to concepts. I will return to the distinction in Section 3.7.
[7] In this chapter I use the term co-occurrence in the broad sense indicating that terms occur within a certain (possibly large) window of each other. Chapter 2, Section 1, explains the use of the term co-association by other authors.

numbers) is constructed from word co-occurrences either by reducing the dimension of the full co-occurrence matrix (count-based methods such as Glove) or using the hidden layer of a shallow neural network trained to predict word contexts. These methods have many advantages in applications: they are computationally fast compared to previous approaches, the similarity of words can be estimated by standard vector-distance metrics, and particular aspects of meaning can be examined by comparing words along a dimension defined by a pair of words chosen by the researcher. However, the actual elements of the resulting vectors do not correspond to actual co-occurrence counts. Direct connection between co-occurrence counts and word representation is lost. Stephen McGregor, describing a system that uses sparse, context-sensitive paradigmatic co-occurrences argues:

> It seems impossible to imagine how a space defined by, typically, dozens to hundreds of purely abstract dimensions could ever be construed as containing the kind of conceptual differentiation that is evidently inherent in the relationship between minds and the world. This is not to say that a number representing the likelihood of two words occurring in the same context should be construed in the same richly interrelated and elaborately differentiated way of Gärdenfors' highly structured, complexly delineated conceptual spaces. Nonetheless, a space of numbers that serve both as anchors for the meaningful positioning of points and also as indicators that can be independently associated with events, even events which are themselves relatively abstract, is somehow more in the world than an essentially indivisible space of mere positions. In particular, in an unreduced base lexical space of sparse, literal co-occurrence dimensions, there remains some hope of constructing contextualised projections by making an informed decision about which dimensions would best serve as the basis for these projections.[8]

In addition, it is not always clear exactly what notion of word similarity is captured by the cosine distance between word vectors. There is an ambiguity even in the phrase 'co-occurs with' – we might count when one word occurs near to another in the same stretch of text (a syntagmatic, or 'first-order' co-occurrence, such as 'the *bark* wore off the *tree*'), or when both words have been observed to occur in separate stretches of text but in the same context (a paradigmatic, or 'second-order' co-occurrence, such as 'the *oak* stood in the wind' and 'the *maple* stood in the wind'). Word association measures based on vector distances between paradigmatic co-occurrences tend to capture words that are similar in the sense that they are easily substitutable for each other. Measures based on literal syntagmatic co-occurrence counts tend to capture words that are related

---

[8] Stephen McGregor, Kat Agres, Matthew Purver and Geraint A. Wiggins, 'From Distributional Semantics to Conceptual Spaces: A Novel Computational Method for Concept Creation', *Journal of Artificial General Intelligence*, 6.1 (2015), 55–86.

or associated generally, but not necessarily similar: *oak* and *maple* are similar; *tree* and *bark* are related.

A word embedding produced by word2vec is the hidden layer of a shallow neural network that is trained either to predict a target word given its context (the continuous-bag-of-words, or CBOW approach) or to predict context words given a central target word (the 'skip-gram' approach). The count-based Glove method also tends to capture paradigmatic associations: the counts are not used directly to measure word similarity; rather, the matrix of counts is reduced to vectors representing words, which can be compared using vector similarity. In practice, for a number of reasons, word2vec and Glove do also capture some syntagmatic relationships: words that are substitutable (or their synonyms and antonyms) also often occur near one another, and generalisations captured by the dimensionality reduction method enhance this effect.[9]

All this might seem esoteric, but the implications for doing the history of ideas are immediate. Is oligarchy more associated with wealth, or government? The answer will be different depending on whether we have in mind a paradigmatic or syntagmatic kind of association. Deciding this is as important for the humanist as the statistician. It remains the case, however, that the ambiguity in kind of association, combined with the mathematical nature of the dimensionality reduction techniques, result in word embedding methods being relatively opaque to humanities researchers in most cases. For this reason, and following the argument put forward by McGregor, in this book we begin the process of measuring word association using direct syntagmatic co-occurrence counts in a particular window.

These direct counts have been shown to correlate well with human word association judgements, and are relatively interpretable to the non-specialist.[10] In summary, it is not really possible to directly trace the relationship between specific word co-occurrence frequencies and word embeddings produced by Glove and word2vec, and as we have seen, both the type of association and robustness of the measurement are somewhat opaque. In contrast, the syntagmatic word-association scores that will be the focus of the following discussion are widely used in corpus linguistics and lexicography and only rely on basic arithmetic operations using word co-occurrence statistics.

---

[9] Omer Levy, Yoav Goldberg and Ido Dagan, 'Improving Distributional Similarity with Lessons Learned from Word Embeddings', in *Transactions of the Association for Computational Linguistics*, III, ed. Michael Collins and Lillian Lee (Cambridge, MA: MIT Press, 2015), 211–25.

[10] Reinhard Rapp, 'The Computation of Word Associations: Comparing Syntagmatic and Paradigmatic Approaches', in *COLING 2002: The 19th International Conference on Computational Linguistics* (2002).

3.4   Expected Co-occurrence

The distinction between paradigmatic and syntagmatic association is not the only difficulty that arises when operationalising word association. Any method that begins by counting co-occurrences quickly runs into the problem that the most frequent co-occurrences for a particular word tend to be words that are generally frequent in the language or corpus overall. In order to mitigate this issue, researchers often step in and remove very frequent words (e.g. of, in, for, the, to, etc., referred to as 'stopwords') from the process. But the problem is deeper than this.

In Table 3.1 we can see that even when the most obvious stopwords have been removed, some function words remain, and making the filter more sensitive would not obviously fix the issue, for example should 'may' be a stopword?[11] Or 'said'? Even ignoring these cases, the list contains some of the most frequent words in the English language: time, people, man, one. This is what results if we naively operationalise the concept of association by equating it literally with a count of

Table 3.1 *The most frequent co-occurrences (after removing the most common stopwords) with the word liberty in a random subset of 3,000 documents (2,198,379 words). Date spread 1790–5. Source: ECCO.*

Focal	Bound	Freq.
liberty	may	2355
liberty	upon	2281
liberty	would	2191
liberty	one	2111
liberty	liberty	1692
liberty	every	1566
liberty	great	1537
liberty	without	1293
liberty	shall	1232
liberty	made	1160
liberty	could	1115
liberty	time	1045
liberty	much	987
liberty	man	941
liberty	people	940

---

[11] All co-occurrence counts in this chapter are from a window of ten words centred ten away words from the target word.

how often words co-occur with each other. Perhaps this seems obvious, but even in the domain of corpus linguistics, there is no consensus on how this bias towards generally frequent words should be corrected for, although there are many heuristics and empirically successful approaches.

Usually, the next step is to compensate for the overall corpus frequency of the co-occurring term by using the notion of *expected frequency*.[12] The expected frequency is an estimate of how often the words would be expected to co-occur by chance, given their general frequencies, if they were independently distributed. The joint probability of independent events is calculated by multiplying their individual probabilities, so the expected frequency is estimated by multiplying the individual frequencies of the two words divided by the size of the corpus. To get a strict probability measurement, it is also necessary to divide by the window size. However, the corpus size and window size are constants across all words, so their effect is only to scale the result by a constant – this part of the calculation does not affect the ordering of word association lists or the relative distance between scores.

A worked example shows how this compensates for the effect of general frequency. Suppose that in a particular corpus, the terms phlogiston, gas, and experiments have the following overall frequencies:

- phlogiston: 13943
- gas: 81685
- experiments: 243518

and the following co-occurrence frequencies as given in Table 3.2.

By raw frequency count, the strongest association is between experiments and gas. However, the observed frequency divided by the expected

Table 3.2 *Co-occurrence frequencies for phlogiston, experiments and gas.*

Word 1	Word 2	Co-occurrence count
phlogiston	gas	8
experiments	phlogiston	65
experiments	gas	256

---

[12] Expected frequency and most of the other measures and statistics described in this section are taken from Stefan Evert, 'The Statistics of Word Co-occurrences: Word Pairs and Collocations', PhD thesis, University of Stuttgart, 2005.

frequency – what we call the raw distributional probability factor (dpf) – is given in the following equations Eq. (3.1):

$$DPF(phlogiston, gas) = \frac{8/N}{13943/N \cdot 81685/N} \simeq 7.02$$

$$DPF(experiments, phlogiston) = \frac{65/N}{243518/N \cdot 13943/N} \simeq 19.14$$

$$DPF(experiments, gas) = \frac{256/N}{243518/N \cdot 81685/N} \simeq 12.86$$

Dividing by the expected frequency increases the salience of the associations that include phlogiston, a relatively infrequent word overall, and down-weights the score for the pairs that include gas, which is much more common overall than the other two words. In one way, this difference is appropriate. Of the cases where phlogiston has appeared, a much higher *proportion* of the occurrences are with experiments than gas. But we should note that this simple statistical adjustment corresponds to a bold claim about conceptual salience: is it really true that terms that are less frequent overall tend to have just as much importance in conceptual association as everyday terms? Another potential problem here is that a very small number of actual co-occurrences (eight) leads to such a high overall score. This feels like false precision. When we look at a full table of co-associations sorted by an observed over-expected measure, it will become more apparent how this issue of false precision derived from low numbers of absolute co-occurrence counts needs to be addressed.

To convert to an information theoretic measure, it is usual to take the logarithm of the observed over-expected calculation, and this association score (sometimes scaled by the size of the co-occurrence window) is known as pointwise mutual information (PMI). As we have noted in Chapter 2, PMI is given in the formula of Eq. (3.2):[13]

$$PMI = log_2 \frac{P(w_1, w_2)}{P(w_1)P(w2)}$$

When used to calculate word associations, we typically consider only positive PMI, as we are usually not interested in terms that are less associated than chance, and in a geometric view of word meaning it does not make sense to include negative distances. Here in Table 3.3 I provide the association table for liberty, sorted by PMI.

As one can see, terms found in Table 3.2 are very different from those in Table 3.1. They are probably more intuitive, but the table is noticeably dominated by terms that have *very* low independent frequencies. In fact, the statistics for this corpus were calculated by only including word pairs

---

[13] Kenneth W. Church and Patrick Hanks, 'Word Association Norms, Mutual Information, and Lexicography', *Computational linguistics*, 16.1 (1990), 22–9.

Table 3.3 *Words with highest PMI score with liberty. Date spread 1790–5, containing 3,000 documents, 2,198,379 words. Source: ECCO.*

Focal	Bound	Freq.	PMI
liberty	montesquieu	12	16.97329
liberty	privi	11	16.88628
liberty	berty	20	16.65744
liberty	venerate	10	16.17193
liberty	definitions	19	16.12064
liberty	unalienable	18	15.99246
liberty	despots	12	15.87468
liberty	fettered	10	15.84651
liberty	dungeons	14	15.81526
liberty	vate	10	15.74115
liberty	infringement	15	15.58700
liberty	enslave	19	15.57207
liberty	congratulations	10	15.55883
liberty	republicans	29	15.45779
liberty	enslaved	21	15.43577

that had a co-occurrence of at least ten (on the basis that less than ten observations of an association is too statistically unreliable), and so most of the associated words are only a few occurrences above this threshold. This is a known issue with PMI – it compensates for the independent frequency a bit too much and scores very infrequent co-occurrences highly, as long as they are above chance. Correspondingly, it excessively penalises words that have high general frequencies.[14] As noted in Chapter 2, in order to compensate for this, recently researchers in natural language processing have adjusted the PMI measure by damping the independent probabilities by a factor by which the independent probabilities are raised to a fractional power, usually 0.75.[15] It has been shown that this particular value minimises the absolute value of the correlation of the resulting score with the word frequencies involved.[16]

[14] Evert, 'The Statistics of Word Co-occurrences'.
[15] Tomas Mikolov, Ilya Sutskever, Kai Chen, Greg S. Corrado and Jeff Dean, 'Distributed Representations of Words and Phrases and Their Compositionality', in *Advances in Neural Information Processing Systems*, XXVI, ed. Christopher J. Burges, Leon Bottou, Max Welling, Zoubin Ghahramani and Kilian Q. Weinberger (2013), 3111–9, https://papers.nips.cc/paper_files/paper/2013/file/9aa42b31882ec039965f3c4923ce901b-Paper.pdf.
[16] Gabriel Recchia and Paul Nulty, 'Improving a Fundamental Measure of Lexical Association', in *Proceedings of the 39th Annual Meeting of the Cognitive Science Society*, ed. Glenn Gunzelmann, Andrew Howes, Thora Tenbrink and Eddy J. Davelaar (2018), https://doi.org/10.17863/CAM.30302.

Table 3.4 *Words with the highest* log-dpf *(smoothed PMI)*
score with liberty. Date spread 1790–5, containing 3,000
documents, 2,198,379 words. Source: ECCO.

Focal	Bound	Freq.	PMI
liberty	liberty	1,692	1.18525118
liberty	berty	20	0.80491126
liberty	montesquieu	12	0.79009278
liberty	privi	11	0.70308140
liberty	definitions	19	0.46231328
liberty	unalienable	18	0.36378127
liberty	freedom	349	0.33685155
liberty	venerate	10	0.23634770
liberty	republicans	29	0.23374480
liberty	dungeons	14	0.15693163
liberty	enslave	19	0.13317371
liberty	despots	12	0.13092541
liberty	frenchmen	25	0.11733238
liberty	enslaved	21	0.09142390
liberty	infringement	15	0.04757358

Accepting that this smoothing is beneficial for distributional probability
measures, it is this smoothed PMI that I will refer to in the remainder of
this chapter as '*log-dpf*'. Here in Table 3.4 are the top associations with
liberty by this measure.

Here one can see that many of the same terms are still there, but several
terms that were very close to the threshold frequency of 10 have dropped
off the list.

Another commonly used score in corpus linguistics is the *t*-score. This
calculation in Eq. (3.3) gives much more weight to the raw number of co-
occurrences; in fact it is based on a statistical calculation of significance
rather than effect size:

$$tscore(w_1, w_2) = \frac{P(w_1, w_2) - P(w_1), P(w_2)}{\sqrt{P(w1, w2)}}$$

In the preceding account of the different ways in which one might
measure association between words, there is an implicit trade-off that
needs to be addressed between the evidence for co-association determined by the raw co-occurrence counts and the researcher's intuition
respecting the robustness of that evidence. Such a trade-off can be
characterised in more strictly statistical terms as the distinction between
significance and effect size.

3.5 Statistical Significance and Effect Size

In statistical terms, PMI is a measure of *effect size* rather than a *significance test*, that is it measures the association above chance given the counts that we have observed, without taking into account how much evidence there is for that effect. This means that small co-occurrence counts can give rise to large PMI scores in cases where the independent frequency of the terms is low.

A common approach in statistics is to estimate what the variance in the data due to noise is, and to use this variance to calculate an interval showing the range of values the association score could have had due to that noise. But with respect to word association scores the research into how to calculate significance tests or confidence intervals is sparse.[17] Here one should note that measures like PMI are designed to calculate the size of an effect, not the significance of the effect. Other measures derived from hypothesis tests, such as *t*-score, place more weight on the observed co-occurrences. One fairly transparent approach is to estimate the uncertainty in the observations of the individual co-occurrence and word frequencies, and plug the upper and lower bounds of these individual frequencies into the word association formulae. The result of this is best presented graphically rather than in a table, and I will return to it in the next section.

3.6 Properties of Association Functions

The association scores that I have discussed so far are strictly metrics or distance functions in the mathematical sense. A metric, or distance function, is a symmetric function that satisfies the triangle inequality and returns a positive real number. That is, for a metric function *score* on words w1 and w2 $score(w_1, w_2)$ is positive, $score(w1, w2) = score(w2, w1)$ (the function is symmetric), and $score(w_1, w_2) \leq ((score(w_1, w_3) + score(w_2, w_3))$ (the triangle inequality).

Neither symmetry nor the triangle inequality are clearly exhibited in human judgements of word association. In the case of the triangle inequality, elements of pairs of highly associated words may not be themselves highly associated, for example the pairs asteroid–belt and belt–buckle have high similarity, but asteroid–buckle has low association. This property is crucial for understanding what is at stake when considering whether to use spatial or network models for visualising the data we generate on word co-association. On a 2D screen, it is not

---

[17] Again, the fullest treatment is in Evert, 'The Statistics of Word Co-occurrences'.

possible to lay out these three words such that asteroid and belt are close together, and belt and buckle are close together, without drawing asteroid and buckle nearer. But if we use a network layout that allows for greater flexibility, this problem is avoided, albeit at the cost of enforcing discrete thresholds to decide which pairs should be connected in the first place.

For the case of symmetry, simple asymmetric word-association functions, such as conditional probability, can be used to generate scores such that $score(w_1, w_2) \neq score(w_2, w1)$. Using these scores would complicate network analysis though, as scores differ depending on whether a term is chosen by the researcher as the focal term, or appears in the resulting list. When applied to network representations, using asymmetric association scores means that directed rather than undirected networks must be used.

These considerations about the nature of co-association and how it is both measured and represented – in tabular form, graphs or scatter plots – are not inert with respect to a digital history of ideas. Indeed, the models we use in the construction of the digital frameworks we adopt have a direct relation to the models the historian of ideas uses in thinking about the ideas and concepts that are the object of their study. If, for example, we take the view that concepts are mental entities, and we want to produce representations that capture the mental associations latent in the corpus, we can choose methods that reproduce human word-association judgements. This would mean using asymmetric functions and perhaps limiting the length of ranked lists of word associations to more closely match the lists produced in human word-association experiments. On the other hand, if we consider concepts in terms of the cultural topology of their structuration, there is no compelling reason to assume that such structures would be identical to the representations that capture concepts considered as mental entities.

3.7   Visualising Word Associations

> In writing about a field of meanings I have often wished that some form of presentation could be devised in which it would be clear that the analyses of particular words are intrinsically connected, sometimes in complex ways. The alphabetical listing on which I have finally decided may often seem to obscure this, although the use of cross-references should serve as a reminder of many necessary connections. The difficulty is that any other kind of arrangement, for example by areas or themes, would establish one set of connections while often suppressing another.[18]

[18] Raymond Williams, *Keywords* (Flamingo, 1966).

So far, I have presented word co-occurrence frequencies and their association scores using what Evert called *n*-best lists: we choose a word of interest, and in a table list the *n* words that are most associated with that word. I will now examine methods of presenting this kind of data directly in terms of spatial distances on the page and connections illustrated in network diagrams.

3.7.1 Tables and Plots

A table of raw co-occurrence data and association scores has several advantages:
- The precise numbers of counts and scores are presented.
- The words in the table can be ordered by counts or by one of the association scores.
- We can easily view scores for several association measures at once.

And disadvantages:
- The words in the table are spaced evenly, even if the differences among the association scores are widely dispersed.
- Space considerations usually limit us to 10–100 rows of associated words.
- We see links between the focal word and its bound words but not links among the bound words.

We can see in Figure 3.1 the differences in association between the terms more clearly if we plot the words with their score as a scatterplot or bar chart.

This way of presenting the data makes it especially easy to compare statistical confidence intervals visually, represented as error bars around the point estimate. The confidence intervals for the association scores are calculated by first obtaining 95 percent confidence intervals for the component joint and independent frequencies, assuming a Poisson distribution, and plugging the extreme upper and lower values into the association formulae.[19] The intuition is that when scores are based on a low number of actual occurrences (both joint and independent counts), the confidence interval is wider.

Another way of visualising the associations between words is to consider word meaning as a space and to place words closer together in this space depending on how closely related in meaning they are. Figure 3.2 shows an example of word meanings represented in a two-dimensional space.[20]

---

[19] Evert, 'The Statistics of Word Co-occurrences'.
[20] Jose Camacho Collados and Taher Pilehvar. 'How to Represent Meaning in Natural Language Processing? Word, Sense and Contextualized Embeddings', blog post, 29 October 2018, https://josecamachocollados.medium.com/how-to-represent-meaning-in-natural-language-processing-word-sense-and-contextualized-embeddings-bbe31bdab84a.

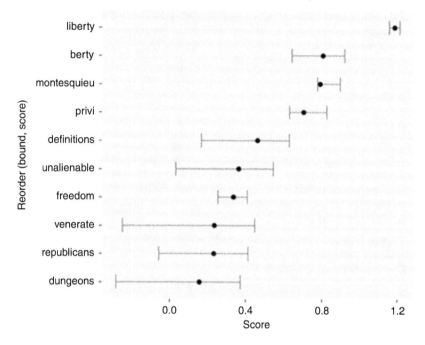

Figure 3.1 Top ten *log-dpf* association scores with the focal term liberty. Date spread 1790–1795, containing 3,000 documents, 2,198,379 words. Source: ECCO.

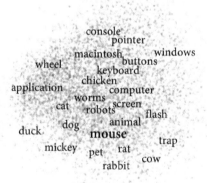

Figure 3.2 Word meanings represented in a two-dimensional space.

As discussed earlier in relation to the triangle inequality, if one only has spatial distances in a low-dimensional plane to indicate association, it is inevitable that terms from unrelated domains may be drawn near each other due to their mutual similarity to a polysemic term. For example, in Figure 3.2, words related to the animal and technological sense of mouse are nearby in semantic space. Network layout algorithms also give rise to this kind of spatial proximity, but the edge links make explicit the forces that are pulling together the terms from separate domains: an edge might be drawn from mouse to rat, and from mouse to keyboard, but not from rat to keyboard directly.

3.7.2 Network Visualisations

As a visualisation method, the network seems to have several advantages.[21] By representing words as points (nodes) connected by lines (edges), connections between all pairs of words can be shown. Furthermore, edge thickness can give some indication of association strength; node size or shape can show properties of the words; and the general conceptual space of interest can be defined by properties of the overall graph, such as viewing a shortest path between two nodes. The disadvantages are that node position does not indicate node relatedness directly (only through the influence of the edges), and the presence or absence of an edge is determined by a hard threshold.

However, the advantage of being able to see common associations between all words associated with a chosen focal term is striking. Consider the plots of words in Figures 3.3 and 3.4 that are scored for association with liberty and rights using the *log-dpf* score.

If we carefully scan through the two lists, we can see that the terms unalienable and despots are held in common. Now let us compare this mode of visualisation with a network constructed from the same data using rights and liberty as search terms, shown in Figure 3.5. The network is built as follows: a global network is constructed first by connecting all pairs of terms in the corpus that have a *log-dpf* score above a certain threshold – in this case, zero. Then, the network is filtered so that an edge only exists between two nodes A and B if *either* A appears above position k on B's n-best list, or B appears above position k on A's list. Remember that relative rank is not symmetric: liberty could be at position

---

[21] Many of the technical terms that I use in this section are from the sub-discipline of mathematics known as graph theory. It is more usual in mathematics to use the term graph for this kind of data structure, while the social sciences tend to use 'network'. As 'graph' has a confusing alternate usage that can refer to any chart, I will use 'network' here.

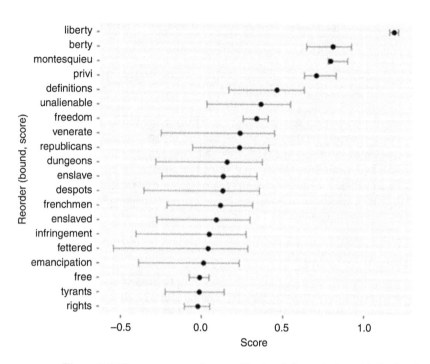

Figure 3.3 Top twenty words scored by *log-dpf* association with the focal term liberty. Date spread 1790–5, containing 3,000 documents, 2,198,379 words. Source: ECCO.

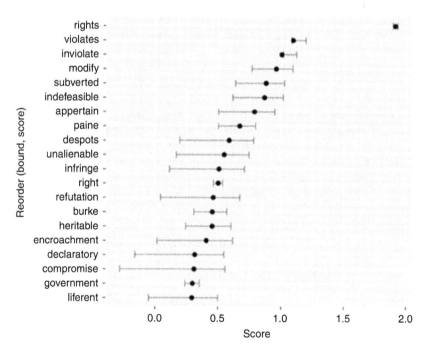

Figure 3.4 Top twenty words scored by *log-dpf* association with the focal term rights. Date spread 1790–5, containing 3,000 documents, 2,198,379 words. Source: ECCO.

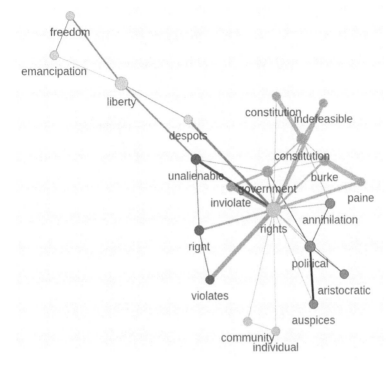

Figure 3.5 A network visualisation with rights and liberty as focal terms, score threshold 0.0 and rank threshold 20. Shading is assigned by a community detection algorithm. Date spread 1790–5, containing 3,000 documents, 2,198,379 words. Source: ECCO.

forty on the list for rights, and rights at position sixty on the list for liberty. Constructing a link if either is above position k on the other's list allows for the graph to remain undirected with a single rank threshold.

Once the global network is built, we visualise only the nodes included in the neighbourhood network for the search terms (i.e. within n steps, with $n=1$ being the default) and all the connections among them. This means that the common material of unalienable and despots stands out right away, and also that we can observe connections among the neighbourhood nodes that do not involve either of the focal terms; for example we can see that government, which is on the list for rights, is also directly connected to burke and constitution. To find these shared words using only n-best lists requires repeatedly taking intersections of the lists for focal terms; the network visualisation not only makes them immediately apparent but draws clusters of terms together spatially, depending on how many connections they have – the network is physically laid out as though it were a system of weighted springs (a 'force-directed' network).

As is often the case when talking about concepts, there is a recursive quality to the question of which representation is most useful. In the same way that we might want to say of political or social concepts that particular formal configurations of them enable us to arrive at an understanding intuitively, with a satisfying sense of having grasped the concept properly, comparing distances between points on a plot or following collections of lines visually is a very different and arguably much richer and more immediate way of apprehending the co-occurrence data than reading words and numbers across lines of tables.

Many ways to layout networks like these are possible, and force-directed networks can be somewhat computationally expensive to draw, leading to different variations that trade-off precision with speed. In Figure 3.5, the edge thickness is displayed in proportion to the *log-dpf* score – the higher the score, the thicker the edge. There is only one type of edge, denoting that the symmetric *n*-best rank and the *log-dpf* scores are above their respective thresholds. This is, in fact, a fairly structurally light network, but it is easy to make it much denser by incorporating, for example, multiple edge types corresponding to different association scores, time periods or window distances.

The choice of thresholds and association score can also influence macroscopic structural properties of the network. The *degree* of a node in the network is the number of edges that it has, and the *degree distribution* of the whole network is the probability distribution of these degrees over the whole network. By loosening the thresholds (decreasing the score threshold and increasing the rank threshold), we end up with a graph shown in Figure 3.6 with a much higher average degree.

Is this more densely connected graph a better representation of how the concepts of rights and liberty were embedded in a set of complex articulations with other concepts at the end of the eighteenth century? It is difficult to say without reference to some source of structural constraints external to the text itself. If the goal were to model human psychological or grammatical constraints, we could set the node degree to approximate human short-term memory capacity, or based on the properties such as locality constraints in transformational grammar. But if we are attempting to visualise how a culture as a whole uses these concepts, the structural parameters are surely very different, and their values were likely to be determined by factors that were generated by patterns of usage and custom which were aggregates of individual human psychological dispositions.

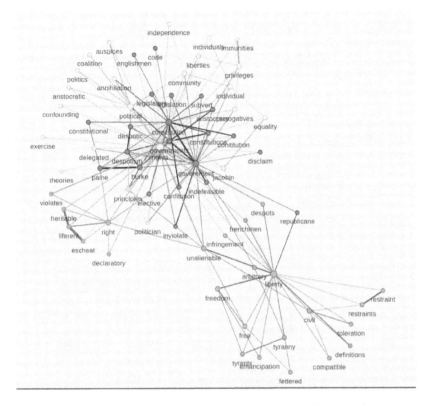

Figure 3.6 A network visualisation with rights and liberty as focal terms, score threshold 0.4 and rank threshold 30. Shading is assigned by a community detection algorithm. Date spread 1790–5, containing 3,000 documents, 2,198,379 words. Source: ECCO.

Just as in cognitive semantics neuroscience is the substrate that theorists attempt to fix their parameters to, in the history of ideas the contingent particulars of the communal knowledge production process comprise the evidence that we need to fix our parameters to. In a single mind, two new concepts can perhaps begin to function together appropriately if a perception brings them together in short-term memory within a small enough number of steps of one another, and especially if that association is reinforced through repetition. But in the culture, this process might be the sending of a letter, the carving of a message, the sailing of a ship, or a bumper harvest; these processes have entirely different sets of parameters, and they are the objects of historical inquiry.

In order to select appropriate values for parameters discussed here (such as edge weight thresholds, co-occurrence distance or word association measure) for use in visualisation, we must have some foundation for these in either mental or cultural constraints. Philosophers often use the term semantics to refer to the properties of logical systems and their referents in work that deals in terms of truth conditions, variable binding and reference ambiguity. In cognitive science, 'semantics' can have a broader meaning that includes general conceptual and common-sense world knowledge. It is in this context that it is appropriate to describe semantic networks as maps of conceptual structures. In addition to familiar taxonomic relations such as hyponymy or metonymy, less essential, more temporally or culturally ephemeral knowledge also forms part of our understanding of a concept, particularly complex and abstract concepts. For example, although aristocracy or tyranny might not be essential components of our knowledge of democracy, these conceptual nodes may be crucial to how the concept operates in particular mental or cultural contexts – that is our knowledge that those three terms are types of government provides us with a context and roles (society, people, force, power); and the concepts are related and distinguished by correspondences and differences among those roles. To think of people as 'wielding' or 'holding' power is not a semantic framing but a conceptual understanding dependent on our world knowledge of how the actions of one group influence, facilitate or constrain those of another. These conceptual relations are not discrete, absolute or essential, but continuous, distributional and contingent. If a word is omitted from a sentence, we can infer some of its properties from our conceptual knowledge of the other words in the sentence. For example: 'The X flowed out of the sink and onto the floor'. Without complete certainty, but with some likelihood, we can infer that X is a type of liquid. This is not merely a lexical relation indicating that 'liquid' could always be substituted in place of X to produce a plausible situation, nor is it grammatical constraint: any noun phrase could fill the slot grammatically. The constraint is not a feature of language but a feature of our conceptual knowledge of the real world. To say 'The house flowed out of the sink and onto the floor' is grammatically correct but does not correspond to the conceptual mapping of real-world scenarios. This is corroborated by the very low incidence of sentences within an English language corpus in which 'house' is the subject of the word 'flow'. In this case the corpus is structured by and represents conceptuality, not syntax, notwithstanding the fact that, say, fictions in the mode of magic realism may well contain sentences in which the opposite is true, that is houses may 'flow' in highly imaginative ways. This is essentially the point of examples like Chomsky's 'colorless green ideas sleep furiously'. As native speakers of English recognise, grammar dictates that the verb 'to chase' must have a noun subject. Semantics suggests that the subject should be an animate agent. Topical association suggests that dog, chase and cat are related, but it is a combination of these kinds of knowledge with broader conceptual knowledge (or simply the contingent structure of the real world) which results in the statistical superiority of 'the dog chased the cat' over 'the cat chased the dog'.

3.8   Conclusion

Perhaps the array of methodological options presented here, alongside the claim that the theoretical concepts we work with when doing DH correspond closely with their operationalisation, leads to a seemingly disheartening conclusion. If a concept as superficially simple as association can be operationalised in so many different ways, how can we hope to communicate findings consistently and with mutual intelligibility? I think that there are two solutions. First, we should acknowledge that at least in the case of word association and conceptual network structure, these concepts are inherently complex and underspecified in the theoretical literature. Historians of ideas and corpus linguists together have to do the conceptual work of defining more precise notions for these terms and finding their appropriate implementations. Second, we should always attempt to use the simplest calculation available that captures only the aspect of the concept that we want to base an argument around. To show an increase in relative association between two concepts over time, a simple scatterplot of relative co-occurrence count over time is all that is needed. For more discrete or structural breaks, thresholding methods in combination with network visualisations may be appropriate. This move towards simple and transparent implementations also smooths work of interdisciplinary collaboration. As this chapter has argued, these collaborations must be thought of as projects where those with complementary skills tackle the same task at the same time, rather than as a production line where specification and assembly are blind to one another.

Part II

Case Studies in the Digital History of Ideas

4   The Idea of Liberty, 1600–1800

Peter de Bolla, Ewan Jones, Paul Nulty, Gabriel Recchia and John Regan

Intellectual historians of early modern and Enlightenment Europe have established a tradition of thought within which many of our contemporary ideas of politics find their roots.[1] Of course, political concepts such as republicanism were not invented in this historical time frame, and most if not all of our contemporary political ideas can trace their histories back to classical times. Notwithstanding such *longue durée* accounts, there is a place for more time-constrained analyses, and the following focus on the 200 years between the start of the seventeenth century and the end of the eighteenth works within a well-delineated tradition of scholarship that gives significant emphasis to this period.[2] This is to note that many of the ideas that contribute to our senses of contemporary social, legal and political life were given explicit and extensive attention during these two centuries in Britain. For present purposes one can call to mind the work of Quentin Skinner, John Pocock and Reinhart Koselleck and the intricate legacies produced by this work as a convenient shortcut for establishing a context for the following observations. This scholarship is not, of course, uncontested, and in common with deep and powerful traditions of intellectual history, it has produced revision and re-calibration.[3] This chapter does not set out to adjudicate any of the local arguments that appear in this tradition; rather, it aims to outline the ways in which a new

---

[1] This chapter uses some material from Peter de Bolla, Ewan Jones, Paul Nulty, Gabriel Recchia and John Regan, 'The Idea of Liberty 1600–1800: A Distributional Concept Analysis', *Journal of the History of Ideas*, 81.3 (2020), 381–406.

[2] This tradition is extensive but see inter alia Quentin Skinner, *The Foundations of Modern Political Thought*, 2 vols. (Cambridge: Cambridge University Press, 1978); John G. A. Pocock, *Virtue, Commerce and History: Essays on Political Thought and History, Chiefly in the Eighteenth Century* (Cambridge: Cambridge University Press, 1985); Crawford B. Macpherson, *The Political Theory of Possessive Individualism* (Oxford: Oxford University Press, 1962); Alan C. Houston, *Algernon Sidney and the Republican Heritage in England and America* (Princeton, NJ: Princeton University Press, 1991); Phillip Pettit, *Republicanism: A Theory of Freedom and Government* (Oxford: Clarendon Press, 1997).

[3] Among others, see Annabel Brett and James Tully, with Holly Hamilton-Bleakley, eds., *Rethinking the Foundations of Modern Political Thought* (Cambridge: Cambridge University Press, 2006).

method for the history of ideas, based upon computational modes of inquiry, might contribute to it.

As its title indicates, this chapter seeks to investigate the idea of liberty across the seventeenth and eighteenth centuries. Throughout, our attention will be directed at its operation within English, and the data upon which our investigations are based has been extracted from the digital archives of printed materials, ECCO and EEBO-TCP, outlined in Chapter 2. Our aim, as in the other chapters in Part II, is to test the efficacy of computational text mining techniques for the history of ideas. An initial observation of the following kind helps orient our approach: let us say that Hobbes had a theory of liberty which directed his thinking with this idea, but did his fellow citizens mirror or adopt this thinking? Of course, we cannot answer that question with very fine-grained detail since those citizens may have thought about the idea in numerous ways that never fell into print transcriptions. Nevertheless, we believe that a full-scale survey of the printed text archive does provide us with valuable insights into the ways in which a culture formulated and used ideas in the past even with the provisos entered (see Chapter 2, Section 2.3) with regard to the construction of the ECCO dataset. Here, as elsewhere in the case studies following, our attempts to track the history of ideas computationally is bound by the data we are working with, essentially the 'official' print culture of the anglophone eighteenth century as represented by the selection decisions made in the construction of ECCO.

One can grasp the trajectory of this endeavour by noting the following: since the publication of Isaiah Berlin's lecture the 'Two Concepts of Liberty' in 1958, intellectual historians and political theorists have debated with some vigour the notion that liberty comes in two different guises. The first, positive liberty, is based upon our freedom to choose what we do. The second, negative liberty, is based upon our accepting constraints upon how we act: freedom *from* slavery, for example. And this debate has a very clear contemporary relevance: it helps us understand our own attempts to work within (or against) what has come down to us as a theory of government and democracy based upon liberalism. The concluding section of this chapter, Section 4.5, outlines ways in which computational methods can shine a light on the emergence or incubation of such a theory, effectively mapping the shifting lexical terrains within which our two terms freedom and liberty operated in English at the end of the eighteenth century. Such an account helps us understand how concepts coagulate or constellate over time and provide the basis for the articulation of complex political ideas. From the evidence of our data mining we believe that any close-grained historical account of what has become a contested but nevertheless widely accepted truth – broadly speaking, the identification of liberalism's triumph over republicanism,[4] or more narrowly, the interdependence of liberty and individual rights – based on English language sources (as this study is, while recognising this as a limitation due to comparability of available datasets) is likely to find the last thirty years of the eighteenth century of particular importance. Indeed, a strongly formulated revision to the prevailing orthodoxy notes that the longer *durée* history of the political idea of liberty is likely to pass over the intense work of conceptual formation and adaptation that occurred in this thirty-year period. The sweep of our argument, then, moves from the well-embedded accounts of liberty both historically and philosophically, that is from Cambridge School accounts and the post Isaiah Berlin philosophical tradition to a data-supported conceptual micro-history that identifies forces active in the last decades of the eighteenth century.[5] It may be useful to note here that in our view 'surface' or 'distant' reading (the terms that have become established for describing methods of interrogating digital text archives through computational means) is not an end in itself. Indeed, the very terms are misleading because machine modes of data extraction are not in any sense 'distant' from the texts to which they are applied: such methods when applied at scale read exponentially closer than humans are capable of doing. Moreover, as Sections 4.4 and 4.5 of this chapter suggest, reading at scale can have the effect of identifying very local effects that otherwise are unperceivable. When we uncover such spikes in a general trend, they should be understood as diagnostic with respect to further interrogation of the underlying data – effectively as an invitation to return to the more generously constructed historical context of our thirty-year period, thereby combining the new methods used here with more conventional modes of the history of ideas. Our hope is to extend and expand the field as it has evolved, not to supplant it. We begin, however, in the pre-history of this emergent political category liberalism, by asking the extent to which the dominant account of two types of liberty (as mapped by Berlin and his interlocutors) might have been recognisable to – say – an English gentleman in 1660.

4.1   Raw Frequency

Our procedure in the following is incremental: we begin with some rudimentary exercises in data extraction from our two datasets before employing some more sophisticated techniques for parsing conceptual

---

[4] See, for example, Pettit, Republicanism, 41–50.
[5] See Quentin Skinner, *Liberty before Liberalism* (Cambridge: Cambridge University Press, 1998).

forms. As the evidence accumulates, we believe a clear picture emerges over the course of two centuries and this picture has some elements in common with some extant accounts that we shall comment upon at the close of the chapter. Let us begin with a very simple inquiry of our data: what did the noun liberty associate with over the first one hundred years of our restricted time period? And how frequently did it do so? Did agents in the seventeenth century speak of 'liberty from servitude'? Did they think of themselves as free from persecution? We can quickly find answers to these questions by searching through the EEBO-TCP dataset in order to find all the uses of the phrase 'liberty from'. The results indicate that liberty was most commonly understood to be *from* sin (or sinne in its variant spelling), with a total of 57 occurrences across the century. The next most common was bondage, with a total of 36 occurrences. Law (24), prison (15), necessity (13), God (12), power (11), king (10), oppression (9), tyranny (9), imprisonment (8) and coaction (8) are the next most frequent terms.

A very elementary comparison with the phrase 'freedom from' helps us begin to see an outline. The same search for this alternative yields the following results: freedom *from* was most commonly attached, once again, to sin (including sinne) – a total of 339 occurrences across the seventeenth century. And bondage was the next most common, with 71 occurrences. Law (55), guilt (49), punishment (47), death (38), arrests (36), evil (35), curse (33), power (31), pain (31), condemnation (30), persecution (27), misery (27) and trouble (25) are the next most common. Here one can see that although the two phrases were applied equally commonly to sin, bondage and law, for the most part they shared very few nouns. This initial inspection of the data leads us to suppose that liberty and freedom certainly shared habits of usage – let us say they operated in a similar ideational terrain – but they were clearly not identical. We shall keep this firmly in view as we begin to investigate the extent to which we can identify two different ideas and concepts – liberty and freedom – at work across the two centuries.

In our second data extraction we have inspected the raw frequency of the two variants of the phrases 'liberty to' and 'liberty from' and compared these with 'freedome from' and 'freedome to' in the first forty years of the seventeenth century (when the variant spelling for freedome was preferred). Table 4.1 presents these data.

As one can see, the data indicate that 'freedome from' was far more common than 'liberty from', and, correspondingly, the frequency of the phrase 'freedome to' is far smaller than 'liberty to': 511 occurrences compared to 3,143. This clearly marks a distinction in the uses for the two words – freedom and liberty – and one might begin to hazard that this

Table 4.1 *Raw frequency of liberty, liberty from/to and freedome, freedome from/to. Date spread 1600–40, containing 7,230 documents, 24.9 million tokens. Source: EEBO.*

Word/Phrase	Raw frequency
liberty	21621
liberty from	234
liberty to	3143
freedome	9482
freedome from	1295
freedome to	511

Table 4.2 *Raw frequency of liberty, liberty from/to and freedom, freedom from/ to. Date spread 1600–1800. Source: EEBO and ECCO.*

Word/Phrase	1600–40	1660–1700	1700–40	1760–1800
	Source: EEBO 7230 documents, 24.9 m tokens	Source: EEBO 24502 documents, 57.6 m tokens	Source: ECCO 55866 documents, 2.6 b tokens	Source: ECCO 118166 documents 6.3 b tokens
liberty	21621	117025	403836	1006661
liberty from	234	1272	2791	5934
liberty to	3143	19913	68788	154122
freedom(e)	9452	29142	96229	304737
freedom from	1285	431	5890	15667
freedom to	511	189	5639	12597

difference is determined by the positive or negative senses of the concept of liberty. Although one could think of freedom in its positive inflection – freedom to choose what one might do – that conception was much more commonly articulated in the verbal expression 'liberty to' do something. Conversely, the negative inflection, liberty from restraint was more commonly articulated in the verbal expression 'freedom from'.

If we now extract the data for these uses across the two centuries, shown in Table 4.2, we can begin to note how the idea of liberty slowly but surely became distinct from the idea of freedom.

These raw frequencies of the phrases indicate clearly that over the two centuries the uses of freedom in both the positive and negative liberty senses evens out: where 'freedom from' in the early seventeenth century is clearly more common than 'freedom to', by the end of the eighteenth century there is no clear preference. The story with liberty is markedly different: 'liberty to' is far more common across the 200 years. If we are to understand liberty as a distinct idea from freedom, these data suggest that liberty was articulated in the positive sense: liberty to act as one wished. In the case of freedom there seems to have been no clear preference for the positive or negative sense.

4.2   Distributional Probability

In our next data extraction we have used a more sophisticated tool for analysing very large datasets of language use. In this case we are using statistical methods for predicting the likelihood of two terms co-associating, as outlined in Chapter 2. Here in Table 4.3 we have constructed the core for the terms freedom and liberty in the last twenty years of the seventeenth century, and we can see that they do indeed very closely resemble each other.[6]

By the end of the eighteenth century, however, the core for freedom has increased to twenty-seven terms (including stopwords) whereas the core for liberty increases to fifty-eight terms (also including stopwords). It is also noteworthy that every term in the core for freedom, 1780–1800, is also in the core for liberty except the following: Patriot, Patriots, Britons, Albion, freemen.[7]

Now if we track the alterations in the shared lexis between our two terms, freedom and liberty, across window size we can see in more granular detail the beginnings of the convergence of the two ideas, shown here in Table 4.4.[8]

Table 4.3 *Core terms for liberty and freedom. Date spread 1680–1700. Source: EEBO.*

liberty 1680–1700, freq.: 68742	freedom 1680–1700, freq.: 16375
liberty	freedom
freedom	bondage
bondage	liberty
	free

---

[6] The method for deriving the core is set out in Chapter 2, Section 2.5.
[7] Slave and slavery appear in the core for freedom but only slavery appears in liberty's core.
[8] Here it should be recalled that the number of terms on a *dpf* list is only very slightly correlated with window size, see Chapter 2, Section 2.4.

Table 4.4 *Number of terms on* dpf *list for liberty and freedom, 1600–40, at spans of 5, 10, 50 and 100; and number of terms shared by each* dpf *list; number of terms on* dpf *list for liberty and freedom, 1660–70, at spans of 5, 10, 50 and 100; and number of terms shared by each* dpf *list. Source: EEBO.*

Span	liberty 1600–40, freq.: 21621	freedom 1600–40, freq.: 549	*n* shared terms
	n co-associations	*n* co-associations	
5	183	443	30
10	116	443	10
50	106	435	5
100	101	453	2
Span	liberty 1660–1700, freq.: 24912	freedom 1660–1700, freq.: 4786	*n* shared terms
	n co-associations	*n* co-associations	
5	177	179	54
10	101	98	21
50	41	76	6
100	39	67	4

One can note that the common terrain between the two terms is populated but at best they share fifty-four terms (at a span of five in the time segment 1660–1700). Here in Table 4.5 we present the data for the eighteenth century using the same forty-year spreads.

It is important to note that at a span of 100 terms the eleven common words in the co-association lists for the time segment 1701–40 contain five 'stop' words – this is to say that there are only six 'content' terms in common. By the end of the century the overlap in lexical terrain between liberty and freedom has been transformed: the forty-three terms that are held in common between the co-association lists at distance 100 represents 51.2% of all of the terms on freedom's list. Or, to look at it from the side of liberty, the 175 common terms at distance 5 comprise 45.6% of the terms in liberty's list in the time segment 1760–1800. The lexical terrain in which the two terms operated had converged by the end of the eighteenth century.

4.3   Common Bound-Lexis

The stability of the lexical terrain within which liberty operates might be thought about in terms of a network or constellation of terms that together comprise the circumscribed semantic space that we call an

Table 4.5 *Number of terms on* dpf *list for liberty and freedom, 1700–40, at spans of 5, 10, 50 and 100; and number of terms shared by each* dpf *list; number of terms on* dpf *list for liberty and freedom, 1760–1800, at spans of 5, 10, 50 and 100; and number of terms shared by each* dpf *list. Source: ECCO.*

Span	liberty 1701–40, freq.: 403836	freedom 1701–40, freq.: 96229	*n* shared terms
	n co-associations	*n* co-associations	
5	276	295	105
10	113	180	45
50	55	91	19
100	44	51	11
Span	liberty 1760–1800, freq.: 417009	freedom 1760–1800, freq.: 120243	*n* shared terms
	n co-associations	*n* co-associations	
5	383	451	175
10	222	275	99
50	133	137	55
100	114	84	43

idea. In the following data analysis, we have constructed the network by identifying which terms are in each other's lists of bound terms, thereby isolating the common bound-lexis to all the terms in the network. Such networks or cliques are generally not large in size, that is they do not number more than a handful of terms – as one can intuit from the observation that as the set size increases the rule that each term must be on each of the other's list is likely to constrain very large sets. This is indeed borne out by the data.

In the early seventeenth century, 1630–40, liberty can be found on the binding list of six other terms, each of which also contain the other terms in the set of seven terms. These terms are liberty, bondage, freedome, slavery, thraldome, servitude and freed. When we inspect the data for the later decade 1690–1700, the largest set within which liberty operates is six terms, and they are thraldom (in the modern variant spelling), bondage, freedom, liberty, slavery and free. Once again, we note the stability of this lexical terrain. When we move to the far end of the eighteenth century, the picture has changed. In the period 1770–1800 liberty is a member of eighty-two sets of eight terms, and the six most strongly associated comprise a set of variations on the following terms: anarchy, aristocracy, democracy, government, liberty, monarchy, republican, tyranny, equality, revolution, republic. Interestingly, however, the profile for freedom is very divergent. In the same time period, the last decades of the eighteenth century, the largest set size within which this term appears is six, and there is only one such set: democracy, freedom, government, liberty, revolution, tyranny. Once again, our earlier data analyses are confirmed: the uses of liberty and freedom converge over the 200 years, and the tight lexical terrain within which liberty operates has, by the end of the eighteenth century, become very evidently established. Whereas the seventeenth century thought liberty in conjunction with slavery – that is it thought liberty as an adjunct of person – by the end of the eighteenth century, liberty had become an adjunct of the state.[9]

This observation should be placed in context with the discussion in Chapter 2 about the constructedness of the datasets we are using. As we know, the selection decisions that have determined the construction of ECCO – compounded by the unstructured and happenstance accretion of data that underlies the current version of it – have failed to capture texts that at some earlier stage in the historico-bibliographical traditions of scholarship were deemed to be 'marginal'. We might note, therefore, that the claim that by the end of the eighteenth century liberty had become an adjunct of the state, should be tempered by the fact that the dataset represents what might be considered to be the 'official' male and white textual record of the period. But this in itself can be helpful with respect to how the idea of slavery was motivated in that textual record. Here it is noteworthy that the co-associations between slavery and terms that can unambiguously be said to have operated within the discourses of chattel slavery – negro, African, planter – are essentially absent from the dataset. The data indicate that, perhaps unsurprisingly, these terms only begin to appear from around mid-century, and only become moderately frequent in the last twenty years of the century, when debates about abolition were given more prominence in political discourse.[10] But perhaps, for the purposes of the present argument, the more important observation is that although this evolution in the architecture of liberty travelled from person to state, the 'official' data support the 'official' understanding that for most of the period chattel slaves were not considered to be persons. Another way of putting this is to note that the idea of slavery was operational within the official discourses that constructed the polis, with all of its exclusions as to who or who did not count

---

[9] As Quentin Skinner notes, Hobbes was the first thinker to effect this change by constructing the state as a particular kind of person. See Skinner, Liberty before Liberalism, 4–5.
[10] The counts are as follows for co-association between slavery and negro(es) at distance five: 1740–60: 25; 1760–80: 168; 1780–1800: 558. The counts for Africa(n) are far lower: 7, 42, 175. It is perhaps an index to the bad conscience of the period's official culture that the co-association between slavery and planter(s) failed to be made until the last twenty years of the eighteenth century, and even then it occurs a mere 25 times at a distance of five within the 73,104 documents, 383 million tokens in the dataset.

(as enfranchised, allowed to speak, own property). This is – perhaps scandalously – borne out by the fact that the anti-British government colonists throughout the period leading up to the revolution, in what became America, consistently characterised themselves as 'enslaved' to the government in Westminster without dropping a beat with respect to the many thousands of persons who were indentured and with whom they shared their world.

4.4   Liberties as Rights

What contribution can the preceding computational and statistical approach to the history of ideas make to the long tradition of inquiry into the foundations of our modern concept of freedom or liberty that underlies the contemporary understanding of liberalism? In this section we shall address this question by focusing on the work of the intellectual historian who, more than any other, has taught us how to read the genealogy of the concept: Quentin Skinner. As is well known Skinner began his long career as a scholar immersed in the traditions of thinking modern political concepts in the late 1960s when he presented his Cambridge lectures that were the basis for *The Foundations of Modern Political Thought*. But it was in the 1980s that he turned most consistently to the historical reconstruction of the various traditions of thinking that developed the idea of liberty.[11]

In his 1984 essay 'The Idea of Negative Liberty', Quentin Skinner gives an historical account of two opposing ideas. One is 'negative liberty', in which the individual's social freedom is guaranteed only by the absence of limiting factors such as state intervention, responsibilities to one's communities and other externalities. In this scheme, liberty can only be defined negatively, as Thomas Hobbes has it at the start of his chapter 'Of the Liberty of Subjects' from *Leviathan*: 'liberty or freedom signifieth (properly) the absence of opposition'.[12] Skinner contrasts this with an ideal of liberty in which the operative factor is the virtue and value of public service. According to this way of seeing things, one is only consummately free when one acknowledges one's social responsibilities and carries out virtuous acts of public service. These contrasting ideas of liberty are named by Canadian philosopher Charles Taylor as the

[11] The best account of the development of Skinner's thought at this time is Marco Guena, 'Skinner, Pre-humanist Rhetorical Culture and Machiavelli', in *Rethinking the Foundations*, ed. Brett and Tully, with Hamilton-Bleakley, 50–72, especially 64–9.
[12] Thomas Hobbes, *The Clarendon Edition of the Works of Thomas Hobbes*, IV: *Leviathan: The English and Latin Texts*, ed. Noel Malcolm (Oxford: Clarendon Press, 2012), 324.

'opportunity concept' and the 'positive exercise concept'.[13] The former relies purely on the absence of constraint and prescribed social objectives (freedom from), whereas the latter involves positive action in the service of the state or community (freedom to).[14] Skinner sets out to demonstrate that the early modern period *combined* these two notions of liberty, writing:

I shall try to show that, in an earlier and now discarded tradition of thought about social freedom, the negative idea of liberty as the mere non-obstruction of individual agents in the pursuit of their chosen ends was combined with the ideas of virtue and public service in just the manner nowadays assumed on all sides to be impossible without incoherence.[15]

In his inaugural lecture as Regius Professor of Modern History in 1997, Skinner returned to this material and subsequently published a short book on the topic entitled *Liberty before Liberalism*.[16] Once again he stressed the combination of negative and positive liberty in the neo-Roman tradition that he claims was dominant in political discourse in England immediately following the regicide in 1649. His aim, in both this short book and the original essay published in 1984, is to revise, even dissolve, our modern assumption that liberty is incoherent outside a theory of rights. Early modern republican writers, he insists, understood liberty from constraint within the context of behaviour that was based in notions of virtue and public service.[17]

---

[13] See Charles Taylor, *Philosophy and the Human Sciences: Philosophical Papers*, II (Cambridge: Cambridge University Press, 1985).

[14] The classic account of this distinction remains Isaiah Berlin, *Two Concepts of Liberty* (Oxford: Oxford University Press, 1958).

[15] Quentin Skinner, 'The Idea of Negative Liberty', in *Philosophy in History: Essays on the Historiography of Philosophy*, ed. Richard Rorty, Jerome B. Schneewind and Quentin Skinner (Cambridge: Cambridge University Press, 1984), 197.

[16] Skinner, *Liberty before Liberalism*. The topic has, of course, been deeply embedded in much of Skinner's work. See, for example, Skinner, Foundations of Modern Political Thought; Quentin Skinner, 'Machiavelli on the Maintenance of Liberty', *Politics*, 18 (1983), 3–15; Quentin Skinner, 'The Paradoxes of Political Liberty', in *The Tanner Lectures on Human Values*, ed. Sterling M. McMurrin (Cambridge: Cambridge University Press, 1985), 227–50; Quentin Skinner, 'Machiavelli's *Discorsi* and the Pre-humanist Origins of Republican Ideas', in *Machiavelli and Republicanism*, ed. Gisela Bock, Quentin Skinner and Maurizo Viroli (Cambridge: Cambridge University Press, 1990), 121–142; Quentin Skinner, 'The Republican Ideal of Political Liberty', in *Machiavelli and Republicanism*, ed. Bock, Skinner and Viroli, 293–309; Quentin Skinner, 'Thomas Hobbes on the Proper Signification of Liberty', *Transactions of the Royal Historical Society*, 40 (1990), 121–51; Quentin Skinner, *Reason and Rhetoric in the Philosophy of Hobbes* (Cambridge: Cambridge University Press, 1996).

[17] Skinner returned to this theme in his *London Review of Books* lecture 'A Third Concept of Liberty', subsequently published in *London Review of Books*, 4 April 2002. There is also a large literature that engages with his argument. See, among others, Pettit, *Republicanism*; Phillipe Van Parijs, *Real Freedom for All* (Oxford: Oxford University

Table 4.6 *Number of shared terms on* dpf *lists for liberty (ie) /benevolence and freedom (e) /benevolence and so on at distance 10 in fifty-year segments. Total number of terms in each list indicated in brackets. Date spread 1600–1800. Source: EEBO and ECCO.*

	1600–50	1650–1700	1700–50	1750–1800
liberty/benevolence	7 (105/520)	7 (98/474)	19 (141/497)	27 (243/566)
freedom/benevolence	20 (502/520)	11 (100/474)	15 (190/497)	35 (290/566)
liberty /magnanimity	1 (105/520)	16 (98/536)	6 (141/612)	25 (243/642)
freedom/magnanimity	13 (502/520)	9 (100/536)	10 (190/612)	36 (290/642)
liberty/charity	2 (105/101)	3 (98/158)	17 (141/309)	29 (243/428)
freedom/charity	5 (502/101)	4 (100/158)	8 (190/309)	27 (290/428)
liberty/generosity	8 (105/505)	10 (98/287)	7 (141/400)	24 (243/487)
freedom/generosity	12 (502/505)	9 (100/287)	13 (190/400)	32 (290/487)
liberty/virtue	1 (105/346)	4 (98/77)	16 (141/196)	47 (243/377)
freedom/virtue	14 (502/346)	2 (100/77)	10 (190/196)	51 (290/377)

If the period in general thought liberty in this way – that is in harness with or articulated around notions of virtue, one would expect the lexical terrain within which the two terms circulated to have intersections or commonalities. Such a common terrain derived from co-association data could, of course, be either supportive or critical of the notion that Skinner proposes, which is to note that co-association in and of itself does not give an index to the senses in which terms qualify each other. Notwithstanding this caveat we can begin by noting that while Skinner's reading of the classic texts – those by Harrington and Sidney prime among them – certainly makes a convincing case, the extent to which this neo-Roman account of liberty penetrated the culture needs to be assessed. A first pass through the datasets we have been using suggests that the overlapping lexical terrain between liberty or freedom and those terms generally used in the period to think virtue (or the virtues) was sparse.[18] In Table 4.6 we

Press, 1995); Daniel Weinstock and Christian Nadeau, eds., *Republicanism: History, Theory and Practice* (London: Frank Cass, 2004); Cécile Laborde and John Maynor, eds., *Republicanism and Political Theory* (Oxford: Blackwell, 2008); Charles Larmore, 'Liberal and Republican Conceptions of Freedom', in *Republicanism*, ed. Weinstock and Nadeau, 96–119.

[18] Table 4.6 should be read in the context of our corpus level inquiry into the size of common lexical lists between two terms. When we constructed baseline data, using terms from each decade of the eighteenth century in the ECCO dataset at distance 10, we found that the number of terms in the common lists of 10,000 randomly selected word pairs have (depending on the decade) median lengths of 5 to 6, and lengths lower than 23 to 32 in 95% of pairs. This is similar to or even higher than the number of terms in common among liberty/benevolence, freedom/benevolence and liberty/magnanimity,

have tracked this overlap across the two centuries by creating *dpf* lists for the indicated terms and then calculating the number of terms each paired list has in common.

The data here would seem to indicate that these virtues – represented here by the lexis that designates them – were not thought about within the same semantic space as either liberty or freedom, and it does not at first glance support Skinner's argument, at least in so far as he supposes the neo-Roman account to have widespread currency. But it does support another strand of his thesis that points out the virtual hegemony of a Hobbesian 'negative liberty'. Moreover, when we inspect the actual terms that appear in these lists – remembering that the number of terms here is very small and entering due caution with respect to generalisations from such sparse data – another strand of Skinner's argument hoves into view. The three terms that appear on the co-association lists for benevolence, magnanimity and generosity in the seventeenth century are slavery, servitude and arbitrary. And these terms fall out of the lists in the eighteenth. It is also noteworthy – given Skinner's insistence that the Hobbesian view has such trouble with the accommodation of a theory of the state as person with a theory of negative liberty that constructs citizenship as effectively independent of the servitude that occurs when arbitrary power is exercised – that the following two terms enter these lists: volition and rights.

We believe this to indicate that the forces which solder rights to liberty really only began to have effects within the conceptual architecture (which we shall investigate in Section 4.5) towards the end of the eighteenth century. For Skinner the *longue durée* account is more persuasive as he draws out the implications of the 'Hobbesian claim that any theory of negative liberty must in effect be a theory of individual rights'.[19] In contrast we see the tectonics underlying the formulation of a linked or constellated set of terms that contribute to a theory of liberty in a slightly broader perspective, as outlined in Section 4.5. Let us keep with Skinner's point as a way of sharpening that observation: note that he claims that '*any* theory of negative liberty' (emphasis ours) must be congruent with,

---

whose common lists have lengths ranging from 0 to 13, depending on decade; their median lengths across decades are 2, 6.5 and 3.5, respectively. Given that this is true across single decades, there is therefore no particular reason to believe that the number of terms in common among liberty/benevolence, freedom/benevolence and liberty/magnanimity over a five-decade span would be substantially higher than the number of terms in common among randomly selected pairs over the same five-decade span – although it is impossible to say this for certain without undertaking this much more computationally intensive version of the analysis. Given that this metric has been created through random selection of paired terms, the baseline is a very low bar for cohabitation of a lexical terrain.

[19] Skinner, 'Idea of Negative Liberty', 218.

Table 4.7 *Number of shared terms (n) on* dpf *lists for liberty/libertie and rights at span of 10 and 100; percentage of terms shared between the two lists. Data source: EEBO and ECCO.*

Span 10	1620–30	1680–90	1720–30	1780–90
liberty/rights	*n*: 3; 1.5%	*n*: 4; 4.7%	*n*: 18; 25.4%	*n*: 44; 42.7%
Span 100				
liberty/rights	*n*: 2; 1.2%	*n*: 0; 0%	*n*: 6; 35.3%	*n*: 24; 63.2%

even inserted within a theory of rights. As we have noted, Skinner is certainly correct in stating that the Hobbesian version of negative liberty quickly became hegemonic and that our history of this idea is to some extent a history of forgetting, of the erasure of different ways of thinking that idea. Noting the linkage of negative liberty and rights, he writes:

As we have seen, this has reached the status of an axiom in many contemporary discussions of negative liberty. Liberty of action, we are assured, 'is a right'; there is a 'moral right to liberty'; we are bound to view our liberty both as a natural right and as the means to secure our other rights. As will by now be obvious, these are mere dogmas. A classical theory such as Machiavelli's helps us to see that there is no conceivable obligation to think of our liberty in this particular way. Machiavelli's is a theory of negative liberty, but he develops it without making any use whatever of the concept of individual rights.[20]

When we inspect the data, we can see how accurate this account of the soldering of liberty to rights is. Here in Table 4.7 we have tracked the shared lexical terrain between liberty and rights across the two centuries.

We take these data to indicate that by the end of the eighteenth century the Hobbesian version of negative liberty was, effectively, the only game in town.

4.5   From Liberty to Liberalism

The data extraction presented so far indicates that the theory of liberty based upon positive individual rights – what Skinner describes above as 'liberty of action' – slowly emerged during the eighteenth century, no doubt framed by practical political action resulting from the two large constitutional events of the second half of the century: the war with the colonies and the British reaction to the French Revolution.[21] In broad

---

[20] Ibid. 218.
[21] See in particular in the vast literature on these topics Jonathan C. D. Clark, *The Language of Liberty, 1660–1832: Political Discourse and Social Dynamics in the Anglo-American World*

brushstrokes these forces have generally been examined within a longer time frame that observes a European shift in political conceptual sensibility, from roughly speaking a late seventeenth century formulation of republicanism to what Skinner takes to be a hegemonic modern concept of liberalism based on subjective rights. The one, liberalism, replaced the other, republicanism: both are seen as opposed or antagonistic to each other. As John G. A Pocock notes, the tradition of republicanism is based upon a completely different set of principles and vocabulary from what emerged in the nineteenth century as the classic account of liberalism.[22] Such a reading is no doubt supported by selective consideration of the major philosophical and political texts within this long period. But when we take a more holistic view from the position of the aggregated archive, another model for the establishment of modern liberalism becomes discernible. This account sees liberalism as effectively the genetic mutation of liberty as it becomes infected by republicanism. And contrary to the longer historical sweep of a pan-European tradition of republicanism, our data analyses based on ECCO suggest a much narrower timescale in which something far more explosive and forceful occurred. This began to happen in the 1770s, and by the end of the century, English language attempts to wrestle with or adapt and alter the concept of republicanism succeeded in transforming the idea of liberty. Republicanism was, effectively, the catalyst for liberalism. The data, therefore, not only support the revision to the Skinnerian account proposed by Andreas Kalyvas and Ira Katznelson;[23] it also allows us to track with considerable granularity the decisive expansion of the lexical terrain that both supported and gave shape to the idea of liberty, essentially providing a window onto its altering architecture as it encountered an increasingly articulated idea of republicanism. And this, we contend, provided the means for the rapid development of what has come to be one of the most consequential Western political concepts since the nineteenth century: liberalism.

Using the same techniques for ascertaining distributional probability outlined in Section 4.2, we can discern the emergence of this lexical terrain by aggregating the co-associated lexis for a target term at three

(Cambridge: Cambridge University Press, 1994); Michael Zuckert, *The Natural Rights Republic: Studies in the Foundation of the American Political Tradition* (Notre Dame, IN: University of Notre Dame Press, 1996); Craig Yirush, *Settlers, Liberty, and Empire: The Roots of Early American Political Theory, 1675–1775* (Cambridge: Cambridge University Press, 2011); Pamela Clemit, ed., *The Cambridge Companion to British Literature of the French Revolution in the 1790s* (Cambridge: Cambridge University Press, 2010).

[22] John G. A Pocock, 'Virtues, Rights, and Manners: A Model for Historians of Political Thought', in Virtue, Commerce *and History*, 37–50.

[23] See Andreas Kalyvas and Ira Katznelson, *Liberal Beginnings: Making a Republic for the Moderns* (Cambridge: Cambridge University Press, 2008), especially 5–17.

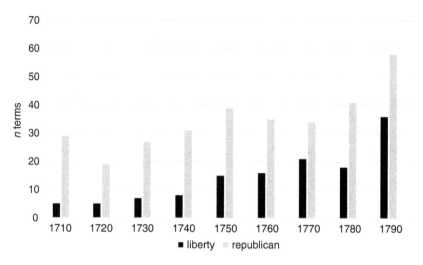

Figure 4.1 Number of terms in the persistent bound-lexical company derived from the common set of terms at distance 10, 50, 100. Counts presented decade by decade 1700–1800. Source: ECCO.

distances: 10, 50 and 100 words away, both before and after the focal term.[24] As our analyses above have already indicated, liberty is a very stable term over the eighteenth century, and its persistent bound-lexical company comprises the following four terms until the 1750s: slavery, volition, tyranny, freedom. Some five more terms enter into this company before that decade and these are servitude, toleration, free, government, licentiousness. The story for republican is very different as can be seen from Figure 4.1, which plots the persistent bound-lexical company for liberty against that for republican with respect to the number of co-associated terms that are common across the three distances.

But it is not simply the fact that the persistent bound-lexical company within which liberty operated began to increase in the decade of the 1750s; it is the overlap in lexis between the company of republican and liberty that provides insight into this process of infection. The terms that comprise that overlap from 1750 are given in Table 4.8.

We interpret the data as indicating that from the 1770s on the idea of liberty, which for over a hundred years had remained stable and resistant to mutation, began to alter under pressure from the attempts within British political theory and debate to conceive of republicanism in

---

[24] See Chapter 2, Section 2.5, where this method for discerning the persistent bound-lexical company of a concept is discussed in detail.

Table 4.8 *Common terms in the persistent bound-lexical company of liberty and republican in each decade from 1750 until 1800. Terms in descending value of dpf. Final row indicates the percentage of the terms within the persistent bound-lexical company for liberty represented by the column. Data source: ECCO.*

1750–60	1760–70	1770–80	1780–90	1790–1800
liberty	despotic	government	arbitrary	despotism
republican	government	despotism	constitution	rights
government	liberty	constitution	government	tyranny
		laws	political	tyrants
		despotic	independence	constitution
		republican	legislative	government
		liberty		equality
				republican
				revolution
				anarchy
				despotic
				citizens
				governments
				republic
				people
				monarchy
				convention
				national
				citizens
18%	17.6%	30.4%	33.3%	51%

a modern dress. This is borne out by the fact that for the first half of the eighteenth century there is no common lexis in the *dpf* lists for liberty and republican at all (the one term in common by 1740 is government, which persists as the single term in common through the 1750s) and that by the end of the century fifty-one percent of liberty's persistent bound-lexical company is held in common with republican's. The following map (Figure 4.2), based upon the same *dpf* information but now expressed within a network graph, indicates that this effort was in large part coincident with the attempts to understand or negotiate the concept of despotism, a word that first appears in English in 1708 but was hardly used for the first fifty years of the century, occurring only 189 times in all English printed text within ECCO up until 1750.[25] During the last decade of the century it appears over 14,000 times.

[25] This observation is based on the ECCO dataset which does not capture *all* lexical use across the anglophone eighteenth century, so to this extent the claim is subject to

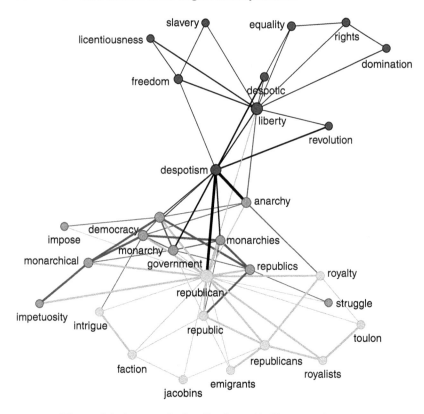

Figure 4.2 A network visualisation with liberty and republican as the focal terms; distance 100, score expressed as *log-dpf* with threshold of 2.6 and rank threshold 20. Date spread 1780–1800. Shading is assigned by a community detection algorithm. Source: ECCO.

We read this visualisation in two ways: firstly, we take the network to represent the tensions between the distinct communities of terms (indicated by different shading), capturing what is identified in Chapter 11, Section 11.1, as both the binding and repelling force between regions in a vector space. In relation to the argument we have outlined, we see the role of despotism as both dragging liberty into proximity with republican and, at the same time, holding the two

qualification. For the first use, see Thomas Cooke, *The Universal Letter-Writer; or, New Art of Polite Correspondence* (London: A. Millar, W. Law and R. Cater, 1708), 123.

apart. This tension, we contend, plays out in our attempts to grasp the lineaments of and contradictions in the modern conception of liberalism as it distances itself (or not) from republicanism. We note in conclusion that the history of these two ideas, liberalism and republicanism, from the nineteenth century to the present-day bears this observation out.

5 The Idea of Government in the British Eighteenth Century

Peter de Bolla, Ewan Jones, Paul Nulty, Gabriel Recchia and John Regan

This chapter complements the previous in a number of ways, but it is important to note that its topic has been determined in the first instance by a curious feature we began to notice as we inspected thousands of *dpf* lists generated by the shared lexis tool. This is to say that without any prior interest in the words which will feature heavily in the following argument, the data returns from the tool indicated that from around the mid-eighteenth century a particular kind of mutual attraction, or binding, began to develop around the terms democracy, aristocracy and monarchy. We were alerted to this because the top four or five terms in the *dpf* lists for each of these terms consistently included the other two terms on lists generated at varying distances and time segments in the dataset. At first, we wondered if our tool was picking up something that operates to a very high degree for all terms in any natural language – say the tendency for terms to co-associate with near synonyms or antonyms – but a corpus-level inspection lead us to conclude that this was not the case.[1] Nevertheless, we were sufficiently intrigued by our initial observations to begin thinking about the ways in which the idea of government was composed over the course of the anglophone eighteenth century. As the scholarship on this topic has long claimed, the accommodations that were necessary for the smooth(ish) transition from an absolute monarchy to the system of democratic government we continue to work with, placed considerable stress on a set of linked terms that include democracy, aristocracy, monarchy, anarchy, republic, liberty, freedom, despotism and tyranny. Indeed, the freighting of these terms in countless debates and arguments across the century might be considered to be in some respects the cause of real-world outcomes such as social unrest, war

---

[1] We developed the data on every clique of three terms in the dataset, using a stricter criterion of inclusion than our initial impressions, and discovered that there are only 175 cliques or mutual dependency sets in all of ECCO, and none of them are unambiguously or overtly cliques containing terms describing a system of government.

in the colonies, imprisonment (think of Wilkes) and the founding of new nations.

Following the modelling of concepts and ideas set out in Chapter 2, we present the following discussion of the theory of government as it came into clear focus over the anglophone long eighteenth century as an exemplification of the utility of this approach. In particular, we depart from the standard history of ideas approach which builds a genealogy of 'great thinkers' who hand down ideas to each other, each putting their own complexion on what came before. In such a model, ideas move from a thinker, or perhaps one 'great text', to another in a chronological chain of transmission: Montesquieu, Harrington, Hobbes, Locke, Rousseau and so on. Our approach is intended to complement this familiar model by using the heuristic set out in Chapter 2, which supposes concepts to be the building blocks of ideas. Thus, we seek to uncover the underlying political concepts formulated in the anglophone eighteenth century that coagulated into clusters and networks – what we call 'bundles' of conceptual forms or ideas – that supported the long project to define and refine the lineaments of what Quentin Skinner designated as 'modern political thought'. We begin, then, with a set of observations on the anglophone eighteenth century understanding of government.

5.1   The Modern Idea of Government

Within the anglophone world of the Enlightenment, the political consensus arrived at in 1688 turned out to be very stable and durable: to this day in Britain we live in a parliamentary monarchy. Over time the lines of force in this conjunction have been subject to scrutiny and attenuation with the first term slowly asserting its priority and unimpeachable authority. Unlike the United States, however, as is repeatedly noted, Britain lacks a document, a written constitution, to which it might refer when parliamentary or governmental authority comes under stress with regard to its legitimacy: all we have is custom and usage. This in itself might make us pause and direct our close attention to *words*, and we shall begin with a brief account of some of these words in their historical constellations, but we wish to indicate that our main purpose is to go beyond mere lexis in order to investigate what we take to be the domain of the conceptual. We shall have more to say about this.

The anglophone Enlightenment's slow cooking of the political theory of parliamentary monarchy entailed pretty consistent attention to the nature of a 'mixed regime' of government that brought into conjunction (with lines of force and attraction that our digital methodology clearly uncovers) the *words* monarchy, aristocracy and democracy – not only words, of course, since their referents are agents in the distributions of power, privilege and politics. We contend that one of the legitimating supports for such action or agency is the *conceptual* conjuncture that was the idea of government, the sign or *techne* of legitimate rule for the time. As a way of getting a quick grip on this mixed regime, we might note that Edmund Burke spent his entire career explaining and promoting its benefit whereby the Crown, Lords and the Commons were jointly and collectively understood to be sovereign. Each could serve as a check on the others with the elected lower house providing one leg of the stool, the hereditary aristocracy another, and the crown the monarchical element. Other writers and thinkers took a different view on some aspects of this triangulation of powers, but our point here is not to follow the intricate debates between individuals or even across texts; rather, we want to observe that this triangulation of words in the first instance – monarchy, aristocracy and democracy – in fact turns out to have a very distinctive signature (which we shall argue is conceptual through and through) in the patterns of distribution of lexis within the culture of the anglophone eighteenth century. Moreover, this apparently commonplace association of the words supervenes upon a deeper conceptual architecture that becomes clear when we subject the massive dataset of ECCO to computational scrutiny. This will be remarked upon in Section 5.2 with respect to our data mining of that archive; here we make the initial observation that 'democracy–aristocracy–monarchy' comprises a 'bundle' of concepts that has very deep foundations in our thinking polities and government within the anglophone tradition from the Enlightenment on.

Our second brief excursus into the uses and histories of words notes this: the word despotism is, until around the decade of the 1740s, almost completely absent from the English language. Although the first use of the word in English was in a handbook for instruction in writing letters penned by the Rev. Thomas Cooke in 1708, in fact the word appears only 189 times in all English printed text up until 1750.[2] During the last decade of the century it appears over 14,000 times. This fact is remarkable given the load the word bears with respect to the geometries of thinking undertaken by the anglophone Enlightenment around the nature of government. Although other European traditions of political thought had long pondered the distinction between tyranny and despotism,

---

[2] This observation is based on the ECCO dataset, which does not capture *all* lexical use across the anglophone eighteenth century, so to this extent the claim is subject to qualification. For the first use, see Rev. Thomas Cooke, *The Universal Letter-Writer; or, New Art of Polite Correspondence* (London: A Millar, W. Law and R. Cater, 1708), 123.

English, it appears, found little use for the word before the 1750s.[3] We should note, however, that once the explosive force of the French revolution against a venal and corrupt aristocracy and a negligent and self-satisfied monarchy occurred, the British were all over the word despotism, applying it not only to the French regime that had been tumbled (a monarchical despotism that Edmund Burke felt the division of powers mitigated) but also to the 'despotism of the people' that ensued. This observation is clearly supported by the fact of the word's frequency, but we shall have a rather more fine-grained analysis to offer which asks us to consider the conceptual knot within which the term operated.

Our third introductory set of remarks seeks to bring to the fore a recurring feature of eighteenth-century conceptual mapping that tests the limits of an idea's internal coherence: how far must one go before, say, freedom turns into slavery? How can we account in structured ways for the complex relationship between a given word (say despotism) and its apparent antonyms (liberty and equality, for instance) and synonyms (tyranny)? At what point can we conclude that a concept fragments or begins to lose coherence? Or extends itself so far as to morph into its opposite as John Brooks, a newly made American, claimed in his observation that 'the extremes of liberty border on despotism'.[4] We think that one way of answering this question, which applies not only to political discourse but also to conceptual usage in general, is to isolate patterns of co-association through computational analysis of large datasets; accordingly, the following sets out to put such methodology into tension with more established forms of intellectual history.

5.2   Data Mining as a Means for Establishing Conceptual Architecture

Let us take an example. The 'language of government' in the anglophone eighteenth century can initially be understood for the purposes of our argument as a network of terms each of which have distinct semantic values. Such networks often contain antonyms, for example, because we often make distinctions between senses through opposition or negation; hence we find that one term co-associates with its opposite (say freedom and slavery). These negation ties are an efficient way of creating and maintaining semantic clarity. Equally we may find synonyms or near-synonyms in a network whose semantic purpose might be to create fine

[3] See Mario Turchetti, '"Despotism" and "Tyranny": Unmasking a Tenacious Confusion', *European Journal of Political Theory*, 7.2 (2008), 159–82; especially 167–76.
[4] John Brooks, *An Oration to the Society of Cincinnati in the Commonwealth of Massachusetts, July 4, 1787* (Boston: Edmund Freeman, 1787), 11.

distinctions between broadly similar values, adding granularity to a larger semantic set (here one might think of the similarities and differences between liberty and freedom). But the ties between words in a network are also determined by larger units of sense making – call these the topics that enable us to rapidly move across and within a cognitive environment (this is one way of describing what we call thinking). An example here would be the binding between liberty and dissenters that we find in the binding list for liberty at distance 70 and in the year spread 1710–30. There is no strictly speaking semantic connection between these two words, but there is a topic or idea connection: dissenters in the period were constrained as to their participation in the political and social life of early eighteenth-century Britain. Hence talk of dissenters was likely to run into the issue of liberty. When mapping these larger networks of bound terms, we speak of the 'company' a term keeps: its proclivities with respect to the number of terms it is predicted to co-associate with, or the preservation of a common set of strongly bound terms over time. This allows us to track how ideas are made up of smaller scale sub-networks we call 'bundles', which are connected to the overall network of considerable complexity that determines the language of government. One of the tools we have constructed (outlined in Chapter 1) enables us to visualise the complex connections between bundles in a larger network and to identify the multiple pathways at different levels of resolution. We can also track these pathways diachronically, thus enabling us to see how ideas change over time.

We turn now to some of the data our custom-designed algorithm produces. In Table 5.1 we present the result of our searches through the second half of the ECCO corpus (1751–1800) for the top twenty-one bound content words most tightly bound at a distance of 100 words from the word government.[5]

In Table 5.1 we can see that our metric of *dpf* ranks the term government as most tightly bound with itself.[6] The terms which follow comprise

---

[5] Note, as set out in Chapter 2, Introduction, that these ranked lists of bound words can be very long, so the issue is where to set a threshold so as to screen out noise but nevertheless identify significant information. Calculating the threshold in the manner there indicated for government (1751–1800) results in 271 terms. For visualisation purposes, we display only the very top of this list here and we have excluded any stopwords.

[6] This is due to the well-characterised phenomenon referred to in computational linguistics as 'burstiness', whereby if a word does appear once, it is much more likely to appear again, that is words appear in bursts. See Rasmus E. Madsen, David Kauchak and Charles Elkan, 'Modeling Word Burstiness Using the Dirichlet Distribution', in *Proceedings of the 22nd International Conference on Machine Learning* (Bonn: 2005), 545–52: 546. Kenneth W. Church and William A. Gale, 'Poisson Mixtures', *Natural Language Engineering*, 1.2 (1995), 163–90.

Table 5.1 *The top twenty-one content words having the highest* dpf *values with focal token government at distance 100 among all documents in ECCO published from 1751 to 1800 (118,166 documents; 6.3 billion tokens).*

Distance 100 (top 21 of 449 total)

Bound token	dpf	N (total)	N (with focal)
government	6377	1346178	32448
governments	4121	83420	2396
democracy	4069	19881	773
monarchical	3299	15609	519
monarchy	3194	114367	2375
executive	2974	66030	1441
aristocracy	2823	14269	414
constitution	2815	466329	6265
republican	2648	38774	847
despotism	2567	24782	579
political	2459	292778	3806
despotic	2424	33141	686
legislative	2363	51430	942
laws	2210	1269863	10745
republic	2174	185536	2358
revolution	2117	206732	2498
anarchy	2105	34305	612
rights	2093	419510	4290
administration	2083	217808	2560
civil	2057	674383	6105
republics	2046	22495	428

the twenty next most highly co-associated words with government at this distance.[7] Getting a sense of the strength of binding between a target word, here government, and its bound pairs is a good place to begin if we want to assess the coherence and stability of a network over time. But we can also develop analyses of the different structures we find in these binding lists and compare them. One such structure we call 'mutual association', whereby the terms very highly bound to one term also feature very close to the top of another term's binding list. Terms held in a mutual-association binding structure are rarely abstractions, but there is one significant outlier to this general observation: across the eighteenth century we find the triad democracy–aristocracy–monarchy

---

[7] The list at a distance of ten words apart contains only one different word, tyranny. We take this to indicate that the language of government in the period operated within a very tight lexical-conceptual network.

in a mutual association structure of binding.[8] Table 5.2 presents the top six bound terms for each.

We interpret this data as evidence for how the period (as represented in and by the ECCO dataset) thought or conceptualised democracy within an underlying structure of binding that tied it to both aristocracy and monarchy. And the same observation applies to the other terms: that is its *mutual* binding. Let us say, then, that when thinking about the nature of government in this period, one would have been very likely to bump into one of the terms in this mutual association structure. Of course, there are other gateways or apertures through which one might think government (as Table 5.1 indicates – one such term was executive). But if we inspect the data for each of the three focal tokens presented in Table 5.2, we can see that the terms most co-associated with government itself include our triad of democracy–aristocracy–monarchy/monarchies, monarchical. Although this surely would come as little surprise to intellectual historians of the period, what is noteworthy is the underlying structure or architecture: it is not that one would have been likely to summon up democracy when thinking with or about the idea of government, but that summoning this term inevitably brings into view the other two. *And this holds true for both of the other terms.* Since each of these terms – as government itself – also has a much longer list of relatively strongly bound other terms, the mapping or intermeshing of all these binding lists quickly becomes extremely complex. One way of getting a view onto that complexity is to set a threshold for the number of ranked terms on a binding list and then to compare the lexis on each list so as to construct a common set. If we do that for the top sixteen terms on each binding list in our triad, once again with the date slice being the second half of the century, we arrive at this common set: democracy, aristocracy, monarchical, monarchy, republics, monarchies, republican, government, governments, despotic, republic, hereditary, despotism, anarchy, tyranny, constitution. One can immediately see a pattern emerging in the co-association data presented so far – the lexis we find in the orbit of the idea of government in the second half of the eighteenth century has considerable stability and coherence, and the mutuality of the binding across the three terms we have identified as a triad persists over a considerable stretch of time.[9] Our aim, however, is to dig deeper into the data so as to more carefully inspect the

---

[8] We have developed data on the entirety of ECCO to ascertain how common this kind of binding structure is and the extent to which it occurs more with concrete terms than abstract. The data is clear: there are 2,852 distinct cliques of three concrete words in which mutual binding occurs as opposed to 1,547 abstract.

[9] The same analysis for the first half of the century comprises the following terms: republics, republic, consuls, plebians, senators, domestic, senate, tribunes, tribune, national.

Table 5.2 *The top six terms having the highest* dpf *values with focal tokens democracy, aristocracy and monarchy at distance 100 among all documents in ECCO published from 1751 to 1800 (118,166 documents; 6.3 billion tokens).*

(a) Focal token democracy (19,881 instances)

Distance 100 (top 6 of 449 total)

Bound token	dpf	N (total)	N (with focal)
democracy	48506	19881	344
aristocracy	15524	14269	85
monarchical	10558	15609	62
patricians	6794	15659	40
republics	6274	22495	49
monarchy	6159	114367	171

(b) Focal token aristocracy (14,269 instances)

Distance 100 (top 6 of 480 total)

Bound token	dpf	N (total)	N (with focal)
aristocracy	47786	14269	202
democracy	15524	19881	85
impeded	5797	13891	24
monarchy	4898	114367	105
republics	4644	22495	28
monarchical	4411	15609	20

(c) Focal token monarchy (114,367 instances)

Distance 100 (top 6 of 331 total)

Bound token	dpf	N (total)	N (with focal)
monarchy	11207	114367	1218
monarchical	7786	15609	179
democracy	6159	19881	171
monarchies	5984	21095	174
aristocracy	4898	14269	105
republican	4620	38774	216

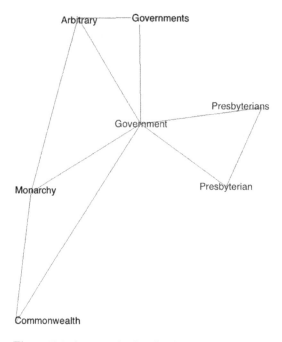

Figure 5.1 A network visualisation with government as the focal term; distance 100, score expressed as *log-dpf* with threshold of 2.6 and rank threshold 20. Date spread 1720–30. Shading is assigned by a community detection algorithm. Source: ECCO.

complexities of these lexical-conceptual behaviours. We now turn to some of the techniques we have established for analysing this complexity through the use of a visualisation method.

5.3   Visualisation of Networks as an Analytic Method

The numbers in Figure 5.1 are derived from the same calculations we have made to discern the *dpf* of terms in our dataset (ECCO). In this case, however, we have exported the data into a network environment that helps us to identify complex patterns of similarity and connection between data points, which are here represented as words in our dataset. The figures are based on screenshots from these network representations displayed in an interactive web app.[10] In Figure 5.1 we can see the lexical environment in which government operated in the 1720s.

---

[10] For a full account of this tool, see Chapter 3.

Here one can see that the term government is connected to six other terms, based upon our code's prediction of its co-association profile. Those terms are, moving from east to north: Presbyterian, Presbyterians, commonwealth, monarchy, arbitrary and governments. By the last decade of the century the network within which government operated had become significantly more complex (see Figure 5.3). Now the terms in the denser network include those in its immediate vicinity, the sub-network outlined in grey: constitution, legislation, subversion, executive, burthens, discontents, Englishmen, abdication, political and magistracy. And this sub-network is bound to the one marked in lighter grey which includes the words: governments, monarchical, nation, polity, people, aristocracy, heredity, nation and democracy. The third sub-network indicated includes: republic, republics, republican, monarchies, despot and despotism.[11]

It is to be expected that these two different ways of slicing into the co-association behaviour of the term government across the period (the first generating the metric of *dpf* and listing bound words in descending order of strength of binding, and the second using a higher dimensional space of a network to visualise nodes and edges that are connected) agree to a very great extent. We *should* find the same lexis because the underlying data are held in common. But the presentational matrix is also a diagnostic tool: we can identify patterns or behaviours by dint of the different ways in which we can inspect the information. And this helps us isolate creases or folds in the data, which drive further investigation. An example of precisely this aspect of the digital method can be seen in the network plot in Figure 5.2.

This plot operates the same thresholds as our previous plots and indicates that the tightly bound company that government keeps in the decade of the 1750s does not include despotism, the term isolated on its own at the right edge of the plot (in light grey). Moreover, despotism has no other terms for company. This accords with the fact that the word in English at this time is very infrequent (commented upon in Section 5.5), but the algorithm is not simply driven by word frequency: the plot is constructed as a representation of the relations or connections between these terms, a heuristic device, which enables us to pose questions about the conceptual supports or architectures for the bundle of terms we are hypothesising comprised the idea of government at the time.

If we turn to Figure 5.3, which presents a visualisation of the data from the final decade of the century, we find that the overall network much

---

[11] Our metric of *dpf* controls for background frequency thereby in part discounting for the fact that the later decades of the century contain more textual information. The takeaway here is that the density of plot indicates a far richer set of co-associations within and across sub-networks: the language of government had become richer.

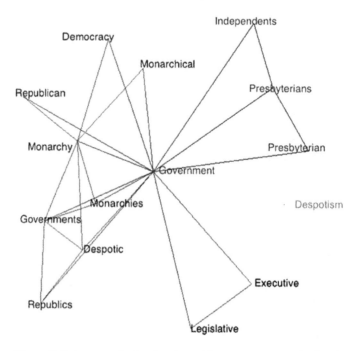

Figure 5.2 A network visualisation with government as the focal term; distance 100, score expressed as *log-dpf* with threshold of 2.6 and rank threshold 20. Date spread 1750–60. Shading is assigned by a community detection algorithm. Source: ECCO.

more closely accords, as it should, with the rank *dpf* list in Table 5.1, and one can note that despotism (the sub-network in grey) has its own quite substantial company including the words tyranny, anarchy and revolution, and that this sub-network has both a direct connection to government and its sub-network and indirect links (via one additional node) to that same network through republican, monarchy, hereditary, anarchy and democracy.

What our visualisation tool has enabled us to see is the steadily increasing bundle or sub-network within which despotism appears as the century moves into its final decades. And its presence in the overall network re-calibrates or adjusts the relations between its constituent parts. One of those adjustments bears heavily upon the conceptualisation of government: the centrality of despotism as a hinge or bridge for liberty and the corresponding marginalisation of tyranny as structural element in a theory of democratic polity. In the next section we present another computational technique for digging deeper into this observation.

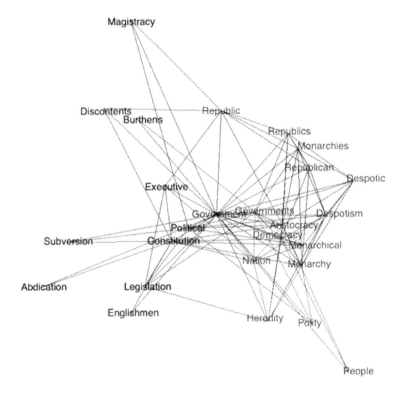

Figure 5.3 A network visualisation with government as the focal term; distance 100, score expressed as *log-dpf* with threshold of 2.6 and rank threshold 20. Date spread 1790–1800. Shading is assigned by a community detection algorithm. Source: ECCO.

5.4   High-Dimensional Conceptual Analytics

As we have seen, the 'language of government', that which supports the idea of democratic polity across the eighteenth century, includes a cluster or bundle of sixteen words. We can assess the extent to which this language swerves towards one term, despotism, or the other, tyranny, over time by calculating the correlations in high-dimensional space between the search term and this list of sixteen bound terms (see Chapter 2 for the explanation of how these Pearson correlations are constructed). Thus, in the early part of the century when the word despotism is very infrequent, we can see here in Table 5.3 that there is very little correlation.

We interpret these calculations as providing evidence for the non-correlation between the lexical contexts within which the word despotism

Table 5.3 *Pearson correlations and cosine similarities between the full* dpf *lists of despotism and selected terms at distance 100 among all documents in ECCO published from 1720 to 1740 (29,332 documents; 1.6 billion tokens; 55 instances of despotism).*

Bound token	Pearson correlation	Cosine similarity	N (total)
government	0.075	0.089	244535
tyranny	0.067	0.083	26446
liberty	0.066	0.081	242331
monarchy	0.066	0.081	23525
governments	0.063	0.077	10733
republic	0.061	0.071	6702
anarchy	0.049	0.059	2646
monarchies	0.048	0.059	3174
constitution	0.039	0.061	59271
republican	0.035	0.045	2490
despotic	0.028	0.035	632
democracy	0.026	0.031	1230
aristocracy	0.025	0.031	581
monarchical	0.018	0.027	2130
hereditary	0.017	0.036	15318
republics	0.005	0.009	379

circulated in the date slice and the lexical contexts for each of the sixteen words in the table. Table 5.4 provides a comparison with tyranny using the same high-dimensional approach and date spread.

In this case we interpret the calculations as indicative of how our bundle of the same sixteen words – what we are characterising as the essence of the idea of government in the period – shares a lexical-conceptual terrain with tyranny to a far greater extent than with despotism. As a way of confirming this correlation we have made the same high-dimensional analysis, once again using the same list of terms, through the search term government, here presented in Table 5.5.

In the period 1720–40 the 'language of government' and its supporting conceptual bundles hardly includes the lexical-conceptual entity despotism – it correlates less than the mean for every term in the dataset. By the end of the century, as we can see from Table 5.6, this had been transformed.

In Table 5.6 we have compared the correlations across the two date slices, 1750–70 and 1780–1800, in order to map the increasing presence of despotism within the constellation of terms that supported the idea of government. We take this as evidence for the fact that not only was despotism becoming more and more central to a theory of government

Table 5.4 *Pearson correlations and cosine similarities between the full* dpf *lists of tyranny and selected terms at distance 100 among all documents in ECCO published from 1720 to 1740 (29,332 documents; 1.6 billion tokens; 26,446 instances of tyranny).*

Bound token	Pearson correlation	Cosine similarity	N (total)
government	0.492	0.662	244535
liberty	0.457	0.651	242331
monarchy	0.320	0.481	23525
constitution	0.312	0.527	59271
governments	0.276	0.421	10733
republic	0.180	0.270	6702
republican	0.166	0.255	2490
hereditary	0.166	0.345	15318
monarchies	0.158	0.266	3174
anarchy	0.139	0.229	2646
aristocracy	0.130	0.169	581
monarchical	0.129	0.197	2130
democracy	0.126	0.171	1230
despotic	0.079	0.140	632
despotism	0.067	0.083	55
republics	0.030	0.064	379

Table 5.5 *Pearson correlations and cosine similarities between the full* dpf *lists of government and selected terms at distance 100 among all documents in ECCO published from 1720 to 1740 (29,332 documents; 1.6 billion tokens; 244,535 instances of government).*

Bound token	Pearson correlation	Cosine similarity	N (total)
liberty	0.681	0.837	242331
constitution	0.554	0.730	59271
monarchy	0.525	0.653	23525
tyranny	0.492	0.662	26446
governments	0.449	0.568	10733
hereditary	0.327	0.498	15318
monarchical	0.309	0.339	2130
democracy	0.260	0.275	1230
republican	0.256	0.335	2490
aristocracy	0.251	0.260	581
monarchies	0.224	0.334	3174
republic	0.219	0.312	6702
anarchy	0.193	0.286	2646
despotic	0.114	0.178	632
despotism	0.075	0.089	55
republics	0.052	0.087	379

Table 5.6 *Pearson correlations (r values) and cosine similarities between the full dpf lists of government and selected terms at distance 100 among all documents in ECCO published from 1750 to 1770 (41,829 documents; 2.2 billion tokens; 346,387 instances of government) and among those published from 1780 to 1800 (73,104 documents; 3.8 billion tokens; 794,588 instances of government). Tokens are sorted by the difference in their Pearson correlation in 1750–70 versus 1780–1800.*

	1750–70			1780–1800			Diff.
Bound token	r	Cosine	N	r	Cosine	N	r diff.
despotism	0.291	0.349	2080	0.602	0.695	19474	0.311
anarchy	0.305	0.423	5529	0.586	0.702	24241	0.282
republican	0.385	0.455	5322	0.600	0.694	29177	0.215
republic	0.503	0.636	44293	0.644	0.753	120722	0.141
governments	0.568	0.662	20037	0.705	0.781	50944	0.137
hereditary	0.437	0.599	26167	0.563	0.702	60356	0.126
constitution	0.652	0.801	102137	0.777	0.872	301651	0.125
despotic	0.427	0.502	7938	0.551	0.677	19295	0.124
democracy	0.318	0.314	3259	0.434	0.491	14081	0.116
tyranny	0.565	0.726	40033	0.662	0.798	80269	0.097
monarchical	0.400	0.435	3697	0.486	0.560	9647	0.086
republics	0.364	0.414	4488	0.438	0.524	14836	0.075
monarchy	0.622	0.717	33093	0.692	0.781	64119	0.070
monarchies	0.295	0.397	7078	0.352	0.485	10294	0.057
aristocracy	0.364	0.375	1918	0.392	0.448	11001	0.029
liberty	0.692	0.843	350222	0.713	0.852	607179	0.021

but that it also provided a kind of negative counterweight to the increasingly fraught concept of liberty, which by the end of the century could no longer be assumed to be the natural purpose or aspiration for any system of government.

5.5   Despotism and the Modern Theory of Government

As we noted in our introduction, the word despotism hardly occurs in English before the 1740s. While it is the case that the word despot does occur, as does despotic, the raw frequencies of occurrence of all three words across the eighteenth century indicate that up until 1750 they were, effectively, not used. Despotic is the most frequent term and it increases in use from mid-century, but from 1775 the frequency of despotism begins to track uses of despotic and in the 1790s overtakes it. This is perhaps striking, given that the English language tends, in the eighteenth

century, to restrict abstractions ending in the suffix 'ism' to tightly specified contexts, mostly religious.[12] And there are only five words with
a frequency greater than 10,000 in our ECCO corpus indicating adher-
ence to a particular system or ideology – atheism, paganism, fanaticism,
patriotism and despotism.[13] The data indicate that among these five
terms up until 1766 atheism was the most common 'ism', but by the
end of the century despotism far outstripped all other contenders.[14]

These statistical trends support what we already know about the politics of the period: the clear spike in 1793–5 can be read as a symptom of
the British counter-revolutionary campaign, its 'war on terror' on home-
grown republican tendencies. Yet the simple rise to prominence of the
individual word despotism, taken by itself, poses broader questions when
we consider the larger conceptual bundle that we established in
Section 5.4. Did this new entrant re-configure the discourse on government, or was it simply drawn into that constellation's ambit? How did it
both open up and close down travel between the bundles of concepts or
ideas that comprised the larger network? Our contention is that it significantly re-mapped the terrain we have been exploring, and in order to
support this claim, we now want to toggle between the large computational patterns investigated in Tables 5.3–5.6 and more localised close
readings that are commonly the evidence base for traditional histories of
ideas.

Intellectual historians have provided extensive and persuasive accounts
of concepts such as tyranny and despotism over historical periods far
broader than that which this chapter surveys. Mario Turchetti, for
example, has surveyed the development and subsequent eclipse of tyranny from early antiquity, arguing for the term's enduring relevance in
our post-totalitarian age;[15] whereas Melvin Richter dates the modern

---

[12] These terms are: scepticism, deism, Judaism, heathenism, libertinism, polytheism, polytheism, Arianism, Calvinism, theism, Methodism, republicanism, stoicism, Hebraism
and Puritanism. David Simpson argues that theoretical abstractions were inimical to
English during this period and that this was one of the ways in which Britain distinguished
itself from its political rival France and the French language. See David Simpson,
Romanticism, Nationalism, and the Revolt against Theory (Chicago: University of
Chicago Press, 1993).

[13] This criterion excludes some highly frequent words that happen to end in 'ism', such as
criticism, schism and mechanism.

[14] These data prompt further speculation about the particular shapes and patterns that
would emerge if overtly religious terms capturing a specific type of observance (say
Calvinism) or its denial (atheism) were tracked in relation to the political concepts we
are investigating here. Work on this is ongoing.

[15] Mario Turchetti has surveyed the development and subsequent eclipse of tyranny from
early antiquity, arguing for the term's enduring relevance in our post-totalitarian age.
See Turchetti, '"Despotism" and "Tyranny"'; Melvin Richter argues, by contrast, that
the semantic fuzziness of tyranny, despotism and so on is a strong incentive *not* to

resurgence of despotism to Montesquieu's *De l'Esprit des lois* (1748), which prefers the term to the then-current tyranny.[16] The distinction between the two synonyms is, Richter contends, comparatively clear-cut: Montesquieu reserves tyranny for republics and uses despotism with respect to nation-states; tyranny designates an individual ruler who may be replaced (hence the cognate tyrannicide), while despotism entails a broader notion of government. Yet the latter half of the eighteenth century, he continues, sees this distinction evaporate. Montesquieu, despite being a pragmatic reformist, unwittingly bequeaths his term to revolutionaries and counter-revolutionaries of all colours and stripes:

By the end of the 18th century, *despotisme* had been used in so many ways, positively and negatively, that it was at once omnipresent and without any single distinctive meaning. Although some theorists continued to distinguish it from *tyrannie*, as we shall find Condorcet doing in his treatment of human rights, these two terms in less specialized general usage ceased to be differentiated.[17]

It is worth pausing over such claims, both for substantive and methodological reasons. In order to substantiate this argument (that despotism travelled from comparative conceptual clarity to increasing fuzziness), we would need to show, firstly, that tyranny and despotism *were* 'differentiated', even in 'less specialized general usage', over the earlier portion of the eighteenth century; and, secondly, that the subsequent confusion of the two terms precluded any relevant conceptual disarticulation. Furthermore, Richter has an even more eye-catching thesis that political terms such these undergo a process of 'whiting out' – a phrase that Richter borrows from the founder of *Begriffsgeschichte*, Reinhart Koselleck – which results in a loss of specificity in meaning, effectively emerging as an ungovernable polysemy.[18]

Such global claims about diachronic change are not easily supported by human-scale reading: Richter, outstanding intellectual historian as he is, works within the traditions and prevailing methodology of the discipline. He closely reads the 'master texts' such as *De l'Esprit des lois*. Now, however, we are able to read at *inhuman* scale, using computational means for tracking lexical behaviour across massive datasets. We believe that such computational methodologies can help place claims established through close reading upon a more secure footing – all the more so when they are used as a supplement to, rather than a replacement of, the close reading of texts. When, indeed, we apply the procedures that we have

re-appropriate such terms for the present age. See Melvin Richter, 'A Family of Political Concepts: Tyranny, Despotism, Bonarpartism, Caesarism, Dictatorship, 1750–1917', *European Journal of Political Theory*, 4.3 (2005), 221–48.
[16] Richter, 'A Family of Political Concepts', 229–30.   [17] Ibid. 231.   [18] Ibid. 244.

outlined, we see clear evidence that the two synonyms concerned (despotism and tyranny) *do* continue (or perhaps even begin) to operate in definably different contexts. These contexts are both shaped by, and in turn contribute to, the broader idea of government that we traced with the mutual association set above.

One of the advantages of the computational tools used here is their provision for a rapid toggling between quantitative patterns of data and the individual texts of which they are comprised. When we switch optics in this fashion, we find that the quantitative trends established in Tables 5.3–5.6 reflect a series of structured ways in which language users employed the idea of government in general, and the emergent notion of despotism in particular. To be sure, there are several instances in which, just as Richter claims, the two terms were used interchangeably. Yet despite this tendency, and despite what any reader of the archive has to acknowledge as the multiplicity of (sometimes mutually exclusive) linguistic contexts in which the term emerges, despotism reveals a number of clear structural trends. All the examples following explore representative contexts in which despotism co-associates with one or more of the terms we have established as operating within the conceptual network of government in the period, and in order to dampen a focus on the texts themselves we have removed their citational traces to the footnotes. When these thousands of linguistic contexts are inspected, decontextualised from the broader argument or theme of the works at hand, three clear structural trends emerge. Despotism, unlike its synonym tyranny, is frequently employed so as to describe (1) a system of governmental *balance*, (2) a theory of governmental *development* and (3) a counter-intuitive affinity between itself and liberty. These tendencies are distinct, albeit that they are often also mutually supportive. We will treat each in turn.

Governmental balance. Despotism, unlike tyranny, is frequently drawn into a broader architecture of government. The logic often runs something like this: despotism is to government as licentiousness is to liberty. The optimal (or least bad) political model, on this view, lies in in the golden middle of these two extremes. Freedom is therefore not an absolute good. Countless examples could be cited; here are but a few: 'privilege and right which constitutes the essence of a free government distinguished on one hand from despotism and on the other from too great licentiousness and anarchy'; 'anarchy my lords is not liberty no more than despotism is government'; 'ill calculated for so large an empire just bursting from the shackles of extreme despotism and liable to fall into the other extreme of licentiousness and anarchy'; 'it is true that no government can subsist in the midst of licentiousness. But, *licentiousness* and *despotism* are only different names for the same thing'; 'natural corruption of liberty is licentiousness; and the necessary correction thereof opens the way to despotism'; 'liberty, subject to no controul, is licentiousness, producing anarchy and confusion, and frequently ending in downright despotism'.[19]

At times, this striking general trend directly permits the disarticulation of despotism *from* tyranny, as when the desire to remove a political evil (i.e. through tyrannicide) involves those mutineers in a travesty of liberty as despotism: 'the people deceived by the charms and delusive attractions of an apparent liberty inadvertently plunge into the most horrid excesses and finish their violent pursuits by establishing a most hateful despotism planned by the very persons who began the tragedy by proclaiming themselves the avengers of tyranny'.[20] The upshot of such examples is that despotism was understood to be a form of government that took its place next to other competing forms such as democracy, rather than a type of tyranny in which the arbitrary rule of an individual was imposed upon the *polis*.

The association of despotism with government therefore clearly poses a potential problem for reformist and revolutionary discourses alike: there is no silver bullet to eradicate despotism as there is for tyranny – tyrannicide. Yet it also offers practical resources: if a theory of government invariably produces the tendency towards despotism, those instruments can be appropriated even by those who believe in liberty. David Hume, for example, viewed political societies as necessary composites: 'we are to consider the ROMAN government under the emperors as a mixture of despotism and liberty, where the despotism prevailed; and the ENGLISH government as a mixture of the same kind, where the liberty predominates'.[21] More positive formulations of this general idea can also be found: 'they may endeavour to ally the peace of despotism with the delights of liberty'.[22]

---

[19] These extracts come respectively from William Coxe, *A Letter to the Rev. Richard Price, D. D. LL. D. F. R. S. &c. upon His 'Discourse on the Love of our Country', Delivered November 4, 1789* (London: T. Cadell, 1790), 44; Charles McCormick, *The History of England, from the Death of George the Second to the Peace of 1783*, 3 vols. (London: C. Cooke, 1795), II, 53; Coxe, A Letter to the Rev. Richard Price, 41; William L. Brown, *An Essay on the Natural Equality of Mankind* (London: T. Cadell, W. Davies and A. Brown, 1799), 145; *The Scotch Preacher, or, A Collection of Sermons*, III (Edinburgh: T. Cadell and J. Dickson, 1789), 333; *Some Hints in Regard to the Better Management of the Poor: In a Letter to a Noble Lord* (London: T. Cadell, 1784), 25.

[20] By John T. Troy, *A Pastoral Instruction on the Duties of Christian Citizens, Addressed to the Roman Catholics of the Archdiocess of Dublin* (Dublin: printed for P. Wogan, 1793), 2.

[21] David Hume, *Essays and Treatises on Various Subjects* (London: A. Millar, 1758), 7.

[22] Jacques-Vincent Delacroix, *A Review of the Constitutions of the Principal States of Europe* (London: G. G. J. and J. Robinson, 1792), 276.

Governmental process. We have already seen that Montesquieu's conceptual disarticulation persists with remarkable force, even into a later historical period and a separate language tradition. The English rendering of *De L'Esprit des Lois* resonates with the efforts of eighteenth-century British political theorists to articulate the exceptionalism of the peculiarly effective reconciliation of competing powers that had emerged since 1688: 'Democracy therefore has two excesses to avoid, the spirit of inequality which leads to aristocracy or monarchy; and the spirit of extreme equality, which leads to despotic power, as the latter is completed by conquest.'[23] The trick they had discovered was to conceptualise despotism as a form of government both in a structural sense, and also as a dynamic process. On this common view, a natural process emerges whereby, say, despotism inevitably leads to democracy; once again, this distinguishes uses of despotism from tyranny since the latter was commonly thought of as a state in which one might find oneself with little chance of being extracted from it. Its temporality was effectively steady state. This should not be understood to indicate that the processual aspect of despotism always led in the same direction; in fact the processes set in motion could be mutually exclusive: they could, for example, support optimistic or even utopian agendas – 'liberty has often sprung from despotism'.[24] So too they could be mobilised for more conservative projects: 'England should *dread* that attachment to liberty which produces such excesses, and consider that if not checked they will soon rise to anarchy and possibly end in despotism'; 'this very Cromwell originally sowed all the seeds of his future despotism in the fertile but disguised hot-bed of *Equality*'.[25] These and many other examples confirm Richter's claim that despotism might be used in a 'bewildering' variety of often contradictory contexts, but they also betray a recognisable mode of thinking in which government is conceptualised with respect to its evolution or change over time: a necessarily unfixed or emergent form of social and political organisation, a *process*.

Affinity of despotism and liberty. These examples already provide evidence for the ways in which despotism and liberty intersect in complex ways. This might involve simple contradiction, affinity-through-opposition (licentiousness is to liberty as despotism is to government) or

---

[23] Montesquieu, *The Spirit of the Laws*, 7th ed. (Edinburgh: Alexander Donaldson, 1778), 140.

[24] Tobias Smollett, *A Complete History of England*, 4 vols. (London: printed for James Rivington, James Fletcher and R. Baldwin, 1754), II, 83.

[25] These extracts come respectively from *Experience Preferable to Theory* (London: T. Payne, 1776), 84; *Liberty and Property Preserved against Republicans and Levellers* (London: J. Sewell, J. Debrett and Hookham and Carpenter, 1793), 10.

process (liberty grows out of despotism, or vice versa). Taken together, such common formulations pave the way for a more extreme conceptual articulation: that liberty or equality is (or can be) despotism (or vice versa). When the newly minted American John Brooks claims, for example, that 'the extremes of liberty border on despotism', he is not suggesting that one extreme is *like* another, or *produces* its opposite; rather, the two terms liberty and despotism share a substantive essence.[26] It is important to state that such formulations are politically agnostic: they can be recruited to serve conservative or revolutionary agendas. We find countless examples of the former: 'such governments according to Polybius terminate in despotism not from the abuse of royalty or aristocracy but from the licence of democracy it seems that the people can no longer be intrusted safely with the exercise of power'.[27] Yet this counter-intuitive affinity between liberty and despotism can also serve very different ends. Richter reminds us of Robespierre's famous declaration that 'the government of the revolution is the despotism of liberty against tyranny', which he takes to indicate the 'whiting out' of meaning.[28] By polemically treating despotism as a political good, Richter claims, Robespierre unwittingly contributes to its general fuzziness. As we have seen above, the phrase certainly is used in a variety of ways, which encompass the structural and the dynamic, the positive and the pejorative. Yet in light of that broader cultural sampling, it is striking just how much Robespierre *retains* a common form of thinking: 'the despotism of liberty' is expressly governmental and contrasts explicitly with an ill – 'tyranny' – that can be directly opposed. When Robespierre equated these two concepts, it was in part because the conceptual fusion was culturally available to him.

This is not to claim that Robespierre directly read Hume's reflections on the compatibility of despotism and liberty, nor to corroborate the sometimes stronger claims made for the cohabitation of both concepts in the more marginal English-language texts that we have surveyed. Our argument rests upon the basis that such linguistic utterances proceed not simply through the desire of a Montesquieu or a Robespierre to alter a given concept decisively – which is to enthrone individuals as the drivers of conceptual change, while often relegating the whole cultural archive to a merely subsidiary or even distorting role. We insist on the far

[26] Brooks, Oration, 11.
[27] See also Alexander Knox, *Essays on the Political Circumstances of Ireland* (Dublin: J. Plymsoll, 1799), 200; Madame de Staël, *A Treatise on the Influence of the Passions, upon the Happiness of Individuals and of Nations* (London: printed for Henry Colborn, 1798), 178.
[28] Richter, 'A Family of Political Concepts', 234.

wider embedding of lexical use in the culture at large, which provides us with information on conceptual change over time. By the end of the eighteenth century, we contend, despotism was not simply one satellite in the fixed constellation of terms used for describing and understanding government – it had become *indispensable* within that constellation. Thus, if we toggle back from the local level to the larger computational patterns that we established in Section 5.4, we can see just how indispensable in Figure 5.4.

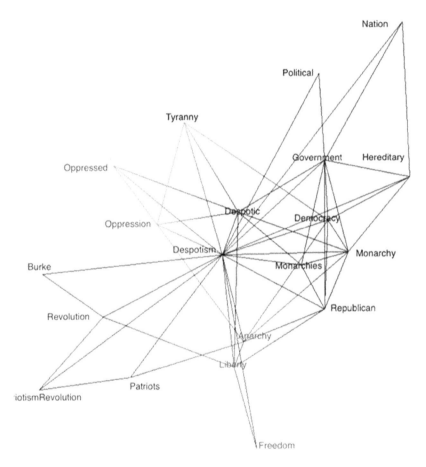

Figure 5.4 A network visualisation with despotism as the focal term; distance 100, score expressed as *log-dpf* with threshold of 2.6 and rank threshold 20. Date spread 1790–1800. Shading is assigned by a community detection algorithm. Source: ECCO.

Figure 5.5 A network visualisation with liberty as the focal term; distance 100, score expressed as *log-dpf* with threshold of 2.6 and rank threshold 20. Date spread 1790–1800. Shading is assigned by a community detection algorithm. Source: ECCO.

It is important to note that our algorithm centres the search term in a plot – hence nothing should be immediately read from the fact that the despotism in the network plot in Figure 5.4 is the largest represented node. However, we take it as significant that despotism draws both liberty and freedom into the network with government. As can be seen from the network plot in Figure 5.5, when we open the network through the search term liberty, we find no connection to government.

We interpret these computationally derived network plots as aids to understanding how the idea of despotism brought into close contact the more established ideas that informed the period's thinking about government – acting as a kind of hinge or bridge to them. As we have already suggested, we can think of despotism as operating like a switching station, sometimes providing an aperture through which liberty enters the larger network and sometimes operating as an antagonist blocking the pathway. And, as Figure 5.5 suggests to us, the liberty network pulls with it the term that will become unavoidable in our own contemporary attempts to think equality, freedom, government: rights. Might we take this as evidence for the observation that in the era of universal rights, say post the 1948 declaration, rights and liberty are interconnected and that this way of thinking has its roots in the later eighteenth-century admixture of government, rights and despotism? In any event, it may be worth recalling this in our contemporary efforts to establish universal human rights.

We might conclude from this exemplary exploration of digital methods that large-scale computer assisted reading of the archive can deepen and strengthen more long-standing traditions of inquiry into the history of ideas. Ideas and the concepts that support and construct them are both distributed across a culture at large and at the same time used by – even on occasion invented by – historical actors. Combining both close and distant reading techniques allows us to inspect the finer grain of the archive and to track larger scale movements both across texts or regions in the archive and over time.

6   Republicanism in the Founding of America

Peter de Bolla

In an essay first published in 1986, the renowned historian of the founding period of America, Joyce Appleby, asked the following question: 'What did Americans in the late eighteenth century mean when they spoke about republicanism?'[1] Her essay was intended to build upon an earlier one, entitled 'Republicanism and Ideology', in which she laid out the central tenets of what became known as the 'Republican thesis', which was itself most strenuously developed by John G. A. Pocock. Appleby notes that in its earliest uses this thesis supposed that 'republicanism referred to a body of ideas said to have animated the men of the revolutionary generation' and that these men were ploughing a furrow first initiated by opposition parties to the British government whose central motivating ideology was the protection of the English constitution from what they characterised as the threat of arbitrary power and endemic corruption within the governing classes.[2] Very quickly, Appleby noted, substantial revisions to the history of the founding era became established that sought to explain the political upheaval of the separation of the colonies from the 'mother country' based upon close reading of classical political theory. This revisionist story was intended to capture what 'men believed in the early Anglo-America world', thereby sweeping 'the colonial house of intellect clean of those wonderfully accessible slogans about no taxation without representation and retrofitted it with a sterner, chaster set of truths about the fragility of civil order and the ferocicty of uncivil passions'.[3] Appleby argued in this essay that in fact republicanism had 'two careers' in the historiography she goes on to outline, essentially drawing together works of revisionist history that quickly established themselves as the new orthodoxy and which would henceforth need to be negotiated in all subsequent histories of the founding era.[4] The first

---

[1] Joyce Appleby, 'Republicanism in Old and New Contexts', in *Liberalism and Republicanism in the Historical Imagination* (Cambridge, MA: Harvard University Press, 1992), 320.
[2] Ibid. 277. This essay was first published in 1985.   [3] Ibid. 278.
[4] The three key texts which set this agenda are Bernard Bailyn, *The Ideological Origins of the American Revolution*, enlarged ed. (Cambridge, MA: Belknap Press of Harvard University, 1992), first published in 1967; Gordon S. Wood, *The Creation of the American Republic*,

'career' entailed the project to develop in detail the governing beliefs of the founding generation and to trace their genealogies, while the second attempted to construct a new model for the history of ideas in which events were in part determined or even caused by abstractions, or ideologies.

Appleby's main argument is that these two rather different accounts of and investments in republicanism in the founding era – the one drawing upon classical and renaissance works of political philosophy for its formulation and committed to a version of civic duty that sought to contain the aggressive self-interests of the citizen, and the second, contrasted with the first, which supported and encouraged enlightened self-interest – sat side by side throughout the turmoil of the founding years. These two versions of this central idea are characterised as

> the chaste and venerable classical republicanism distilled by Harrington for English needs and updated by Montesquieu for eighteenth-century readers, [and] the liberal republicanism that contemporaries traced to the inquiries of Bacon, Newton, Locke, and Smith.[5]

Appleby claims that the fault-lines between the two can be easily traced in the late eighteenth-century and nineteenth-century debates between Federalists and Jeffersonians. In the thirty-plus years since this revisionist history became so well established, new avenues of inquiry have sought to widen the optic and to contextualise the formation of the first modern republic in a more geographically expansive way – essentially bringing to the party the many issues that are now commonly interrogated through the lens of transatlantic studies – and also in relation to the settled cultures the colonists first encountered in North America.[6] But in spite of these newer approaches, it remains the case that for most historians of the period the question from Joyce Appleby with which I began – 'What did Americans in the late eighteenth century mean when they spoke about republicanism?' – continues to have interest. The only problem with this, however, is that if or when they spoke about republicanism as an

---

1776–1787 (Chapel Hill: University of North Carolina Press, 1969); and John G. A. Pocock, *The Machiavellian Moment: Florentine Political Thought and the Atlantic Republican Tradition* (Princeton, NJ: Princeton University Press, 1975). For a good overview, in which Pocock's 'linguistic turn' in his writings of the 1970s is noted, see Daniel T. Rodgers, 'Republicanism: The Career of a Concept', *Journal of American History*, 79.1 (1992), 11–38, which also provides an extensive account of the varying fates of the term republicanism in the historiography of the founding of the American Republic.

[5] Appleby, 'Republicanism', 323.

[6] See Craig Yirush, *Settlers, Liberty, and Empire: The Roots of Early American Political Theory, 1675–1775* (Cambridge: Cambridge University Press, 2011).

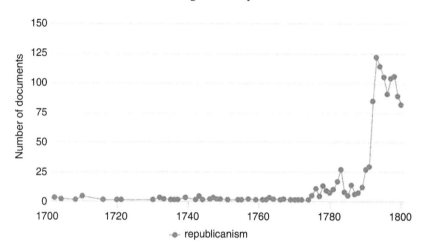

Figure 6.1 Number of documents per year containing the word republicanism, 1700–1800. Total number of documents: 202,191. Source: ECCO graphing tool.

identifiable set of principles or paradigms, as a theory or system of politics and government, they elected not to use the word for almost the entire eighteenth century, as can be seen from Figure 6.1.

In contrast to approaches which seek to answer Appleby's question by reading closely the 'master texts' of political theory, or through the minute inspection of letters, whether exchanged between well-marked and established major figures (such as the Founding Fathers) or less well-known actors in the struggle for independence, this chapter explores the formation of a political concept, republicanism, by toggling back and forth between close and distant reading methods. It begins by unearthing the contexts in which the term was used up until around the mid-century, essentially utilising very traditional modes of close reading the very few occasions where the word is present in the textual record of the period represented by ECCO. It then inverts the lens in order to explore how some of the tools developed by the Cambridge Concept Lab can complement such close reading. While it is more than apparent that writers across the length of the British eighteenth century thought with and through the concept republic and they were energetically interested in both the historical forms it had taken and its contemporary uses and expressions, for the most part debate and discussion took place without a seeming need to formulate the abstraction republicanism, which might operate as a container or place-holder for the set of principles or beliefs that could be said to underpin a political theory.[7] Throughout, then, I shall be trying to ascertain if there may be compelling candidate terms or phrases that stood in the place of the abstraction, republicanism, essentially mapping the contours and close history of a political idea for which there was, for most of the century, no single word. And, in the closing pages, I shall ask why, by the end of the century, the word found its uses and began to employed in ways that were consistent with what Appleby and other scholars of the founding period have taken to be the motivating political concept that drove the colonists towards independence.

In order to provide a very broad brush context for my initial observation about the sparsity in use of the term republicanism across the anglophone text base for the eighteenth century and its increasing uptake from the 1780s on (reaching a peak of usage in 1793, where it occurs in 122 documents), we can compare the relative frequencies of some other candidates for political concepts (monarchy, anarchy, etc.) and some abstractions used to designate beliefs (patriotism, atheism, etc.) in the last ten years of the century.[8] Thus among the total documents for this decade (73,104) we find monarchy (in 11,084 documents), republic (11,070), anarchy (8,456), patriotism (6,695), despotism (5,991), democracy (3,844), atheism (3,575) and republicanism (985). And to give one further context, it is noteworthy that in the most widely circulated contemporaneous history of the founding era, *The History of the American Revolution* by David Ramsey, the term appears on only one occasion.[9]

Given the sparsity of use of the term republicanism until the 1780s, it is possible to inspect each use and its associated context from the start of the century. The seven texts in which it appears up to 1710 are all religious in character, whereas some of the twelve texts between 1710 and 1747 have a more overtly political purpose and orientation.[10] In *The loyal: or,*

---

[7] In a fine essay Mark Philp makes this point, noting that there may have been two very different ways in which users of the English language in the period mobilised the term: on the one hand he notes that republican simply referred to someone who had anti-monarchical views. On the other, Philp tries to ascertain when the term might have had a very different resonance, picked up and promoted by Quentin Skinner in his characterisation of 'republican liberty'. Although Philp is at pains to register his agreement with Skinner's dissection of the concept of liberty, he wonders whether the argument 'can be sustained in the analysis of texts in the late eighteenth and early nineteenth centuries'. See Mark Philp, 'English Republicanism in the 1790s', *Journal of Political Philosophy*, 6.3 (1998), 235–262; 235.

[8] See Chapter 6 for a discussion of 'ism' words in the period.

[9] See David Ramsey, *The History of the American Revolution*, new ed., 2 vols. (London: printed for John Stockdale, 1793), I, 353.

[10] This religious inflection may well have persisted into the colonial era of founding, an observation made by Philp, 'English Republicanism', 251. See also Ruth Bloch, *Visionary*

revolutional tory, for example, the Whigs are said to have 'stretch'd the principles of Whiggism to those of unbounded *Republicanism*'.[11] In all there are ten uses of the term up to 1747 in the ECCO dataset that can unambiguously be read as referring to a species of political persuasion or commitment, sometimes with a clear negative spin ('republicanism, anarchy and confusion'), but in all of these cases the precise content of this persuasion or ideology is not provided.[12] One can conclude from this initial inspection that although the term was available it had no significant currency up through the middle of the century. This is indeed explicitly stated in a document of 1747 that bears some more careful scrutiny. Horace Walpole, who was a significant member of the political culture of the time – unlike the authors of the texts reviewed so far – wrote *A letter to the Whigs* that year. Here we find a use of the word republicanism embedded in a very eye-catching claim that will set the tone for much of what is to follow.

We need to reconstruct the salient features of the context in which this claim is made in order to get a first sense of how the term republicanism was operationalised in mid-century English political culture, at least within that segment of it that could be assumed to comprise the natural audience for a political spat of the type Walpole was engaged in. His letter was a reply to George Lyttleton's *Letter to the Tories*, which he penned on 9 June 1747 and subsequently published as a pamphlet.[13] The author's argument is essentially that the Tories, of whom he counts himself a member, should strenuously disengage themselves from the Jacobites in order to make themselves contenders for office. This, he states, requires them to demonstrate loyalty to the Hannoverian court. In the course of this argument he also suggests that the liberty of the press be curtailed, and this is the immediate prompt for Walpole's rejoinder, which spends its first ten pages viciously exposing the danger and hypocrisy of his opponent's suggestion.[14]

Republic: Millennial Themes in American Thought, 1756–1800 (Cambridge: Cambridge University Press, 1985).

[11] *The loyal: or, revolutional tory. Being some reflections on the principles and conduct of the Tories; shewing them true friends to the present establishment, some of the capital pillars of the constitution, and worthy of royal trust and confidence. By a friend to the church and constitution* (London: printed for J Wilford, 1733). The same text also makes the conjunction between religion and politics as it characterises those who support 'Popery' as 'reduced' to 'heathenism in Religion and Republicanism in government', 55.

[12] See *A Scourge for the Dissenters, or, The Fanatick Vipers* (London: printed for F. Cook, 1735), 13.

[13] The pamphlet was published anonymously and is signed 'J.H' at its close. The attribution to George Lyttleton, who was a Whig, has become conventional.

[14] I am grateful to Jonathan Clark who has pointed out to me that Lyttleton's purpose in assuming the character of a non-Jacobite Tory was tactical.

The real work of Walpole's text, however, is to examine the contradictions in Lyttleton's position and to vilify his characterisation of the political culture of the time. This is the first clear and explicit mapping of that culture I have found in the ECCO dataset in which a set of ideological positions associated with the term republican are placed in tension with a number of politically freighted terms such as Whig, Tory, Jacobite and Patriot. Ventriloquising Lyttleton, Walpole sardonically notes that according to his Tory opponent, Patriots have 'weaken'd the Protestant Cause, and have been doing the work of the Jacobites'.[15] This had supposedly come about because the Patriots 'left the Tories in the Lurch, and have patch'd up with the Whigs'.[16] In characterising this landscape, Walpole notes that Lyttleton outlines a 'Progression of Principles' that stretches from 'the highest pinnacle of Jacobitism, to the lowest Level of Heterodoxy and Republicanism'.[17] In order to make up one's mind at the ballot box, Lyttleton, according to Walpole, proposes a kind of hexagonal structure for political allegiance: 'a False patriot, a Tory, a Church-Whig, a Dissenting-Whig, a Republican, a Jacobite'.[18] It is important to register that Walpole is borrowing from his opponent's text and is seeking to dismiss his opinions. Given this it would be a mistake to assume that one might be able to reliably gauge the senses in which Walpole uses the terms republican and republicanism, both of which occur just once in his text. And as I have pointed out, on both occasions he is borrowing the language of his opponent, so it is certainly plausible that Walpole had no investment in the terms at all. But there is a moment in Walpole's text where something more helpful to my task occurs.

On page thirty-six Walpole writes, referring to page ten of Lyttleton's text: 'If they are not Jacobites, this paragraph will let us in the Secret of who are the Republicans, whom we find so often mention'd in the letter before me.' Walpole is either reading very strongly here, or he is over-egging the pudding since Lyttleton uses the term republicans on only three occasions in his letter to the Tories. In fact, Walpole observes four pages earlier:

Jacobites he has determined shall be one party, under whom he intends shall list the dissenters (p. 16) republicans, another set of men that nobody knew existed

---

[15] Horace Walpole, *A Letter to the Whigs. Occasion'd by the* Letter to the Tories (London: printed for M. Cooper, 1747), 39.
[16] Ibid. 38.   [17] Ibid. 40.
[18] Ibid. 40. This hexagonal mapping of the political culture might be usefully contrasted to the more oppositional structure that maps a 'court' against a 'country' party in the period. It might be also noted that what distinguishes republican from the other terms is its anti-monarchical inflection.

till he discovered them, and a few Whigs (p. 17) the other, when he has got the Tories to court, are to be Hannoverians, after his own example.[19]

Reading across these two texts, which create an intricate political landscape of the late 1740s, one is able to discern a kind of conceptual engineering in process. If we are to take Walpole at his word (one should take care to note that this is far from the only way we ought to read him, given what is known about his political, religious, ethical, social and aesthetic interests), he was unaware of a faction known as 'republican' until he read Lyttleton. But over the course of his critical interaction with his *Letter to the Tories*, it is Walpole, not his opponent, who coins the term republicanism, which – again reading from one perspective only – might now be taken to refer to an identifiable set of principles or political commitments. Did Walpole recognise himself in his own repackaging of Lyttleton's sketch of the political landscape in the phrase – his not Lyttleton's – 'the lowest level of Heterodoxy and Republicanism'? Perhaps, but it is also possible that he simply assumed the term republicanism was merely derogatory and without any real substance in terms of political ideology.

The negative spin to the term is certainly evident in the next text to use the term, Edward Bentham's *A letter to a fellow of a college*. Here the Tories are vilified for taking the topics for their conversation from the 'very dregs of republicanism'.[20] And in 1754 in the second volume of Bolingbroke's *Works*, the negative conjunction of republicanism and Jacobitism is also made.[21] In 1771 the term is attached to those who profess heterodox religious beliefs by David Williams, who notes that 'the dissenters were fond of the influence of the people, even to republicanism and democracy'.[22] But it is only in 1776, the year of the Declaration of Independence, that one can find uses of the word republicanism that explicitly and unambiguously refer to a political doctrine, and even here the evidence is paltry as it can be found in a mere five documents.[23] One

---

[19] Ibid. 32.

[20] Edward Bentham, *A letter to a fellow of a college. Being the sequel of* A letter to a young gentleman of Oxford (Oxford: printed for S. Birt and Mary Senex, 1749). Bentham was engaged in a defence of Oxford dons against the accusation that they predominantly held Jacobite sympathies.

[21] Henry St. John, *The Works of the Late Right Honorable Henry St. John, Lord Viscount Bolingbroke*, 5 vols. (London: published by David Mallett, 1754), II, 83.

[22] David Williams, *The Philosopher: In Three Conversations. Part III* (London: printed for T. Becket, 1771).

[23] These are A. M. *Reflections on the American contest: in which the consequence of a forced submission, and the means of a lasting reconciliation are pointed out, communicated by letter to a member of parliament, some time since, and now addressed to Edmund Burke, Esq.* (London: printed for J. Bew, 1776), in which 'republicanism' is said to comprise of 'Roman ideas of domination', 32; Ambrose Serle, *Americans against liberty, or, An essay on the nature and*

of these, a popular digest, indicates that 'the true principles of republicanism are at present so well understood'.[24] This may or may not have been the case, but the evidence from the printed record makes that look very unlikely if 'well understood' is taken to mean widely accepted and known. Let us pause for a moment to register that at least on the basis of this evidence, it is unlikely that Americans of the founding generation meant anything at all by the term republicanism, to return to the question posed by Appleby and quoted in my opening paragraph. As we can see, the printed record in ECCO provides no evidence for a well-formed and widely distributed concept of republicanism in the years leading up to the Declaration of Independence, at least if one assumes that this political ideology is most likely to have been available through the uses of the word itself. There is a counter argument to be noted here, remarked on in Section 6.3, which assumes that the dataset I have been using is too selective: it does not, for example, contain letters, diaries or notebooks that were circulating within the colonies over the years in which the independence movement gathered steam. But as I shall argue in Section 6.3, the problem persists once one inspects such documents and it becomes clear that the colonists could not have located the supports for an ideology that later writers and political theorists, and even more pointedly historians of ideas in our own era, would have recognised as republicanism or found its politico-philosophical architecture in the writings in English that were published at the time. The word, for all intents and purposes, was simply not current.[25]

6.1   Conceptual Modelling

I now turn to some of the computational methods and techniques outlined in Chapter 2, in order to disturb my emerging picture: was the concept of republicanism used and available to anglophone political culture during the founding period but known under a slightly different

---

principles of true freedom, shewing that the design and conduct of the Americans tend only to tyranny and slavery, 3rd ed. (London: printed for James Mathews, 1776), in which the colonists are said to be attempting to 'establish Republicanism', 23; James Macpherson, *The History of Great Britain, from the Restoration, to the Accession of the House of Hannover*, 2 vols., 2nd ed. (London: printed for W. Strahan; and T. Cadell, 1776), II, 468, in which the Whigs are said to embrace republicanism; *The Remembrancer, or, Impartial Repository of Public Events. For the Year 1776*, II (London: printed for J. Almon, 1776); Charles Inglis, *The true interest of America impartially stated, in certain stictures [sic] on a pamphlet intitled Common sense. By an American* (Philadelphia: printed and sold by James Humphreys, 1776), in which it is claimed that 'Britons never could bear the extremes, of either monarchy or republicanism', 52.

[24] *Remembrancer*, 126.
[25] Linguists would recognise this as an issue for 'onomasiological' inquiry.

rubric? This is to address what is implied and on first inspection seems improbable in the claim made above, namely that the radical political traditions of late seventeenth-century England, in which the benefits and disbenefits of a republic were so strenuously debated, had a very short half-life: by the time of the founding these formulations of republican ideology were buried in an increasingly distant past.

Although, as we have seen, republicanism is a very rare word in the archive of eighteenth-century print represented by ECCO, this is not the case for the terms republic, republican and republicans. One place to start, then, is to inspect the clusters of associated terms around these words in order to ascertain if there might be a candidate word or expression that effectively operated as the place-holder for the abstraction republicanism. I shall begin by using the Lab tools in order to calculate the Pearson correlations between the *dpf* lists for each paired term in Table 6.1; thus 'republican/term X'. Candidates for 'term X' are taken from the top sixty co-associates for republican in each of the twenty-year time slices across the century, and I shall restrict these candidates to those terms with an overt political slant.[26] It should be pointed out that such a selection criterion will reproduce the hypothesis I am testing, namely that the abstraction republicanism, referring to a set of principles determining a particular form of government, must have emerged from the debates and discussions around, and have been motivated by, the term republican. This is to say, I am assuming that republican was used in, or implied, the phrase republican government. As we shall see, this hypothesis is insensitive to the other sense of the word republican which refers not to a form of government but to a kind of person (and for the moment let us beg the question as to whether such persons must have held to the principles of republicanism). My initial inquiry, then, seeks to determine the extent to which term A (republican) and term B operate in each other's lexical environments, and thus help to identify possible terms for further investigation with respect to the emergence of the abstraction republicanism. Where the Pearson correlation is high, I take it as a clue for that further work.[27]

I interpret the data as indicating that the terms most likely to appear in close context to republican over the entire century are monarchy, monarchical and government. This should hardly surprise us as the word republican during the anglophone eighteenth century is most commonly distinguished from the word that designates the form of government that had prevailed over centuries in England and Britain: monarchy.

---

[26] Thus, for example, I have not included terms such as contenting or mocked, which appear within the top sixty co-associates for the period 1701–20.

[27] See Chapter 2, Section 2.4, for the corpus-level statistics indicating a weak correlation between term frequency and number of bound terms.

Table 6.1 *Pearson correlation between terms, 1701–1800.* Dpf *calculated at distance 10. Source: ECCO.*

	1701–20	1720–40	1740–60	1760–80	1780–1800
republican/monarchical	0.281	0.533	0.556	0.576	0.594
republican/liberty	0.139	0.148	0.210	0.234	0.359
republican/slavery	0.129	0.094	0.166	0.174	0.211
republican/democracy	0.062	0.078	0.188	0.186	0.381
republican/aristocracy	0.056	0.077	0.297	0.254	0.382
republican/despotism	−0.002	0.045	0.127	0.277	0.413
republican/patriots	0.112	0.094	0.095	0.127	0.246
republican/anarchy	0.165	0.164	0.243	0.243	0.390
republican/despotic	0.018	0.025	0.354	0.418	0.414
republican/whig	0.158	0.083	0.095	0.074	0.107
republican/presbyterians	0.118	0.116	0.107	0.174	0.175
republican/independents	0.085	0.096	0.103	0.177	0.177
republican/royalists	0.055	0.095	0.137	0.114	0.318
republican/freedom	0.091	0.086	0.139	0.167	0.295
republican/commerce	0.023	0.026	0.056	0.099	0.152
republican/commonwealth	0.140	0.201	0.274	0.258	0.273
republican/monarchy	0.210	0.348	0.468	0.500	0.603
republican/constitution	0.119	0.158	0.220	0.292	0.431
republican/rights	0.121	0.108	0.115	0.162	0.323
republican/atheists	0.150	0.091	0.033	0.050	0.064
republican/zealots	0.114	0.147	0.100	0.099	0.078
republican/revolution	0.197	0.115	0.112	0.173	0.400
republican/dissenters	0.160	0.088	0.089	0.094	0.136
republican/principles	0.220	0.142	0.169	0.215	0.339
republican/tyranny	0.139	0.174	0.218	0.235	0.348
republican/government	0.267	0.307	0.415	0.425	0.546
republican/tories	0.213	0.141	0.161	0.084	0.105

As one might expect, the semantic energy surrounding the word republican seeks to distinguish it from other, similar or contrasting words. But perhaps the most significant data in Table 6.1 is the substantial convergence of the lexical terrains for the terms republican/despotic and republican/despotism. As the table indicates, over the course of the century the Pearson correlation moves from −0.002 for despotism in the first twenty-year segment to 0.413 in the last, and from 0.018 for despotic to 0.414. This will be further commented on in Section 6.2. On initial inspection, two further terms whose values in the table indicate substantial increases over the century merit attention: aristocracy (from 0.056 to 0.382) and democracy (0.062 to 0.381).

One further observation prompts a second set of data intended to address the issue of confirmation bias outlined above: the Pearson

Table 6.2 *Vector subtraction of* dpf *lists for republican, 1701–20, minus 1780–1800.* Dpf *calculated at distance 5. Source: ECCO.*

Bound token	Increase in *dpf*	Increase in N (with focal)
fawning	8027.4	11
traced	6665.0	7
opposers	6211.2	12
positions	5365.2	11
audacious	5103.0	8
listening	5068.5	2
exclaim	5043.2	9
spawn	4956.8	6
schemes	4858.6	16
abhors	4611.8	7
disbanded	4351.0	8
blasphemous	3963.3	5
ensure	3838.9	2
whigs	3739.4	1

correlations that fall in value across the century are all for paired terms that can be said to refer to person: atheists, zealots, Whig, Tories. When we inspect the data from a vector subtraction of the *dpf* lists for republican taken from the opening twenty years of the century and the closing, the alteration in orientation in the uses of the concept I remarked above is clearly evident (see Table 6.2).[28]

At the beginning of the century the most common co-associated lexis with republican refers to qualities of person: fawning, audacious, listening, blasphemous. By the end of the century the picture is remarkably different as we can see in the orientation towards government and its different forms in Table 6.3.

Here one can see that the most common co-association for republican is government – nearly 2,500 instances.

6.2   Mapping the Environment for the Emergence of Republicanism

The Lab tools enable one to create extremely complex maps of the intersecting clusters of terms that operated across the eighteenth century based on the evidence of the printed text dataset ECCO. These maps are

---

[28] See Chapter 2, Section 2.6, for an explanation of vector subtraction.

Table 6.3 *Vector subtraction of* dpf *lists for republican, 1780–1800, minus 1701–20.* Dpf *calculated at distance 5. Source: ECCO.*

Bound token	Increase in *dpf*	Increase in *N* (with focal)
monarchical	22416.0	353
monarchies	9153.7	93
government	7066.9	2439
republican	6084.3	368
monarchy	5661.4	380
acrimonious	5117.6	33
kingly	4748.7	48
fleetwood	4740.4	29
governments	3957.5	152
democracy	3639.5	47
despotic	3542.6	58
paine	3466.6	71
despotism	3416.3	57
courtier	3368.5	53

created by using a simple set theory protocol, by which one establishes the lexis held in common across any number of *dpf* lists for different terms, the so-called intersection.[29] In order to reduce random variables, all the lists must be generated using the same window size – in the following a distance of ten has been set. As the sample size increases, adding more terms and their *dpf* lists, the common set of terms – lexis held in common for every *dpf* list – decreases in number (as one can easily intuit since the criterion that term X must appear on every other term's list makes the threshold for commonality higher and higher as the number of *dpf* lists increases). Thus, if one constructs the common set between republican and Presbyterian in the decade 1710–20, the number of terms in common is thirty-four. Each time one adds another term into the geometry, thereby raising the bar, the number of common terms falls. If, for example, I add dissenter to what is now a three-sided or triangular plot the number of common terms falls to eleven. Of course, the selection of the terms plays a significant role in determining this common set, again as

[29] This technique mirrors a procedure for tracking changing meanings outlined by Hila Gonen, Ganesh Jawahar, Djamé Seddah and Yoav Goldberg, 'Simple, Interpretable and Stable Method for Detecting Words with Usage Change across Corpora', in *Proceedings of the 58th Annual Meeting of the Association for Computational Linguistics*, ed. Dan Jurafsky, Joyce Chai, Natalie Schluter and Joel Tetreault (Stroudsburg, PA: Association for Computational Linguistics, 2020), 538–55.

Table 6.4 *Common set derived from the top eight terms by Pearson correlation value in each time segment in Table 6.1. Source: ECCO.*

1740–60	dpf	1760–80	dpf	1780–1800	
democracy	131638.6	democracy	116165.1	republican	50835.88
monarchical	71380.14	aristocracy	78640.67	despotism	47913.83
aristocracy	67039.49	monarchical	68073.32	democracy	46316.63
republican	55715.44	republican	66632.51	monarchical	42406.24
monarchy	45076.82	despotism	51792.83	monarchy	41940.4
government	24993.31	monarchy	49696.78	aristocracy	38342.05
governments	23165.94	anarchy	39119.73	anarchy	37000.58
popular	16748.5	despotic	36444.47	despotic	32469.64
tyranny	14970.4	governments	32167.19	government	30590.55
arbitrary	10734.97	government	30646.04	revolution	26595.35
absolute	9891.502	constitution	18644.12	governments	25337.67
laws	9836.949	arbitrary	13797.24	constitution	23906.48
liberty	8125	laws	12088.06	tyranny	22569.9
power	7701.37	absolute	10919.07	republic	20767.48
people	6821.353	political	10654.92	arbitrary	16432.61
		liberty	10162.06	hereditary	15994.66
		power	9275.298	subversion	15051.45
		faction	8911.236	liberty	13997.05
		civil	8866.554	rights	13620.69
		sovereign	7989.519	france	12969.88
		people	7899.491	political	12888.27
		govern	7592.165	popular	12665.64
		authority	7356.794	freedom	12083.94
		privileges	7055.205	principles	11882.73
				usurpation	11060.35
				civil	11052.83
				people	10233.98
				system	10073.97
				faction	9885.61
				nation	9577.53
				the	8802.997
				established	8750.998
				of	8728.969

one can easily intuit. For example, if I were to construct the triangular plot with the terms republican, Presbyterian and a term I imagine to have very little connection to these first two, carriage, then the number of common terms falls to one (in this case supporters).

The following data in Table 6.4 have been constructed by plotting the common set between the top eight terms by Pearson correlation value in the twenty-year segments indicted in Table 6.1. The common set in

Table 6.1 for the top eight terms in the first segment, 1701–20, which are monarchical, anarchy, Whig, monarchy, revolution, principles, government, Tories, is one: republican. The set for the second twenty-year segment is the same: republican (the top eight terms from which this common set has been established are: monarchical, monarch, government, commonwealth, tyranny, anarchy, constitution, liberty). From 1740, however, the number of terms in each common set for the following three twenty-year segments substantially increases and there is a clear emergence of a vocabulary that relates to specific types of government, as shown in Table 6.4.

In the light of the following section, it is noteworthy that the term principles only enters the common set in the last twenty years of the century, but perhaps the most perspicuous aspect of this table is the increasing presence of terms that might easily fall within the discourse of government and its underlying political ideology.

6.3   The Founding Era: Crucible for the Invention of the Idea of Republicanism?

As we have seen the word republicanism is too infrequent within the printed archive of eighteenth-century texts to make the question posed by Appleby, with which I began, easily answerable using computational methods. Now I want to return to the more familiar techniques of close reading in order to press harder on a line of inquiry introduced earlier: were the political commitments and ideologies encapsulated in the term republicanism articulated in a phrase or a term other than it (republicanism)? We have, in fact, already encountered an extract from *The Remembrancer* in 1776 that provides a good candidate for such a term: principles. The hypothesis, then, is that republicanism understood as a set of political commitments was available to the period under the rubric republican principles.[30]

The first time in the printed dataset ECCO that these republican principles were explicitly outlined and referred to as republicanism occurred in 1779 in a text by the pro-monarchy American Charles Inglis in his *Letters of Papinian: in which the conduct, present state, and prospects of the*

---

[30] A search across ECCO reveals that other possible candidate phrases such as 'republican ideas', 'beliefs' or 'theories' were simply not used. A very small incidence of 'republican notions' occurs, but this amounts to fifty-eight uses for the entire century, and on many occasions it is used in combination – hence 'republican notions and antimonarchical principles', *The high Church mask pull'd off, or, Modern addresses anatomized. Designed chiefly for the information of the common people* (London: printed for A. Baldwin, 1710), 5; or 'republican principles and notions', Catherine Macaulay, *The History of England from the Accession of James I to the Revolution*, 8 vols. (London: printed by A. Hamilton, 1781), VI, 3.

American Congress are examined published both in New York and London in 1779. This text responds to Thomas Paine's *Common Sense*, first published in 1776, in a long diatribe against one whom he calls variously in his earlier and more immediate reply to Paine 'our republican author' or 'republican guide'.[31] This first attack frequently pushes the button of republican as a derogatory term even if there is also a shadowy sense that a set of principles motivated persons so designated. But in the *Letters*, which had been first published in two newspapers, the *Royal Gazette* and the *New-York Gazette*, the explicit conjunction between republican principles and the abstraction republicanism is made. Inglis puts it like this:

Indeed some of your [referring to Paine] European friends have asserted that neither the Congress, nor their adherents were tinctured with republicanism … The principles which you published to the world, and on which you attempted to justify your rebellion, were perfectly democratic: swarms of zealots started up in every province to vindicate those principles, and carry your measures into execution – measures directly calculated to establish a republic, and banish every vestige of monarchy – measures to which you have since invariably adhered. After this, to deny that the American rebels were infected with republicanism, is at once a violation of truth, an insult on our understanding, and an injury to you.[32]

And the second time – followers of Pocock may smile – it has an explicitly Machiavellian tenor as he characterises the American republic in which a 'deep rooted republicanism' and

democratic levelling principles, ever unfriendly to monarchy had spread their baneful influence far and wide. Actuated by these, your adherents were disposed to revolt … The effects of your ambition, and of those Machiavelian methods, come next to be considered.[33]

If this marks the moment at which, at least within the colonies, the abstract idea of republicanism became fully articulated as a political concept, one should not jump to the conclusion that anglophone American political culture hereafter found good use for it. The data from the Early American Newspapers collection, for example, indicate that although the first occurrence of the term is in 1774, there are only sporadic uses (fewer than five) until 1786, when it occurs fourteen times.

I noted in the introduction to this essay that claims about the availability of grounding concepts for the founding generation based on the full

---

[31] The earlier text is Charles Inglis, *The true interest of America, impartially stated, in certain strictures on a pamphlet intitled Common Sense* (Philadelphia: printed and sold by James Humphreys, Jun. 1776)

[32] Charles Inglis, *Letters of Papinian: in which the conduct, present state and prospects, of the American Congress, are examined* (New York: printed by Hugh Gaine, 1779), 75.

[33] Ibid. 76.

dataset of ECCO may be too insensitive to the more local and immediate contexts within which the colonists developed their political ideology, and I suggested that a different dataset might be more useful. I have accordingly constructed a corpus from a substantial collection of colonial writings in order to test this, but the picture that emerges is remarkably similar: republicanism occurs nineteen times in the dataset, and republican principles a mere thirty-four times.[34]

The conclusion that I think should be drawn from the data points towards a more nuanced reading of the eighteenth-century mobilisation of the political concept of republicanism and its presence within colonial debate and discussion. The evidence from the printed text archive of the founding period indicates that the colonists did not reach for a ready-made political abstraction that later became known as republicanism. On the contrary, it makes much more sense to argue that they were searching for a way of understanding how and under which principles a new polity could be formed which re-oriented the conceptual cluster monarchy–democracy–aristocracy that had for nearly a century provided the foundations for thinking government in the anglophone world.[35] They were both searching for and attempting to construct a new conceptual cluster into which republicanism, understood as a *system* of government and polity, was only later inserted.[36] I find no evidence that supports the hypothesis I raised in Section 6.3, which asks if that theory of government, the abstract idea of republicanism, was bound up in the phrase republican principles or any other candidate phase, notwithstanding Charles Inglis's

---

[34] This level of incidence is so low as to be almost non-existent since the corpus comprises nearly 2 million words from the following Liberty Fund online resources (see 'Titles', Online Library of Liberty, https://oll.libertyfund.org/titles): Max Farrand, ed., *The Records of the Federal Convention of 1787*, 3 vols. (New Haven, CT: Yale University Press, 1911); Charles S. Hyneman and Donald Lutz, eds., *American Political Writing during the Founding Era, 1760–1805*, 2 vols. (Indianapolis, IN: Liberty Fund, 1983); Ellis Sandoz, *Political Sermons of the Founding Era, 1730–1805*, 2 vols., 2nd ed. (Indianapolis, IN: Liberty Fund, 1998); David Ramsay, *The History of the American Revolution*, 2 vols., ed. Lester H. Cohen (Indianapolis, IN: Liberty Fund, 1990). In the *Records of the Federal Congress*, where one might expect to find significant reference to 'republican principles', in fact the phrase is uncommon, occurring only ten times. This should be compared to the very frequent use of the word principles, which occurs over 200 times.

[35] On this very persistent cluster see Chapter 5.

[36] Anglophone uses of the word in this sense were most commonly directed at understanding the post-revolution situation in France. See, for example, Thomas Paine's observation that 'system of Republicanism' should not be considered to be adaptable only to small countries, Thomas Paine, *Miscellaneous articles. Consisting of A letter to the Marquis of Lansdowne. A letter to the authors of the republican. A letter to the Abbbey Syeyes. Thoughts on the peace, and the probable advantages thereof. First letter to Mr. Secretary Dundas. Letter to Lord Onslow. Second letter to Mr. Dundas. A letter to the people of France. &c. &c.* (London: printed for J, Ridgway, 1793), 9.

observation. The data from my sub-corpus of colonial texts indicate that republican principles were not low-hanging fruit to be easily picked as arguments for and against separation ignited the colonies; rather they become, *ex post facto*, back formations, constructed principles *after the founding*. They were identified with the clarity of hindsight and used in the ongoing project to build the republic's institutions and legislative practices: principles that were in fact made in the hot house of the revolution, not invoked as historical truths which could be mobilised as justifications for it.

Perhaps no one was more influential in promoting that back formation than the third president of the United States, Thomas Jefferson. On the occasion of his first inaugural speech, he gave to the republic's future the 'essential principles of our Government' that have subsequently provided shape and contour to the politics of modern republicanism, principles which it is sad to note have not always been as closely followed as Jefferson hoped and intended. This is his elegant list:

Equal and exact justice to all men, of whatever state or persuasion, religious or political; peace, commerce, and honest friendship with all nations, entangling alliances with none; the support of the state governments in all their rights, as the most competent administrations for our domestic concerns, and the surest bulwarks against anti-republican tendencies; the preservation of the General government in its whole constitutional vigor, as the sheet anchor of our peace at home, and safety abroad: a jealous care of the right of election by the people, a mild and safe corrective of abuses which are lopped by the sword of revolution where peaceable remedies are unprovided; absolute acquiescence in the decisions of the majority, the vital principle of republics, from which is no appeal but to force, the vital principle and immediate parent of the despotism; a well disciplined militia, our best reliance in peace, and for the first moments of war, till regulars may relieve them; the supremacy of the civil over the military authority; economy in the public expence, that labor may be lightly burthened; the honest payment of our debts and sacred preservation of the public faith; encouragement of agriculture, and of commerce as its handmaid; the diffusion of information, and arraignment of all abuses at the bar of the public reason; freedom of religion; freedom of the press; and freedom of person, under the protection of the Habeas Corpus; and trial by juries impartially selected. These principles form the bright constellation, which has gone before us and guided our steps through an age of revolution and reformation. The wisdom of our sages, and blood of our heroes have been devoted to their attainment; they should be the creed of our political faith; the text of civic instruction, the touchstone by which to try the services of those we trust; and should we wander from them in moments of error or of alarm, let us hasten to retrace our steps, and to regain the road which alone leads to peace, liberty and safety.[37]

[37] Paul L. Ford, ed., *The Works of Thomas Jefferson*, 12 vols. (New York: G. P. Putnam's Sons, 1904), IX, 197–9, https://oll.libertyfund.org/titles/757.

It would be foolish to imagine that his substantial learning, reading and experience did not provide the scaffolding for the articulation of these principles; he had not found them neatly listed in a book, nor even in a canon of texts or authors who had conveniently mapped out the politics of republicanism. In fact, in common with the political culture of his time, he hardly ever used the word republicanism in the texts he penned – both letters and documents – throughout his long life.[38] But by 1801, on the occasion of his becoming the third president, the compact list of principles, which he took to be at the core of the concept of a modern republicanism, had come to represent the extraordinary achievement of the founding generation and to articulate the investments it had made in the truly remarkable experiment of creating the institutions that were to put their ideas into practice. It was only then, with hindsight, that Jefferson could claim that the nation had been built upon the struggle to realise these republican principles: he was participating in the construction and dissemination of a myth of the founding. That myth, which purports to describe the flowering of a republicanism with its roots sunk deep into a tradition of political philosophy whose most recent apologists were English radicals of the late seventeenth century, has turned out to be extraordinarily tenacious. What actually happened through those founding years was rather more untidy, prosaic, incoherent. As the data indicate, the very slow formation and mobilisation of the political idea of republicanism in its English guise during the century in which the American Revolution occurred involved various geometries in which religious conviction, patriotism, support for the Stuart succession and suspicion of any form of centralised power were made to jostle and cohabit with each other. All manner of dress was given to the identity republican, which meant that it could simultaneously be painted with the brush of anarchy and of liberty, depending on where one placed one's convictions. Republicanism, however, was noticeably absent from the political consciousness of the founding generation.

---

[38] The first use in *The Works of Thomas Jefferson* is in 'Notes on Virginia' of 1782, in which it occurs a single time; thereafter the word occurs in correspondence thirty-eight times up to 1798. But by the turn of the century another inflection to the term republicanism had come to surface in American political discourse that articulated the deep division between those who argued strenuously for a strong executive power, the Federalists, and those who wished to see the executive constrained by a very tight interpretation of the constitution, the republicans. So, for example, when Jefferson uses the term republicanism in a letter to Levi Lincoln on 25 October 1802 he meant to contrast it to federalism, thereby referring to the more narrow political context of the early republic, *Works*, IX, 397.

7   Enlightenment Entanglements of Improvement and Growth

Peter de Bolla, Ryan Heuser and Mark Algee-Hewitt

The economic concept of growth is a relatively recent invention.[1] In fact, it can be traced to a very specific moment when the Congress of the United States commissioned the Russian-American economist Simon Kuznets, who would go on to win the Nobel Prize for economics, to gather data on income across the States in 1932. Kuznets had been a member of the National Bureau of Economic Research since 1927, and he took charge of the bureau's work on the national income accounts in 1931. The work that he oversaw produced detailed statistics on what became known as the Gross National Product (today more commonly referred to as the Gross Domestic Product), and this was quickly adopted as the most accurate measure of the total value of an economy. Although it was not an intended outcome of his method, Kuznets effectively enabled the creation of a world ranking for economic efficacy and success measured in terms of the rate of growth of an individual national economy, and to this day competitive advantage within the global economy is based on the measure of an individual economy's rate of growth, thereby making growth the single most important desideratum of modern global economies. While there have been moments since 1932 when economists, policy makers and political commentators have broken with this orthodoxy and wondered if growth should be the primary economic objective, for the most part it has been the only game in town.

Economic historians, however, have long considered the building blocks for our modern concept of economic growth to have a deeper history, and they commonly point to William Petty's work on 'political

---

[1] This is not intended to be contentious; it merely follows the standard way in which economists (as opposed to economic historians) since the 1930s have made a distinction between what is known as 'classical economic theory' and modern *theories of economic growth*. The latter are often taken to have become central to economic modelling following the publication of Roy F. Harrod, 'An Essay in Dynamic Theory', *Economic Journal*, 49 (1939), 14–33. On this see Frank H. Hahn and Robin C. O. Mathews, 'The Theory of Economic Growth: A Survey', *Economic Journal*, 74 (1964), 779–902.

arithmetic' in late seventeenth-century England as a signal moment in the development of statistics for representing the value of an economy.[2] Further elaborations of this economic measure took place over the next 150 years, contributing to the most significant nineteenth-century models of the economy and to economic theory that we commonly associate with the names of David Ricardo and Karl Marx.[3] But it would take another century or so before accurate statistical modelling of the size of an economy based on good quality data became possible, in great measure owing to Congress's invitation to Kuznets. At that moment the concept of economic growth had finally found its day.[4]

This chapter makes a cut into the long historical gestation of a concept, essentially asking the following question: can we look inside an idea – in this case the notion of economic growth as we have come to understand it – and identify its DNA, the essential building blocks out of which it is composed? And we propose to answer this question by using our computational tools to identify the historical material from which the modern idea of economic growth was made. We contend that this material, call it the sub-structure of the idea, is to be found in the period between Petty and Marx, during the long eighteenth century, in which inquiries into political economy came to have such resonance.[5] One salient feature of this period is the fact that although the term growth was available and used in describing the increase (howsoever determined) in many kinds of matter (for the most part organic), it was not used in the modern economic sense of a continuous increase in the total output of an economy over long periods of time. Notwithstanding this fact, economic historians have found evidence in the writings of the period for models of the economy that attempted to take account of its overall size and sustainability, and argue that something like our modern notion of economic

[2] See Adam Fox, 'Sir William Petty, Ireland, and the Making of a Political Economist, 1653–87', *Economic History Review*, 62.2 (2009), 338–404; Paul Slack, 'William Petty, the Multiplication of Mankind, and Demographic Discourse in Seventeenth-Century England', *Historical Journal*, 61.2 (2018), 301–25.
[3] For a good overview of this long history with respect to the British economy, see Joel Mokyr, *The Enlightened Economy: An Economic History of Britain 1700–1850* (New Haven, CT: Yale University Press, 2009); and for the role of growth in this history of economic thought, see Walt W. Rostow, *Theorists of Economic Growth from David Hume to the Present: With a Perspective on the Next Century* (Oxford: Oxford University Press, 1990).
[4] Such a day would come more than once: the evolution of the Organisation for European Economic Cooperation into the OECD in 1961 is certainly another contender. See Matthias Schmelzer, *The Hegemony of Growth: The OECD and the Making of the Economic Growth Paradigm* (Cambridge: Cambridge University Press, 2016).
[5] For a good account of Petty's contribution to political economy, see James H. Ulmer, 'The Macroeconomic Thought of Sir William Petty', *Journal of the History of Economic Thought*, 26.3 (2004), 401–13.

growth operated in these classical formulations of political economy.[6] This will be commented upon in Section 7.4; here we note the shape and form of an argument we encountered in the previous chapter, namely that concepts may operate in historical contexts when the label for the concept was not immediately accessible or current. There the discussion of the concept of republicanism in the era of the founding of the United States made the hypothesis that such a concept was captured by or contained in *other words* current at the time. In this case economic historians have most consistently claimed the candidates for those words to be progress and opulence.[7] We shall argue, however, that another term needs to be included in this cluster and that without it the foundations for the modern concept of economic growth would lack its most important support. That term is improvement.[8]

In the following we have used our tools to identify a set of entanglements or clusters of concepts coalescing across the eighteenth century, as the idea of improvement was used to explore and explain the development of agriculture, the arts, manufacture, trade and knowledge. Our investigations of these uses allow us to detect a fault line in the *concept* of improvement that, we shall argue, provided the basis for the emergence of a way of thinking about production, labour and the economy in general that is compatible with twentieth-century modelling of the growth in value of national economies. This fault line can be characterised as the distinction between qualitative and quantitative improvement, that is improvement as betterment distinguished from improvement as an increase in something countable. Furthermore, we shall argue that

---

[6] See Walter Eltis, *The Classical Theory of Economic Growth* (London: Macmillan Press, 1984).

[7] As will become clear below, when Adam Smith began to work out what some economic historians claim to be a putative theory of economic growth, he used the phrase 'the progress of opulence' to characterise the increase in value of an economy. See Anthony Brewer, 'The Concept of Growth in Eighteenth-Century Economics', *History of Political Economy*, 27.4 (1995), 609–38; 610.

[8] We do not wish to imply that this term has completely escaped the notice of economic historians. Anthony Brewer notes that this stress on improvement features in Adam Ferguson's *An Essay on the History of Civil Society* (1767), which can be seen as a precursor to Adam Smith's conceptualisation of 'progress' in his *Wealth of Nations*. Brewer also suggests that the immediate milieu within which both Ferguson and Smith circulated was likely to have conceived of economic growth in similar terms. See Anthony Brewer, 'Adam Ferguson, Adam Smith, and the Concept of Economic Growth', *History of Political Economy*, 31.2 (1999), 237–254; 238, 249. And Paul Slack's study of the seventeenth-century uses of the term in a period that increasingly became 'information rich' is also a magisterial exception. See Paul Slack, *The Invention of Improvement: Information and Material Progress in Seventeenth-Century England* (Oxford: Oxford University Press, 2015).

notwithstanding the fact that 'to improve' could mean 'to make good use of, or to turn a profit' as early as the sixteenth century, it was only in the mid-eighteenth century that it began to be used in more narrowly financial or monetary contexts, meaning 'to enhance in monetary value'.[9] And as we shall see, the play between the qualitative and quantitative senses of improvement became a resource for Adam Smith's conceptualisation of the ways in which an economy might be said to grow in our modern sense, thereby prompting his speculations about the causes of such growth. This play can be understood as a kind of affordance within the term improvement from its very first uses in the language, which encompass both a sense of process and completed action.

Notwithstanding this very long history of usage, we believe that our method uncovers a kind of mutation in the noun that appears most persistently around the early decades of the eighteenth century. And we think of this mutation as a kind of shadow grammar emerging in the noun as its sense as 'process' began to turn towards or even into its gerund form 'improving'. We have more to say about this in the following section. We also identify a second mutation, in this case more identifiably semantic, that became instrumental in Adam Smith's account of the progress of an economy in his *Wealth of Nations*. For most of the period under investigation here, the anglophone eighteenth century, 'improvement' required an object – 'improvement of' something – that could be either concrete, say improvement of the land, or abstract, say the improvement of knowledge. The mutation or development that we identify most closely in Smith, however, resulted in uses of the word without an object. This new sense, 'improvement in and for itself', has a complicated conceptual and semantic history that was grounded in the term's long-established use as betterment. For most of that history uses of the word would have made little sense if the question 'betterment of what?' lacked an answer, but when this requirement for an object began to lose some force, it became possible to conceive of betterment as an end in itself. One might think of this as a kind of soldering of the two senses within the word improvement: process became the end, and a kind of concrete abstraction had been minted. This, we shall argue, enabled Smith to make a key breakthrough in coming to understand how economies might grow, in our modern economic sense. Part of our story, then, concerns the forces that bear upon conceptual formation as we seek to inquire into the difficult question: how do concretions mutate or evolve into abstractions, or to put that

---

[9] The Oxford English Dictionary gives us 'to make good; turn to profit' (1539); 'to enhance in monetary value' (1750); 'to make greater in amount or degree' (1771).

in more technically conceptual terms, what is the process by which noetic concepts are formed?[10]

Our larger argument, however, is that the fault line we identify in improvement is deeply embedded in what eventually became our modern economic concept of growth, a part of its DNA, and this is why, from time to time, when debates and discussions of the benefits of growth take centre stage they stall or stumble over whether economic growth is always for the good. Perhaps the most significant heretofore was the moment at which the 'limits to growth' became a hot-button topic for economists in the early 1970s.[11] It is likely to return as economies across the world chase what continues to be the primary target for a post-pandemic recovery: growth. We believe, however, that in common with that earlier moment in the 1970s economists, politicians and concerned citizens will challenge such an easy panacea and begin to articulate contrasting models of economic growth which will, once again, reveal the fault line in its DNA.

7.1   Eighteenth-Century Uses of Improvement

We shall begin in a relatively rudimentary manner by gathering together some observations on the ways in which the period used the term improvement. This will create a lexicographical context for our subsequent computationally aided characterisation of the architecture of the concept. We can quickly glean some of the outlines of that context from the dictionaries and encyclopaedias published in the period. This enables us to get a feel for how the noun improvement negotiated its two senses of process and completed action. The most frequently reprinted and revised book of this kind throughout the century was Ephraim Chambers's *Cyclopaedia*, whose full title gives us a quick handle on its ambitious reach and range.[12] When it was compiled there seems to have been no substantial use of the term improvement in the sense of what we earlier called a concrete abstraction, that is as a kind of state or desideratum in and for itself without an

---

[10] For a fuller discussion of noetic concepts, see Peter de Bolla, *The Architecture of Concepts: The Historical Formation of Human Rights* (New York: Fordham University Press, 2013), 33–47.

[11] For a good account of the central players in this argument, see Paul Sabin, *The Bet* (New Haven, CT: Yale University Press, 2014).

[12] *Cyclopædia, or, An universal dictionary of arts and sciences; Containing The Definitions of the Terms, And Accounts of The Things signify'd thereby, In the several Arts, Both Liberal and Mechanical, And the several Sciences, Human and Divine: The Figures, Kinds, Properties, Productions, Preparations, and Uses, of Things Natural and Artificial; The Rise, Progress, and State of Things Ecclesiastical, Civil, Military, and Commercial: With the several Systems, Sects, Opinions, &c. among Philosophers, Divines, Mathematicians, Physicians, Antiquaries, Criticks, &c. The Whole intended as a Course of Antient and Modern Learning. Compiled from the best Authors, Dictionaries, Journals, Memoirs, Transactions, Ephemerides, &c. in several Languages*, 2 vols. (London: printed for James and John Knapton et al., 1728).

object: improvement without qualification. This is evident from the fact that there is no standalone entry for the term in any of its editions or subsequent revisions. The word is, however, used on twenty-eight occasions throughout the two-volume first edition, and on almost all of these occasions it is unambiguously marked as a noun referring to a completed action. But on eight occasions it is not so clear if the noun refers to a finished state or a process of getting better, and on three of them where it is used in conjunction with a gerund, one can identify a kind of pressure towards its gerund form improving. Thus, where Chambers notes that the French Academy was 'established for the improvement and refining of the language', there is an implication that he is referring to a continuous process, thereby pushing the noun improvement towards the gerund improving.[13]

Our second compendium, Samuel Johnson's *Dictionary*, provides a slightly later window onto the semantic history of the term.[14] In this case improvement appears in a number of entries. Accrue, for example, is defined as 'to be added, as an advantage or improvement, in a sense inclining to good rather than ill'; and under the entry for advancement it is offered as a synonym. But the greater majority of entries in which the word appears are concerned with agriculture. The first definition in the entry for cultivation, for example, reads as 'the art or practice of improving soils' and the second as 'improvement in general; promotion; melioration'. The entry for manurement gives us 'cultivation and improvement'. This slant towards husbandry and agriculture is reinforced in the works of reference produced in the years following the publication of Johnson's *Dictionary*, most of which simply follow Johnson's lead. Richard Rolt, in his *A new dictionary of trade and commerce* (1761) notes that the land in Africa has 'a rich soil capable of the greatest improvements'.[15] And Nathan Bailey's *An universal etymological English dictionary* (1761) includes an entry for culture that harks back to Chambers while including another sense with respect to manners and learning: it reads as 'husbandry, tillage, improvement, good education'.[16] His 1763 edition of the same work has the most exotic entries,

---

[13] See Chambers, *Cyclopaedia*, I, 13. A similar effect occurs in his observation that Spencer 'contributed not a little to the improvement and refining of the tongue', I, 310.

[14] Samuel Johnson, *A Dictionary of the English Language: in which the words are deduced from their originals, and illustrated in their different significations by examples from the best writers* (London: J. & P. Knapton, 1755).

[15] Richard Rolt, *A new dictionary of trade and commerce, compiled from the information of the most eminent merchants, and from the works of the best writers on commercial subjects, in all languages* (London: printed for G. Keith, 1761), 3.

[16] Nathan Bailey, *An universal etymological English dictionary; Comprehending The Derivations of the Generality of Words in the English Tongue, either Ancient or Modern, from the Ancient British, Saxon, Danish, Norman, and Modern French, Teutonick, Dutch, Spanish, Italian; as also from the Latin, Greek, and Hebrew Languages, each in their proper Characters* (London: printed for T. Osborne et al., 1761), 233.

however, where we find agricolation defined as 'the art of husbandry, improvement of land'; and another term destined for obsolescence imprudiamentum, which is defined as 'improvement of land by husbandry'.[17]

There is a secondary stream to the uses for the word that more easily connects to the evolution and development of an economic concept of growth. Thus, in *The new royal and universal English dictionary* the entry for profit reads as: 'gain, pecuniary advantage. Advantage; accession of good. Improvement; advancement; proficiency'; and the entry for 'to profit' reads: 'to improve. To make improvement'.[18] And it is also useful to note, in light of the following discussion, that Samuel Johnson identified a sense for the term improvement that leans heavily towards quantification, although the entry in which this occurs is for its close antonym, decline: 'contrary to increase, improvement, or elevation'.

In the light of the following analyses, it is perhaps noteworthy that the first time a dictionary included a definition of improvement combining the uses found mainly in the context of agriculture with those that were attached to education and learning was in 1780 when Thomas Sheridan included the following in his standalone entry for improvement: 'melioration, advancement from good to better; instruction, edification; effect of melioration'.[19] The feature of this definition we wish to highlight is the implication of a kind of concrete abstraction in the notion of 'advancement from good to better' whereby improvement is both qualitative – 'good' – and at the same time quantitative – 'better'. This will be further explored in Section 7.5, the final section.

7.2   The Conceptual Core of Improvement in the Anglophone Eighteenth Century

We now turn to some computational and statistical methods, outlined in Chapter 1, for parsing the changing conceptual core for improvement across the eighteenth century. In the period 1700–20 we find that the following three words comprise the core: improving, improve, trade. We take this to indicate that early in the century there was already a clear economic freighting to the concept of improvement, as the appearance of

[17] Nathan Bailey, *An Universal Etymological Dictionary* (London: printed for T. Osborne et al., 1763), 38, 438.

[18] J. Johnson, *The new royal and universal English dictionary. In which The terms made use of in Arts and Sciences are defin'd; The words are explained in their Various Senses; The accent properly placed, to facilitate the true Pronunciation; The parts of speech denoted; and The spelling throughout reduced to an uniform and consistent standard. To which is prefixed, A grammar of the English language*, 2 vols. (London: printed for A. S. Millard, 1763), II, 152.

[19] Thomas Sheridan, *A General Dictionary of the English Language* (London: J. Dodsley et al., 1780), 519.

Table 7.1 *Terms in the core for improvement, 1720–40, derived from lexis common to all* dpf *lists at all distances, 10–100. Terms in decreasing rank order of* dpf. *Source: ECCO.*

1720–40
improvement
improvements
husbandry
gardening
clover
improving
culture
manure
improved
improve
tillage
useful
knowledge
trade
moral

trade in the core indicates. During the following twenty-year segment of the century, however, the core of the concept began to alter and evolve as terms predominantly associated with husbandry and agriculture enter the *dpf* list. Table 7.1 shows the terms that comprise the core for 1720–40.[20]

We can note that trade is still within the core, but a new orientation towards working the land is evident. The last term in the list, moral, might at first be considered to be evidence for very standard accounts of the period's investments in 'moral improvement', but this needs to be qualified by the fact that moral only appears in the core for improvement in this twenty-year segment. And although the term knowledge appears in this list, as it does in every list from 1720 on, this co-association that makes the conjunction between improvement and education and learning has a weak *dpf* score, which is commented upon following Table 7.4. We interpret the data for the following twenty-year period, 1740–60, as an index to the strengthening orientation of improvement towards agricultural practices: trade, as can be seen in Table 7.2, dropped out of the core.[21]

---

[20] The terms in italic allow one to quickly identify terms that are common to this and the following two lists.

[21] This break in the link between improvement and trade over the course of the rest of the century supports the hypothesis that arguments with respect to the 'decay of trade' became increasingly prevalent. See Richard A. Kleer, 'The Decay of Trade: The

Table 7.2 *Terms in the core for improvement,*
1740–60, derived from lexis common to all dpf
lists at all distances, 10–100. Terms in
decreasing rank order of dpf. *Source: ECCO.*

1740–60
improvement
improvements
manure
improving
improved
improve
husbandry
clover
culture
useful
knowledge

In the following twenty-year segment, 1760–80, shown in Table 7.3, there is a significant increase in the number of terms in the core to thirty-six, over half of which are associated with husbandry and cultivation (the terms in italic are common to Tables 7.1 and 7.2; those in bold are the new terms to the core associated with agriculture).

Thus, taking into account the terms that occur in more than one core date slice across the entire century, the picture is very clear: although trade lies within the core at the start of the century, it quickly disappears as first husbandry and manure enter and persist from 1720 to 1740, and then agriculture, industry, farms, cultivation and manufactures enter and persist from 1760 to 1780, as shown in Table 7.4.

It can immediately be seen that knowledge, even if it appears on every list from 1720 on, is consistently at the bottom, bar that for 1720–40. And with the exception of the twenty-year segment 1740–60, the *dpf* scores for knowledge are consistently approximately half the value of the highest scoring term.[22] We take these diagnostics to indicate that the orientation towards agriculture consistently predominates over the course of the century.

Politics of Economic Theory in Eighteenth-Century Britain', *Journal of the History of Economic Thought*, 18.2 (1996), 319–46.

[22] The scores (per thousand) are: 1720–40: husbandry (19.4), knowledge (7.4); 1740–60: manure (12.8), knowledge (8); 1760–80: cultivation (17), knowledge (8.5); 1780–1800: agriculture (24.8), knowledge (11).

Table 7.3 *Terms in the core for improvement,*
1760–80, derived from lexis common to all dpf
lists at all distances, 10–100. Terms in
decreasing rank order of dpf. *Source: ECCO.*

1760–80
improvement
improvements
cultivation
improved
improving
agriculture
manure
marle
premiums
husbandry
improve
draining
soils
crops
culture
acre
tillage
farms
cultivating
cabbages
farmers
industry
manufactures
turnips
advantages
of
society
knowledge
cultivated
farm

7.3   The Conceptual Network of Improvement across the Anglophone Eighteenth Century

We now turn to a different method for ascertaining the signature of the concept of improvement and its associated contexts of use across the century. In this case we have used the tool which produces network visualisations of the co-association data from ECCO described in

Table 7.4 *Terms appearing in more than one core list for improvement in each twenty-year segment, 1700–1800. Cores derived from lexis common to all* dpf *lists at all distances, 10–100. Terms in decreasing rank order of* dpf. *Source: ECCO.*

1700–20	1720–40	1740–60	1760–80	1780–1800
trade	husbandry	manure	cultivation	agriculture
	culture	husbandry	agriculture	cultivation
	manure	culture	manure	husbandry
	knowledge	knowledge	husbandry	manure
	trade		culture	farms
			farms	industry
			industry	manufactures
			manufactures	culture
			knowledge	knowledge

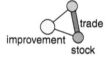

Figure 7.1 A network visualisation with improvement as the focal term; distance 100, score expressed as *log-dpf* with threshold of 2.6 and rank threshold 20. Date spread 1700–10. Shading is assigned by a community detection algorithm. Source: ECCO.

Chapter 3.[23] Here we have taken advantage of the tool's capacity for providing a more granular inspection of the century as it plots the information decade by decade. The following graphs (Figures 7.1–7.4) are based upon *dpf* scores derived from a window or distance of 100 terms between focal and target term in order to capture what we think of as the most conceptual associations between them.[24] And the construction of the graphs uses the following filters: the input data has been limited to the top twenty terms in each co-association list, and the score threshold has been set at 2.6. Lastly, we have restricted the graphing tool to drawing connections to a single node. Figure 7.1 shows the network visualisation for the concept of improvement in the first decade of the century.

This visualisation, built upon a different window index from the data presented in the previous section, nevertheless captures similar

[23] See Chapter 3, Section 7.2, for a full description of the graph's presentational features.
[24] For a discussion of the use we make of varying window sizes, see Chapter 2, Section 2.1.2.

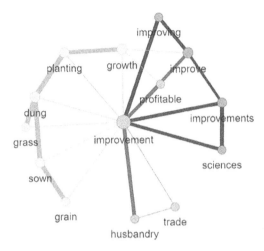

Figure 7.2 A network visualisation with improvement as the focal term; distance 100, score expressed as *log-dpf* with threshold of 2.6 and rank threshold 20. Date spread 1720–30. Shading is assigned by a community detection algorithm. Source: ECCO.

information: at the opening of the century improvement was conceptually associated with trade. Already by the second decade of the century, however, the tool provides evidence for an alteration in orientation of the concept towards husbandry and agriculture. As the following network visualisations gain in complexity, we interpret them as capturing something significant to the history of the conceptual formation we are tracking: the increase in the number of nodes and edges is not only a function of the network math – it also reflects a greater complexity in conceptualisation. That complexity, here represented in Figure 7.2 as linked clusters of terms, we model as a kind of conceptual density that helps us understand the architectures that support ideas, and hence to construct more granular histories of ideas.[25]

We interpret this visualisation as indicating that the density of the concept improvement – here represented in Figure 7.3 as a fractured spoke with one non-radial connection (growth ↔ profitable) – has significantly increased from the previous decade, and, in relation to the larger argument we are pursuing, it is noteworthy that the term growth is included in the network. We also note that the sub-network within which growth appears (marked in grey) is clearly oriented towards

---

[25] See the discussion of models in Chapter 2, Section 2.1.2.

Figure 7.3 A network visualisation with improvement as the focal term;
distance 100, score expressed as *log-dpf* with threshold of 2.6 and rank
threshold 20. Date spread 1740–50. Shading is assigned by a community
detection algorithm. Source: ECCO.

agriculture. In the following decade the network visualisation represents
a more complex cluster of terms as the number of nodes and edges
connecting and connected to growth increases. We also note the entry
of manufactures into the network.

While the sub-network within which growth appears includes the same
number of terms as the previous visualisation, its connection to the root
network constructed through improvement is now far more complex.[26]
Here we can see the terms acre, manure, oats, plough, wheat, cows, turf
are now included in a new sub-network that contributes to the overall
increase in density for the concept improvement. But it is perhaps most
significant that in every decade from 1750 on growth drops out of the
networks built from improvement as the focal term. Thus, when we build
the network from the focal term growth for the last decade of the century,

---

[26] See Chapter 3, Section 7.1, for the technical explanation of how the network has been
constructed.

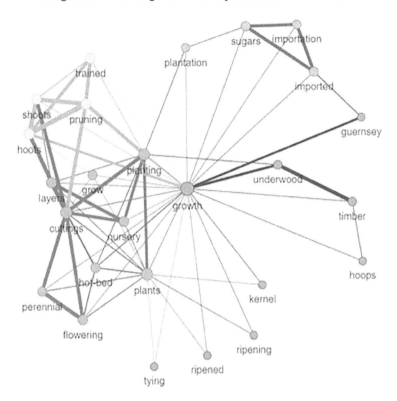

Figure 7.4 A network visualisation with growth as the focal term; distance 100, score expressed as *log-dpf* with threshold of 2.6 and rank threshold 20. Date spread 1790–1800. Shading is assigned by a community detection algorithm. Source: ECCO.

we find in Figure 7.4 that it is composed almost entirely of terms relating to horticulture. If the foundations for the modern economic concept of growth are to be located in the eighteenth century, it is clear that we need to look elsewhere for them.

One further observation regarding the conceptual foundations for the modern concept of economic growth can be entered here. When we do a vector subtraction of the *dpf* list for growth 1780–1800 minus 1701–20, thereby capturing the evolution of the concept growth across the eighteenth century, we find in Table 7.5 that among the terms that most closely associated with growth by the end of the century are the following, all of them clearly indexed to colonialism: plantations, plantation, America, importation, colonies.

Table 7.5 *The top twelve terms having the highest* dpf *values with growth at a distance of 10 generated by a vector subtraction of* dpf *list 1780–1800 minus* dpf *list 1701–20. Source: ECCO.*

Bound token	Increase in *dpf*	Increase in N (with focal)
plantations	7434.2	913
hoots	5961.2	98
imported	5018.7	1176
cuttings	4890.9	150
plantation	4807.3	294
pruning	4553.1	92
America	4163.1	1422
flowering	4028.8	269
pursuant	3957.3	269
importation	3841.4	424
colonies	3645.8	639
hot-bed	3406.4	103

7.3.1   Entanglements: Improvement/Growth/Increase

If growth would seem to have no observable conceptual articulation so as to make it useful for understanding the behaviour of the entire economy during the eighteenth century – which is to say, if it is not a good candidate for one of the foundations for the modern idea of economic growth – might it nevertheless sit somewhere within the orbit of concepts that are better candidates? In this section we trace the entanglements between three terms that, we contend, supported the construction of our modern idea of economic growth. Those terms are improvement, growth and increase, and we shall see how the quantitative use of improvement began to alter the concept growth as it became entangled with the concept increase. This network visualisation in Figure 7.5 built from inputting all three terms into the tool indicates that from the decade of the 1720s such an entanglement was taking place.

As can be seen in Figure 7.5, the link from the cluster around improvement to that around increase is through growth, and notably the single node connecting the growth cluster to that of increase is plantation. Once again, the role played by colonialism in the foundation of the modern economic concept of growth is worth dwelling upon as the altering of senses of plantation from its agricultural or horticultural uses to what the Oxford English Dictionary gives us as 'a company of settlers or colonists' (1715) reflects the establishment of the

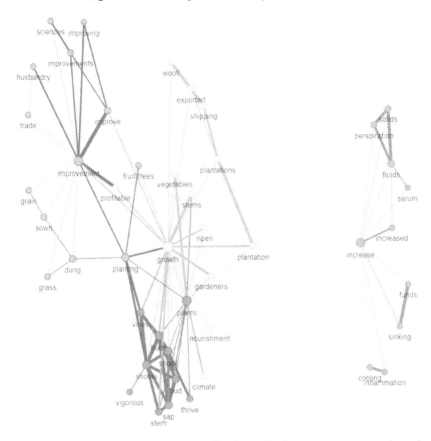

Figure 7.5 A network visualisation with improvement, growth and increase as the focal terms; distance 100, score expressed as *log-dpf* with threshold of 2.6 and rank threshold 20. Date spread 1720–30. Shading is assigned by a community detection algorithm. Source: ECCO.

institutions of an imperial economy whose growth was based on the trade in goods and people. The visualisation for the same focal terms in the decade 1740–50 presented in Figure 7.6 gives further support for an underlying colonial slant to their entanglement as manufactures, importation and exports enter the network.

In the following section we turn to the period's most eminent economic thinker, Adam Smith, in order to test the hypothesis that improvement began to take on a sense of economic quantification.

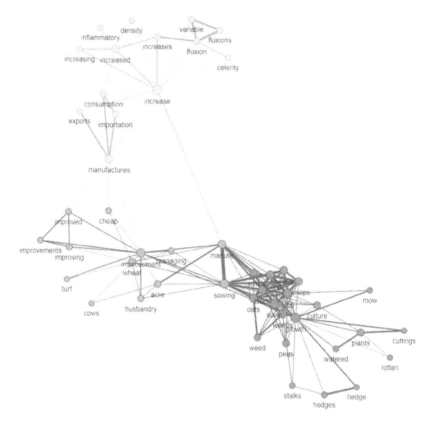

Figure 7.6 A network visualisation with improvement, growth and increase as the focal terms; distance 100, score expressed as *log-dpf* with threshold of 2.6 and rank threshold 20. Date spread 1740–50. Shading is assigned by a community detection algorithm. Source: ECCO.

7.4   Improvement between Abstraction and Quantification: The Case of Adam Smith

Economic historians argue that in so far as commentators on political economy in the long eighteenth century found use for a concept of growth, they applied it most consistently to the size of the population. Indeed, even if writers such as Francois Quesnay, David Hume, James Steuart, Anne Robert Jacques Turgot and Adam Smith differed in their views about the precise mechanism for the sustainability of an economy, they were united in their conception of the size of the population as endogenous, believing it to be essentially self-correcting as the pressure of resources – food and so forth – was exerted on human reproduction. Given that eighteenth century political economists also understood that the size of the population was directly related to the value of the economy, it is not immediately evident that they could also have developed a modern concept of economic growth, that is one which assumes a continuous and unlimited expansion of the economy.[27] Here it is useful to note that classical economic theory held that the increase in population size is a consequence of capital accumulation, not its cause, notwithstanding the fact that accurate data on the size of the population was unavailable to eighteenth-century political theorists.[28] In Smith's modelling, however, this consequence of capital accumulation was understood to be one of the elements of a dynamic economy as population growth created a larger labour pool that, according to the principle of the division of labour, led to greater efficiency and productivity.[29] Hence, as Anthony Brewer notes, Smith can be said to have been the first writer to embrace something close to our modern economic concept of growth.[30]

Smith's thinking, however, did not occur in a vacuum. Although the term growth had yet to be used in the modern economic sense, writers such as Josiah Child anticipated the generation of Hume and Smith in his observation that Britain had become richer, but unlike Smith he thought that the mechanism for such increases in wealth was simply trade.[31] The other arena in which a putative modern economic concept of growth can be identified is agriculture, whose decline or advancement was commonly understood to be connected to the size of the population. Writers often took an historical viewpoint, contrasting their own period with ages past, and the argument was often made that progress from a simple state to one in which luxury was a desideratum created the mechanism for change and hence improvement or growth. Such arguments were often based on the contrast between the finite resource of productive land and the infinite capacity for manufacture to expand.[32] These observations, however, were not used to support a model of the economy that indicated its natural

---

[27] Smith noted that the 'most decisive mark of the prosperity of any country' is 'the increase in the number of its inhabitants'. See Adam Smith, *An Inquiry into the Nature and Causes of the Wealth of Nations*, 3 vols. (Dublin: printed for Whitestone et al.,1776), I, 103; and see Brewer, 'The Concept of Growth', 609–38, 610, 611.
[28] See David V. Glass, ed., *The Population Controversy* (Farnborough: Gregg, 1973).
[29] See Eltis, Classical Theory of Economic Growth, 101.
[30] See Brewer, 'The Concept of Growth', 609–38, 631–4.
[31] For a good account of political economy in the generation before Smith and Hume, see Terence Hutchison, *Before Adam Smith: The Emergence of Political Economy, 1662–1776* (Oxford: Basil Blackwell, 1988).
[32] See Brewer, 'The Concept of Growth', 609–38, 625 n. 31.

tendency was to grow in the modern sense. Although Smith considered that the 'progress of opulence' was 'natural' – that is the economy could be expected to continuously 'improve' – he nevertheless held to the view of his contemporaries that when seen in its fullest guise, the economy could advance no further, that is to say he believed that the natural tendency of the economy was to stasis.[33]

As we have noted in Section 7.2, during the eighteenth century the term improvement was most frequently used in conjunction with terms referring to agriculture or husbandry. But there was also a more general sense in which the period expressed its aspirations for betterment across a very wide range of activities. The many societies that were established for the encouragement of arts and manufactures throughout the century were essentially 'improvement' initiatives.[34] Such organisations were based in many cities and in all regions of the country, and they often awarded medals or prizes to those who successfully achieved progress in the fields promoted by the various societies. There was a widespread sense that to be alive at that time was to be witness to the improvement of the world in which one lived. The term also had a more narrowly moral sense, in which the improvement envisaged was in behaviour. One can find many works across the century – both fictional and non-fictional – that announce such a project.[35] One might expect this moral sense to frequently feature in Adam Smith's treatise *The Theory of Moral Sentiments*, but in fact he uses the word only once in the entire work. It occurs in the following context: 'when a patriot exerts himself for the improvement of any part of the public police'.[36] But in the *Wealth of Nations* the word is used on over 300 occasions, and the most common context for those uses concerns the improvement of the land: improvement, for Smith, referred first and foremost to an agricultural or farming intervention.[37] It meant something like 'more efficient exploitation of the land'.

---

[33] On this see Eltis, Classical Theory of Economic Growth, 70.

[34] See David Spadafora, *The Idea of Progress in Eighteenth-Century Britain* (New Haven, CT: Yale University Press, 1990), 76–8.

[35] See, for example, Jane Barker, *The entertaining novels of Mrs Jane Barker ... written for the improvement of some young ladies of quality* (London, 1743); *The Beauties of Thought ... calculated for the improvement of the minds of readers of every class* (Bridlington, 1793); *The Candid Disputant ... calculated for the improvement of all virtuous, charitable, and well-dispos'd minds* (London, 1751).

[36] Adam Smith, *The Theory of Moral Sentiments*, 4th ed. (London: W. Strahan et al., 1774), 274.

[37] The most common co-association with 'improvement' is 'land' or 'lands', which combined total fifty-two occurrences. This should not be surprising when one takes into account the distinctively Scottish project to 'improve' the land in its pursuit of what was called 'opulence'. This project had been in full flow from the early decades of the

There is, however, an interesting tension in his uses of the word, which can be observed in the distinction between improvement as an abstraction simply referring to something getting better, in whatever capacity, and improvement as an increase in the quantity of something. As we have noted earlier in this section, this distinction between abstraction and quantification is a feature of the entanglements of growth and improvement in the dataset of ECCO from around the mid-century onwards. Such a tension arises in, for example, Smith's observation that it is possible to acquire 'great fortunes' from manufacture and the 'raising of rude produce by the improvement and cultivation of land'.[38] Although this putative improvement might occur by claiming more land for agricultural exploitation – hence an increase in the extent of land used for farming – it seems most likely that Smith had in mind an improvement in the techniques and practices for such exploitation.[39] In fact the phrase 'improvement and cultivation of the land' is repeated on enough occasions throughout the *Wealth of Nations* to be considered to be the primary semantic context for Smith's use of the term improvement.[40] Although on most of these occasions it would be difficult to claim that such improvement was gained by an increase in the number of anything as opposed to a qualitative amelioration, there are some instances of use where this is not so cut and dried. In the following text, for example, the immediate context in which improvement is used suggests, even if

eighteenth century, at least since 1723 when the Honourable Society of Improvers was formed. See T. C. Smout, 'Problems of Nationalism, Identity and Improvement in Later Eighteenth-Century Scotland', in *Improvement and Enlightenment*, ed. T. M Devine (Edinburgh: John Donald Publishers, 1989), 45–72; T. C Smout, 'Where Had the Scottish Economy Got To by 1776?', in *Wealth and Virtue: The Shaping of Political Economy in the Scottish Enlightenment*, ed. Istvan Hont and Michael Ignatieff (Cambridge: Cambridge University Press, 1983), 45–72; 68–9; Neil Davidson, 'The Scottish Path to Capitalist Agriculture 3: The Enlightenment as the Theory and Practice of Improvement', *Journal of Agrarian Change*, 5.1 (2005), 1–72; Michael Ignatieff, 'Primitive Accumulation Revisited', in *People's History and Socialist Theory*, ed. R. Samuel (London: Routledge, 1981), 130–5; Anand C. Chitnis, 'Agricultural Improvement, Political Management and Civic Virtue in Enlightened Scotland: An Historiographical Critique', *Studies in Voltaire and the Eighteenth Century*, 245 (1986), 475–88; Nicholas T. Phillipson and Rosalin Mitchison, eds., *Scotland in the Age of Improvement* (Edinburgh: Edinburgh University Press, 1970).

[38] Smith, Wealth of Nations, I, 187.

[39] See also *Wealth of Nations*, III, 211: '[A tax] may be imposed in such a manner as to vary with every variation in the real rent of the land and to rise or fall with the improvement or declension of its cultivation'; II, 210: 'The purchase and improvement of uncultivated land'.

[40] See, for example, *Wealth of Nations*, I, 247: 'the improvement of the powers of labour in producing food by means of the improvement of the cultivation of land'.

only by sequence and association, that improvement is countable because the other two terms, wealth and population, are:

This balance of produce and consumption is entirely different from what is called the balance of trade. It might take place in a nation which had no foreign trade, but which was entirely separated from all the world. It may take place in the whole globe of the earth, of which the wealth, population, and improvement may be either gradually increasing or gradually decaying.[41]

Perhaps unsurprisingly, we find this tension between the abstraction of improvement and its sense of being susceptible to counting when the verb increase is present – very often, in fact, in the orbit of Smith's discussion of the propensity for wealth to increase. Thus, he says that 'as riches, improvement, and population have increased, interest has declined'.[42] And again, noting that an increase in precious metals 'arose from the increase of wealth and improvement';[43] or that commodities become more expensive as society 'advances in wealth and improvement'.[44] On these occasions it is easy to read improvement by association with countables, as if the *amount* of improvement in and for itself might be quantifiable. Such a sense is also present to the locution Smith uses quite frequently, 'the progress of improvement', where 'progress' can be read as 'increase'.[45]

On other occasions Smith seems to have in mind a *process* when he refers to improvement, as in the following:

In every state of society, in every stage of improvement, corn is the production of human industry ... In every different stage of improvement besides, the raising of equal quantities of corn in the same soil and climate, will, at an average, require nearly equal quantities of labour.[46]

Or when he notes that France 'has been much longer in a state of improvement and cultivation' than Great Britain.[47] A similar sense is conveyed in his contention that at the accession of Elizabeth 'the country was much more advanced in improvement, than it had been about a century before'.[48] And at one point this process is conceived of in terms of the mechanism of the market itself:

If by the general progress of improvement the demand of this market should increase, while at the same time the supply did not increase in the same proportion, the value of silver would gradually rise in proportion to that of corn ... If, on

---

[41] Smith, *Wealth of Nations*, II, 320.   [42] Smith, *Wealth of Nations*, I, 137.   [43] Ibid. 288.
[44] Ibid. 325.   [45] See Ibid. 222, 263, 265, 325, passim.
[46] Ibid. 281. The same locution is used at I, 281. See Robert E. Prasch, 'Ethics of Growth in The Wealth of Nations', *History of Political Economy*, 23.2 (1991), 337–51; 341, for discussion of the tension between improvement as process and end point.
[47] Smith, *Wealth of Nations*, III, 341.   [48] Smith, *Wealth of Nations*, II, 110.

the contrary, the supply by some accident should increase for many years together in a greater proportion than the demand, that metal would become cheaper and cheaper ... But if, on the other hand, the supply of that metal should increase nearly in the same proportion as the demand, it would continue to purchase or exchange for nearly the same quantity of corn ... These three seem to exhaust all possible combinations of events which can happen in the progress of improvement.[49]

In this characterisation of the 'progress of improvement' Smith effectively lays the ground for the construction of the modern economic concept of growth, even if he does not use the word.[50] And he builds further on these foundations a little later in the same volume where he describes the differences between kinds of 'rude' produce, noting with respect to scarce goods unsusceptible to human industry, that under the conditions in which there is 'progress of wealth and improvement' these goods will increase in price that 'seems not to be limited by any certain boundary'.[51] Smith here identifies an economic process or mechanism in which 'progress' of wealth and improvement leads to an ever increasing price for natural commodities such as rare gemstones, which one might represent schematically: progress in X causes rise in price of Y. Although it is clear that Smith is applying a model of demand and supply, he is also exploiting the 'play' we earlier identified in the concept of improvement in order to construct a recursive system: progress in size or quantity necessarily leads to progress as 'betterment', and betterment necessarily leads to an increase in quantity or size. Although it would take another 150 years before the statistical means for assessing the total size of an economy became available, Smith had conceptualised the basic structure of economic growth. As he noted in an earlier observation in his *Wealth of Nations*: 'since the time of Henry VIII, the wealth and revenue of the country have been continually advancing, and, in the course of their progress, their pace seems rather to have been gradually accelerated than retarded'.[52]

7.5   Conclusion

As we noted in the introduction to this chapter, we think it likely that the race for economic growth post the COVD-19 pandemic will be intense across the global economy. There may, however, be calls for a reconsideration of the wisdom of such policy, along the lines of the

---

[49] Smith, *Wealth of Nations*, I, 265.
[50] Although the term growth is used on thirty-one occasions by Smith in the third edition of the *Wealth of Nations*, he never assigns the modern economic meaning to it.
[51] Smith, *Wealth of Nations*, I, 325.   [52] Ibid. 132.

'limits to growth' arguments of the early 1970s. Here we do not wish to enter into strictly economic arguments, about the possibility, for example, of building the national and even the global economy with different desiderata. Rather, we wish to highlight the long-range effects of the entanglements of growth and improvement. Conceptual formation and evolution can have very long periods of gestation. In the case to hand, we have discovered what might be thought of as a conceptual resource in the entanglements of growth and improvement in the eighteenth century. This resource lay dormant, as it were, for over 150 years, before the concept of economic growth became fully articulated in and through the lexical item growth. Once it became established the sense of betterment associated with improvement lay in the kernel of the concept, muted for the most part, but nevertheless tightly bound in its DNA. We contend that, even putting aside technical economic arguments and theories concerning growth, uses of the concept at the present time silently invoke and assume that growth is good, that 'going for growth' is necessarily for the good of an economy. This is because the concept's long gestation occurred within its entanglements with improvement. Should we wish to change that, find new uses for growth that are less destructive of finite resources and more attuned to economic cooperation and cohabitation, we will need to edit the concept's DNA.

8   The Idea of Commercial Society: Changing Contexts and Scales

John Regan

In contrast to the chapters in this book that begin with investigations of the distribution of lexis in the corpus ECCO, this chapter takes a long-standing scholarly discussion centred on a key social and economic concept for the eighteenth century – commercial society – as its point of departure. My main purpose is to investigate the correlations between the history of an idea as it has been articulated in traditional intellectual histories and a corpus-based approach using some of the methods outlined in this book.

The Cambridge political theorist and intellectual historian Istvan Hont argued in his posthumously published Carlyle Lectures that the term commercial society was used by Adam Smith in ways that were distinct from any of his peers. Smith, Hont claims, 'stretched' the term in order to 'make it a theoretical object for moral and political inquiry'.[1] This chapter engages with this argument using computational methods for interrogating datasets of varying sizes. The first, a custom-produced Adam Smith corpus (hereafter 'Adam Smith'), will be compared with a Scottish Enlightenment corpus (hereafter 'Scottish Enlightenment'), both of which have been extracted from the larger ECCO dataset. For the second of these datasets, I have used a list of publishers' names collated from existing scholarly enquiries by Richard B. Sher (*The Enlightenment and the Book*) and Andrew Hook (*The Glasgow Enlightenment*) to construct a dataset that enables one to inspect and interrogate what might be thought of as the distinctively *Scottish* history of ideas in the period within which Smith wrote his seminal works.[2]

---

[1] Istvan Hont, *Politics in a Commercial Society* (Cambridge: Harvard University Press, 2015), 3.
[2] Richard B. Sher, *The Enlightenment and the Book: Scottish Authors and Their Publishers in Eighteenth-Century Britain, Ireland, and America* (Chicago: University of Chicago Press, 2006); Richard B. Sher and Andrew Hook, eds., *The Glasgow Enlightenment* (East Linton: Tuckwell Press, 1995).

The main thrust of the approach I shall take is a tripartite comparative analysis, tracking the architecture of the concept of commercial society across the two datasets and comparing the 'Adam Smith' and 'Scottish Enlightenment' ideas to that found in the larger 'British' eighteenth century collection. I intend to ascertain the extent to which Smith did, as Hont argues, use the term idiosyncratically, through the identification of the component parts of its clustered lexical imprint – in the first instance located in Smith's own writing, then in the Scottish Enlightenment corpus before comparing both to the fuller (although limited by the selection decisions outlined in Chapter 2) ECCO dataset. This method allows us to stress test Hont's assertion that Smith deployed the concept of commercial society idiosyncratically by charting the extent to which the features of Smith's thinking were adopted by his contemporaries, firstly within the Scottish context and secondly within anglophone culture of the period at large as represented by ECCO.

Using a measure of lexical co-association that is detailed in Chapter 2, Section 2.1, I will present data about the distribution of lexis that can only be grasped through the application of digital tools to historical natural language datasets. To be sure, my aim is decidedly *not* to debunk or contradict what we know about the concept of commercial society from the various traditions of close reading that ground intellectual history. Rather, it is to open up three new pathways into an ostensibly familiar territory in late Enlightenment political economy. In doing so I shall put considerable pressure on the claim made by Hont that Smith 'stretched' the phrase commercial society, thereby constructing a distinctive 'theoretical object'. In other words, I shall be seeking to answer the questions: where did the idea of commercial society come from? Did Smith structure it idiosyncratically? Or did his use of the concept gain wider traction in the period?

We can only answer these questions by discovering and thinking about the actual words Smith used to articulate concepts such as real versus nominal value, or the labour theory of value, which would be refashioned by David Ricardo and would of course be adapted by Karl Marx. We must establish, on the basis of evidence, the actual, real vocabulary in which he articulated the distinctions between factors such as money and corn rents, theories of value, and numerous agronomic concepts feeding into Smith's understanding of what is commonly referred to as 'commercial society'. Reconstructing the real, rather than assumed, lexical lineaments of these by-now ostensibly familiar ideas is crucial if we are to test Hont's theory of the distinctiveness of Smith's possession of the concept.

8.1   'It Is Just Barely There': 'Commercial Society' across Three Corpora

In beginning our digital investigation of the distinctiveness of Adam Smith's concept of commercial society, it is of course important to understand Hont's main suggestions about that distinctiveness. In *Politics in Commercial Society* Hont places Smith's work in the context of his contemporary Jean-Jacques Rousseau and argues that neither Rousseau nor Smith adequately outlined the form of government that was most appropriate for the functioning of 'commercial society'.[3] Moreover, while Rousseau and Smith shared ground when it came to the ethical foundations of their moral philosophy (Rousseau's esteem for self-love and Smith's celebrated theory of sympathy in *The Theory of Moral Sentiments* seem to Hont roughly compatible), their respective theories on distributive justice and government were inchoate and at odds.[4]

Hont is not alone in noting the drama of convergence and divergence between Rousseau and Smith more widely, including for example their affinities with regard to issues such as the importance of the rhetorical power of language.[5] But Hont's particular interest is in engaging with each writer's historical understanding of the origin and progress of the social contract, which leads them to different positions on the type of state that fits the commercial nature of modern society. The main disagreement Hont perceives between them is on whether commercial society should be built upon contractarian principles that enshrine in law the concept of private property and the commercial practices entailed by this. Smith, after David Hume, argues that unwritten convention should supplant contract; that human society should (indeed throughout history does) construct conventions of behaviour, which then, much later, may be codified in law.[6]

---

[3] Charles Griswold explores this in a chapter entitled 'On the Incompleteness of Adam Smith's System', in *Adam Smith Review*, II, ed. Vivienne Brown (London: Routledge, 2006), 181–6.

[4] See Edward S. Cohen, 'Justice and Political Economy in Commercial Society: Adam Smith's "Science of a Legislator"', *Journal of Politics*, 51.1 (1989), 50–72.

[5] The best studies of this act of the drama are Mark Salber Philips, 'Adam Smith, Belletrist', in *The Cambridge Companion to Adam Smith*, ed. Knud Haakonssen (Cambridge: Cambridge University Press, 2006), 57–78; Stephen McKenna, *Adam Smith: The Rhetoric of Propriety* (New York: University of New York Press, 2005); Benoît Walraevens, 'Adam Smith's Economics and the *Lectures on Rhetoric and Belles Lettres*: the Language of Commerce', *History of Economic Ideas*, 18.1 (2010), 11–32.

[6] Smith's inheritances from Hume in this context are illuminated by Paul Cheney's 'Constitution and Economy in David Hume's Enlightenment', in *David Hume's Political Economy*, ed. Margaret Schabas and Carl Wennerlind (London: Routledge, 2009), 223–42.

In this broadly organic, non-contractual view, the late progress of mankind sees law and the modern state given definition by a natural tendency towards commerce, and by the collective, gradual realisation that modern society must enshrine in law the protection of private property. Presenting a stadial history that is typical of his age and intellectual milieu, Smith argues that the progress of man to commerce is the driver of modern liberty and the rule of law. This optimistic, gradualist stadial narrative is at variance with Rousseau's profound scepticism about any system in which private property is of integral legal importance – Rousseau argues that history has demonstrated time and again that when private property and the law were mutually determining, humankind tended towards exploitation. Having laid out some of the broad lineaments of Smith's theory of commerce in the context of human progress, let us now begin our digital investigation.

No digital study of the discourses within which Smith and Rousseau presented their ideas can proceed without a sound investigation of the words that characterise such discourses, and I shall begin by looking closely at the terms that Smith used in his writings about political economy. I intend to avoid replicating assumptions about what Smith wrote based on inaccuracies as to the words that he actually used in his publications. Let us consider some examples. As de Bolla et al. observe in Chapter 7, Smith wrote about opulence rather than wealth as the goal of the improvement of Scottish land. This 'progress' was towards an opulent commercial society rather than capitalism; what Smith characterised as an optimal conjunction of agricultural and urban centres of commerce. Because these clarifications attempt to capture what Smith specifically intended in his use of the words he deployed in his articulation of the key concepts of the new commerciality, they are germane to the objective of articulating what commercial society meant to him.

In the 'Adam Smith' corpus, the word commercial appears 73 times in total; the word society appears 560 times. This disparity is mirrored in the historical tranches of the two other corpora under investigation. In the relevant 1750–1800 time slice of 'Scottish Enlightenment', commercial occurs 10,365 times and society occurs 115,057 times. Naturally, frequencies for ECCO for the relevant historical period are several orders of magnitude greater – commercial occurring 82,610 times and society occurring 748,515 times. One way of presenting these disparities is to note that there are 7.6 times as many uses of the word society as there are of commercial in 'Adam Smith'; in the 'Scottish Enlightenment' corpus there are roughly 11.1 times as many; and in ECCO there are approximately 9 times as many uses of society as there are of commercial.

These numbers give a rough first sense that the proportionate frequencies of each word in Smith mirror the proportions of their uses in the 'Scottish Enlightenment' and ECCO corpora for this fifty-year time period.[7] First inspection of the data appears to indicate that Smith's consideration of society is not only, or primarily, conditioned by the adjective that forms one of the most familiar concepts associated with his understanding of political economy, but it also accords with how the word is used in the two larger corpora. What is more surprising, however, given the widespread assumption within Smithian scholarship about the central importance of the concept of commercial society, is that Adam Smith only uses the phrase *twice* in his entire corpus. Both of these occasions are in *The Wealth of Nations*. The first is in the chapter 'Of the Origin and Use of Money':

Division of labour being established, every man lives by exchanging. When the division of labour has been once thoroughly established, it is but a very small part of a man's wants which the produce of his own labour can supply. He supplies the far greater part of them by exchanging that surplus part of the produce of his own labour, which is over and above his own consumption, for such parts of the produce of other men's labour as he has occasion for. Every man thus lives by exchanging, or becomes in some measure a merchant, and the society itself grows to be what is properly a *commercial society.* (emphasis mine)[8]

The second occurrence of the phrase in *The Wealth of Nations* is in 'Article II: Of the Expence of the Institutions for the Education of Youth':

Notwithstanding the great abilities of those few all the nobler parts of the human character may be in a great measure obliterated and extinguished in the great body of the people.
    The education of the common people requires, perhaps, in a civilized and commercial society, the attention of the publick more than that of people of some rank and fortune.[9]

The first passage is as succinct a summation of the crucial, ameliorative 'exchange' component of Smith's concept of commercial society as one could hope to find. The second, describing how human potential can be squandered by the careless dissipation of attention and various types of labour among young people, maps less easily onto the more familiar

---

[7] Note that here I do not necessarily assume equivalence between either of these datasets and how these terms would have been used by the populace of the nations within Britain more widely.

[8] Adam Smith, *An Inquiry into the Nature and Causes of the Wealth of Nations*, 2 vols. (London: W. Strahan and T. Cadell, 1776), I, 27.

[9] Adam Smith, *An Inquiry into the Nature and Causes of the Wealth of Nations*, 3 vols. (Dublin: printed for Messrs. Whitestone, Chamberlaine, W. Watson, Potts, S. Watson, 1776), III, 138.

articulations of the concept – let us say its canonical shape or structure – in which society is considered to operate a system of negotiations of value and price embodied in the material realities of the abstraction of money. No matter how familiar the lineaments of the concept of commercial society seem to be to us now, the notable infrequency of the actual phrase in the original texts presents us with a problem: how can we assess the veracity of Hont's claim that Smith's concept of commercial society was distinctive if the phrase itself is vanishingly rare in what he published?[10] Even as he argues for the specialness of the concept to Adam Smith, Hont admits that this sense is based on virtually no textual evidence:

commercial society is Smith's own term; perhaps nobody else used it in quite the same linguistic fashion, even if strong theoretical affinities with it did exist. It is Smith's own use of this expression that validates it historically. But this validation is not outstandingly strong. It is just barely there.[11]

It is perhaps noteworthy that in more recent critical treatments of Smith's analysis of political economy, we find a superabundance of the phrase. For example, in Edward S. Cohen's 1989 article on the concept of justice in Smith, the author uses the phrase commercial society thirty-eight times. In 'Morality and Sociability in Commercial Society', Robin Douglass uses the phrase fifty-seven times.[12] This comparison between primary and secondary texts indicates something significant: that the afterlives of the concept commercial society in political theory create a lexical shorthand that is markedly incommensurate with Smith's own use of the phrase. Theorists and critics use the lexical tag commercial society in a way that suggests it loomed large in Smith's writing. But it simply did not.

Despite this significant infrequency of the phrase in the Smith corpus, we may nonetheless recover the lexical environments in which the phrase's two component words (commercial and society) circulated, thereby removing the temptation to elide or conflate the historical discursive context with its reception and later operationalisation in the history of ideas. Let us return to Hont's headline claim that commercial society is Smith's term for a 'fundamental type of society'. One avenue of inquiry,

---

[10] In addition to the Smith publications that are searchable using the computational method outlined above, I searched all individual digital versions of Smith texts on the Online Library of Liberty. Adam Smith, Online Library of Liberty, accessed 20 October 2020, https://oll.libertyfund.org/person/adam-smith. The two instances of the phrase commercial society discussed in this section are the only ones occurring anywhere throughout the corpus.

[11] Hont, *Commercial Society*, 3.

[12] Cohen, 'Justice and Political Economy', 50–72; Robin Douglass, 'Morality and Sociability in Commercial Society', *Review of Politics*, 79.4 (2017), 597–620.

in common with the method set out in Chapter 7 of this book, is to test the hypothesis that the absence of the phrase commercial society does not indicate that the *idea* was not current; it merely indicates that different words were used to express or interrogate it. In the following section of this chapter, I intend to search for these different words and thereby to address Hont's claim that Smith proposed there might be a 'fundamental type' of society.

8.2 The Particularity of Smithian Commerce

A good start can be made by investigating the nouns that were qualified by the adjective commercial in Smith's writing. Table 8.1 shows the nouns that occur immediately after the seventy-one instances of the adjective commercial within *The Theory of Moral Sentiments* and *The Wealth of Nations*.

Can we identify the presence of a dominant conceptual architecture across a variety of noun-adjectival phrases? Prima facie, the answer seems to be yes: the word commercial is situated in two discrete, seemingly consistent semantic domains. The first is the vocabulary of

Table 8.1 *Nouns following commercial in* The Theory of Moral Sentiments *and* The Wealth of Nations.

Nouns following commercial in The Wealth of Nations (59 total instances)	n	Nouns following commercial in The Theory of Moral Sentiments (12 total instances)	n
world	10	policy	4
system	9	information	1
countries	9	politics	1
country	6	intercourse	1
state	5	system	1
nations	3	regulations	1
towns	3	countries	1
policy	2	interests	1
relations	2	freedom	1
regulations	2		
projects	1		
benefits	1		
dealings	1		
interests	1		
spirit	1		
advantages	1		
treatises	1		
states	1		

geopolitics: world, state, states, country, countries, nation, nations, towns. The second most coherent semantic field consists in a vocabulary of commercial apparatuses: regulations, policy, relations, projects, benefits, treaties. And in concert with these parts of what would have been a notably Polybian conception of mixed government after 1688, one can also note the language of negotiation: advantages, dealings and intercourse. On the evidence presented so far, the word slants towards geopolitics just as much as it slants towards the processes and institutions of nascent free-market capitalism.

Hont claims that Smith's concept of commercial society is distinctive because it is a 'theoretical object'. He argues that the concept stands out because it abstracts from particulars to make wider assertions about a 'fundamental type' of society. He makes a distinction between the two writers' possession of the concept of society, arguing that Rousseau's esteeming of ancient city-states as cynosures for modern government in the stage of development labelled 'commercial', is attributable to his Genevan background. Rousseau, Hont argues, projected the ancient city state onto his native Geneva as he modelled a putative modern government, one that was produced in the stage of societal development he called 'commercial'. Smith on the other hand presents no such model – ancient nor modern – that might be replicated. In fact, he perceives there to have been a comprehensive break with ancient Europe, which makes examples from antiquity inadmissible. Indeed, for Smith there is no modern state which is fitting to the new conditions of commerciality. According to Smith man's progress towards commerce needs no such model anyway: a modern commercial society emerges from within the stadial operation of commercial progress. Hont's stress on Rousseau's espousal of the importance of a physical and geographical context for a theory of government, however, should not be taken to imply that Smith was indifferent to concepts of place or their utilisation in his putative theory of commercial society.

Here we encounter a significant problem in Hont's argument about the theoretical distinctiveness of the concept commercial society (again, if we wish to designate it as such – about which more later). This is that *The Wealth of Nations* is deeply concerned with environmental, physiocratic and geopolitical particularities. It is this particularity that repeatedly undercuts any sense that Smith is constructing an abstract or primarily theoretical conception of commerce: something evident from the company that our two constituent search terms keep in his corpus. The text of *The Wealth of Nations* is a virtual compendium of specific case studies in how the physical and topographical conditions of particular places produce particular types of commercial conditions. Individual cases within this compendium are too numerous to mention, but a brief survey will suffice to convey how important geographical particularities were to Smith. Some of Smith's areas of inquiry are: the decline in the demand for labour in Bengal, the price of corn in the Netherlands, the relative opulence of countries cultivating rice rather than corn, the cheapness of labour in England when compared to North America, the particular conditions of commercial administration in various colonies, the more particular, profound knowledge required in farming as opposed to most forms of manufacture owing to physiocratic conditions. As afore-mentioned, this particularising treatment of environmental conditions cuts profoundly against Hont's characterisation (which I would contend is canonical) of commercial society as a generalising, theoretical concept of a fundamental type. Contra Hont, and in line with Smith's organic and non-prescriptive, non-contractarian view of the correct form of government, each geopolitical specificity is recognised and mapped: real conditions take the place of abstractions or theories in the vast majority of cases. Just as there is hardly any presence of the phrase commercial society to speak of in Smith's corpus, we now see that what is said to be 'commercial' in Smith is more particular than 'theoretical', to use Hont's adjective.

The importance of the particular rather than the abstract is supported by my observation with respect to the counterweight in the semantic context for commercial society: geopolitical entities – world, town, nation, country. Smith, as we now know, declined to use the phrase commercial society, and his mapping of the terms commerce and society was almost equally distributed between *particular* ideas of place and ideas of transaction. But when he brought the two together, he used a different phrase than commercial society: he made the conjunction with system. Looking back on the publication of *The Wealth of Nations* in 1776, he referred to it as a 'very violent attack I had made upon the whole commercial system of Great Britain'.[13] More will be said about 'commercial system' below.

Smith's concepts of commerce are more aligned with his intellectual milieu than Hont claims. In 1770, Sir James Steuart published *An Inquiry into the Principles of Political Oeconomy*, capturing one of the common ways in which the concept of commercial countries is constituted by the great, significant turn towards interest and other promissory forms of financial interaction which drive the improvement of countries such as Scotland:

In countries where trade and industry are in their infancy, credit must be little known; and they who have solid property, find the greatest difficulty in turning it into money, without which industry cannot be carried on . . .

[13] *Correspondence of Adam Smith*, ed. by Ernest C. Mossner and Ian S. Ross (Oxford: Oxford University Press, 1987), 208.

Under such circumstances, it is proper to establish a bank upon the principles of private credit. This bank must issue notes upon land and other
securities, and the profits of it must arise from the permanent interest drawn
for the money lent.

Of this nature are the banks of Scotland.[14]

Steuart's theory of capital broadly aligns with Smith's: where there is
a scarcity of material money, usually in the form of precious metal in
coins and other less easily transmissible objects, 'private credit' will take
the place of these objects to drive progress. By focusing on the particular
conditions of Scotland after the Seven Years' War, Steuart argues that
Scotland's economic shift from cumbersome mercantilism to lean commerciality was entirely driven by a readiness to 'lend upon mortgage',
something that was not available from institutions such as the Bank of
England. Of course, this resembles Smith's theory of capital: money
stock that is not used to satisfy the immediate needs and wants of any
one person or 'society', but which is held back until it can be used to
acquire additional revenue. One form of money supplies immediate
demand, and the other is used to speculate and so to accrue more
money.

Steuart's avowed aim is to expand a concrete, and distinctively
Scottish, reliance on private capital to energise other more ostensibly
opulent countries: 'By this I flatter myself to do a particular service to
Scotland, as well as to suggest hints which may prove useful, not only to
England, but to all *commercial countries*, who, by imitating this establishment, will reap advantages of which they are at present denied' (emphasis
mine).[15] There are at least two points of relevance here. The first is that
Steuart claims that precisely because of a shortage of cash attributable to
a sluggish movement of money around rural areas, the Scottish system
has abstracted money into a system of what is here considered a highly
desirable, incredibly efficient and mobile idea of money: capital. In other
words, the particular, situated, located conditions of post-war Scotland,
with its relative poverty but also its remarkable perceived commercial
potential, are those which allow and indeed encourage the proliferation
of a private credit system which did not necessitate the presence of actual
cash.

Secondly, it is notable that at precisely the moment when Steuart gives
definition to this less material conception of how value might be trans-
ported and transacted, he cannot avoid a sense of its actual instantiations,

---

[14] James Steuart, *An Inquiry into the Principles of Political Oeconomy: Being an Essay on the
Science of Domestic Policy in Free Nations* (Dublin: James Williams and Richard
Moncrieffe, 1770), 356.

[15] Steuart, *Inquiry*, 357.

referring to the private credit expansion of Scotland as 'this establishment'. No matter how abstracted this theory of capital is from the metal realities of cash that so captivated Smith in *The Wealth of Nations*, its author evidently relies upon a concept of the establishment. The actual, the real and the established are the ideas that underwrite a more ideational idea of money that aligns with Smith's theory of capital. When we attend to the grammatical aspect of the word establishment – either noun or verb, even implied gerund – we can begin to see the architectural lineaments of this complex idea of commerce. Reading along these lines, establishment can refer to both an institution and a form of action. This establishment can be understood not only as an idea of an institution but also of a real, actual action: the establishment of capital and all that this entails.[16]

Steuart's example is important not because it aligns perfectly with Smith's vision of what a commercial country is (indeed it does not do so entirely) but because both Steuart and Smith describe the new commerce and the capital that drives it with repeated, significant reference to actual locations: real establishments and institutions. Their primary reference points are things in the world rather than abstract concepts. Examples of geographically determined commerce are littered throughout Smith's corpus, but here we come to perhaps the most crucial point of distinction between how Smith uses the term commercial and how it is used in Steuart and very widely throughout ECCO.

In a passage near the end of the second volume of *The Wealth of Nations*, Smith describes how, in Wales and the Highlands of Scotland, 'revenue' gathers in old families and is not distributed readily through the system: 'I cannot help remarking it, that very old families, such as have possessed some considerable estate from father to son for many successive generations, are very rare in commercial countries.'[17] Far from embodying a muscular and spry new commerciality, rural Scotland and Wales are places where money becomes stuck. By contrast, 'In commercial countries, therefore, riches, in spite of the most violent regulations of law to prevent their dissipation, very seldom remain long in the same family.'[18] Again, the particular case of Scotland as a place through which money moves only sluggishly produces the apparatus of capital. It might be objected here, with respect to Hont's argument about a 'theoretical object', that Smith is in fact employing a *theory of how money works* – call it 'capital'. But capital only emerges in Smith, and in Steuart, through

---

[16] This way of thinking about the relation of word types to conceptualisation resonates with the study presented in Chapter 7, in which de Bolla et al. write that a 'shadow grammar' for the word improvement begins to appear as its use changes: '"process" began to turn towards or even into its gerund form "improving"'.

[17] Smith, *Wealth of Nations*, II (Dublin, 1776), 207. [18] Ibid.

Table 8.2 *Instances of phrase,*
1750–1800. Source: ECCO.

Phrase	frequency
commercial countries	321
commercial country	1022
commercial system	311
commercial state	413
commercial policy	284
commercial dealings	231
commercial relations	131

particular, real, non-theoretical conditions. Far from stretching the real into the theoretical, Smith is at pains to capture as much as he can of the real and the particular.

As we have seen, the nouns used in conjunction with commercial in the Smith corpus refer, in significant numbers, to geopolitical particulars. I now want to ascertain if this context can be considered the real basis of Smith's 'distinctive' conception of commercial society (leaving to one side for the moment the issue of whether Hont's notion of commercial society was in fact conveyed by a different phrase in Smith's works) by investigating the other two corpora. When we run the query commercial as a Boolean search through the ECCO Historical Texts official interface for the period 1750–1800, the term occurs immediately before a noun on 15,437 occasions. My first comparison between these results and the terms we found in the Smith corpus – that is comparing the same noun-adjective phrases – indicates the following frequencies for the period 1750–1800, here presented in Table 8.2.

We can only gain a sense of whether Smith's use was broadly concurrent with or aberrant from the general use of the adjective by finding out whether these numbers are notably high or low in the context of uses of commercial in the ECCO corpus. What comes to light is that these uses are not particularly common in the corpus when compared with some other co-associations: commercial intercourse, for example, accounts for 1,456 of the 15,437 occurrences.

8.3   Limited Companies and the Question of Distinctiveness

Comparing what has emerged so far in 'Adam Smith' to what we find in 'Scottish Enlightenment' and ECCO, the first point to note is that Smith's vanishingly rare use of the phrase mirrors how it was used in both corpora. There are a total of eighty-five instances of the phrase commercial society in the whole of the vast ECCO dataset. Of these, eighty-three occur in the 1750–1800 time slice of ECCO, and twenty of these occurrences are accounted for by editions of Smith's *The Wealth of Nations* themselves. And, as we have already noted, the phrase in fact occurs on only two occasions in the entire text. Of the remaining sixty-three, one is a direct response to (or perhaps more accurately, version of) Smith's text: Jeremiah Joyce, *A Complete Analysis or Abridgement of Dr. Adam Smith's* Inquiry into the Nature and Causes of the Wealth of Nations.[19] It is notable that only one occurs in a text within the 'Scottish Enlightenment' corpus: James Beattie's *Elements of Moral Science*. Beattie uses the phrase to frame a discussion of external intervention in markets: 'In commercial society, it is sometimes necessary to fix, for certain commodities, a *pretium legitimum*, or legal price, which cannot be exceeded. This is particularly the case with those things in regard to which the seller has it in his power to take advantage of the buyer.'[20] And overall, the sixty-three non-Smith occurrences most commonly invoke a type of state intervention that is required in order to buttress the efficient functioning of markets.

At first glance it might be assumed that the uptick in uses of the phrase commercial society in the final quarter of the century in the ECCO dataset was caused by the reception of Smith's works. And indeed, this would seem to be the silent assumption in much of the scholarship on Smith and his economic theories. Should this be the case one would expect to find a correspondence or overlap between the two very rare uses of the phrase in Smith's *Wealth of Nations* and its wider distribution in the full ECCO corpus. But in fact, on close inspection of the sixty-three uses in texts by authors other than Smith, it becomes clear that a much weaker – even totally distinct – conceptualisation is in play that refers to a society with a relatively small number of members whose activities are in some sense commercial. This concept warrants more attention than it has received.

If we look at the two pre-1750 uses of the phrase in the ECCO dataset – in fact located in one text and its subsequent second edition, first published anonymously in 1728 and then under the author's name the following year – this alternative 'weak' sense is very evident. Thus, in *The Academical, or Week-Day's Subjects of the Oratory, from July 6, in the First Week, 1726, to August 31, 1728*, we find the phrase commercial society

---

[19] Jeremiah Joyce, *A Complete Analysis or Abridgement of Dr. Adam Smith's* Inquiry into the Nature and Causes of the Wealth of Nations (Cambridge: Benjamin Flower, 1797).

[20] James Beattie, *Elements of Moral Science*, II (London: T. Cadell, 1790), 294.

being used to refer to a certain constituency within society, that is to a subset of society understood to represent the totality of persons. Among the miscellany of topics, the author outlines 'a plan for a new commercial society of the trading, landed and money'd interest: domestick and foreign; to survey each, and their connexion, and real and imaginary bottom, in all articles: not only to subsist and flourish within itself, but to command a leading power over all rivals, in each of those interest, at home and abroad'.[21]

A caveat should be entered here: such sparse data cannot support a secure claim about the uses of the phrase over the first fifty years of the eighteenth century. But the inflection or slant of the phrase towards this sense of a subset of society as a whole does map onto the uses of the phrase following the publication of *The Wealth of Nations*. Across these uses it is clear that the majority refer to a relatively small constituency of men whose interests coalesce in a legally recognised commercial institution of limited size. Examples of this conception abound throughout 'Scottish Enlightenment' and ECCO: Eberhard August Wilhelm von Zimmerman's *A Political Survey of the Present State of Europe* from 1787 suggests that a single company, the East India, is a 'commercial society' and that 'time must show, whether the provisions of Mr Pitt's bill will be an adequate cure of the evils which have affected the prosperity and stability of this extraordinary commercial society'.[22] The phrase names a company rather than a whole nation's interactions in Abbé Reynal's *A Philosophical and Political History of the Settlements and Trade of the Europeans in the East and West Indies* of 1783, and in the anonymous *Second Report from the Committee of Secrecy, Appointed to Enquire into the Causes of the War in the Carnatic* of 1781.[23]

Some more representative examples suffice to capture the tenor of the wider uses across the corpora being examined here. The first comes from Robert Watson's *The History of the Reign of Philip the Third, King of Spain* of 1792:

A fund, amounting to more than six million of florins, was immediately subscribed for by the merchants in the principal maritime towns, and managers were

---

[21] *The Academical, or Week-Day's Subjects of the Oratory, from July 6, in the First Week, 1726, to August 31, 1728* (London, 1728), 11.

[22] Eberhard August Wilhelm von Zimmerman's *A Political Survey of the Present State of Europe, in Sixteen Tables; Illustrated with Observations on the Wealth and Commerce, the Government* (London: C. Dilly, 1787), 211.

[23] Abbé Reynal, *A Philosophical and Political History of the Settlements and Trade of the Europeans in the East and West Indies*, 5 vols. (London: W. Strahan; and T. Cadell, 1783); *Second Report from the Committee of Secrecy, Appointed to Enquire into the Causes of the War in the Carnatic* (London, 1781).

appointed, under whose direction all the trade to India was henceforth to be carried on. This company being the first regular commercial society, of which we read in history, has served in some measure as a model, to all the trading companies that have been created in modern times.[24]

In 1781, Philippe Fermin writes about the efficacy of government administration in a colony; he contrasts this not with commercial society as a general concept of human relations in the commercial stage of development, but merely with actual private companies:

An attention so important, and so essential to the prosperity of this colony, demands certainly the care of the state. An administration of this nature requires an authority and an activity which can never be found in an exclusive company, or in any commercial society whatever.[25]

This indicates that Fermin thinks of 'exclusive company' as generically or conceptually identical to commercial society, where the term society (as in mutual society) means the same thing as company.

James Macpherson (chief confector of the Ossian phenomenon) outlines a different idea of commercial society in which the stress is placed on the persons who comprise such a society, the nobility. He depicts it as a coming together of like-minded commercial people who all fall into the social and political category of the nobility:

Our nobility and gentry, with a spirit becoming Britons, either serve in our constitutional defence, the militia, or with their influence and purses exert themselves, in raising new corps. The greatest commercial society, in the kingdom, has set a noble example to their fellow-subjects, by a unanimous and powerful aid to the state, in the present emergency.[26]

In this conception, the nobility is itself the commercial society: a cynosure of civic mindedness to which other 'societies' within the populace might turn for guidance. A similar conception is evident in 1790, when George Griffin Stonestreet writes of commercial society as an actual institution that requires a literal support or underwriting, such as insurance.[27] Reflecting on the precarious state of commercial intercourse in the context of the frequency of fires in London,

---

[24] Robert Watson, *The History of the Reign of Philip the Third, King of Spain*, 2 vols. (Basel: J. J. Tourneisen, 1792), I, 218.

[25] Philippe Fermin, *An Historical and Political View of the Present and Ancient State of the Colony of Surinam in South America* (London: W. Nicoll, 1781), 99.

[26] James Macpherson, *A Short History of the Opposition during the Last Session of Parliament* (London: T. Cadell, 1779), 56.

[27] Two other uses (among a great many) of the phrase which support the idea of commercial society as a more 'concrete' concept occur in Abbé Reynal, A Philosophical and Political History, II, 174. Anonymous, *Second Report from the Committee of Secrecy*, 342.

Stonestreet identifies insurance as a necessary buttress for the procedure of commercial society.[28]

Surveying the sixty-three uses of the phrase across the 'Scottish Enlightenment' and ECCO corpora, it is difficult to identify any, at all, that seem to resemble Hont's 'theoretical object' that characterises exchange and interaction between persons who inhabit the same space, call it the polis or *societas*. This is so notwithstanding the one use to be found in Cato's *An Essay on the English Constitution* of 1770: 'Our acquisitions on the continent, require a great military force, which is incompatible with every principle of a commercial society. The country, from whence you pretend to draw the articles of trade, is ruined, and the inhabitants become your enemies.'[29] A close survey of all uses of the phrase commercial society within ECCO, as well as within our subcorpus *Scottish Enlightenment*, indicates that it is difficult to sustain an argument that Smith, or indeed anyone else, minted an abstract political concept which sought to capture the specific nature of a kind or type of society in general. It is difficult to defend the hypothesis that Smith 'stretched' the use of the phrase to make it do such 'theoretical' as opposed to particular work.

Another view onto Smith's use of the terms can be gleaned by using the measure of lexical co-association outlined in Chapter 2. And the data here indicate that there is no lexical overlap between the terms highly co-associated with commercial and society in the entire Smith corpus.[30] And then, when we compare this with the two other corpora, we find substantially the same thing: only one word – civilisation – occurs on both lists of associated terms here. On this evidence, Smith's tendency not to use the words in similar contexts is concurrent with the uses of these words across what can broadly be characterised as his intellectual milieu. Once again, the data indicate that far from using the phrase commercial society in a distinctive, idiosyncratic manner, Smith swam in the same waters as his contemporaries: his conceptual mapping of both commerce and society fully accorded with the prevailing tendencies of his times.

But if the picture provided by 'Scottish Enlightenment' publications seems persuasive, the view across the wider, much larger ECCO corpus seems even more compelling: there is no overlap – that is not a single word – between the strongest contexts for commercial and society in the historically relevant section of the ECCO corpus. The same is true for the

---

[28] George Griffin Stonestreet, *Reflections Occasioned by the Frequency of Fires in the Metropolis; with Thoughts on Measures for Adding to Public Security* (London: G. G. J. and J. Robinsons; J. Debrett; J. Whieldon; and J. Sewell, 1790), 6.

[29] Cato, *An Essay on the English Constitution* (London: J. Almon, 1770), 94.

[30] See Tables A8.1 6 in the Appendix.

words' contexts in 'Adam Smith'. We are discovering that commercial and society are simply not words that occurred in the same semantic domains in the corpora under investigation.

Let us take stock of some of the salient observations that have been made so far, before proposing some ways in which it may possible to gain greater granularity with respect to how Smith conceptualised commerce. We have already ascertained that Smith hardly ever used the phrase commercial society, but what is coming into focus now is that given the absence of lexical overlap between the two terms in the candidate phrase, we need to look elsewhere, to other terms and phrases, in order to capture how he thought about society.

We have also discovered that relative to the number of occurrences of the terms commercial and society in both the ECCO dataset and the sub-corpus 'Scottish Enlightenment', we can judge the use of the phrase within the period as a whole to be infrequent. And in the majority of instances where we do find uses in both 'Scottish Enlightenment' and ECCO, it refers to something transactional rather than ideational. This is to say that it names a concrete process, an exchange of things in the world rather than an idea or 'theoretical object'. So, to gather together these observations with respect to Hont's claim of distinctiveness, my first observation is that the phrase can hardly be said to be distinct on account of the fact that Smith in effect never used it. Moreover, this scarcity also occurs in the larger datasets. Although it can be argued that Smith used the phrase as a theoretical object on one occasion, this is not replicated across the sixty-three uses we found in the larger corpora. And, as we have seen, the two constituent words in the phrase hardly keep any company at all: they operate in distinctively separate lexico-semantic contexts in each of the corpora.

8.4   Conclusion: 'Commercial System' at the Fault Line between the Particular and the Theoretical

In Chapter 7, de Bolla et al. propose an understanding of conceptuality that is useful as we draw this inquiry to a close. Their argument runs as follows:

concepts may operate in historical contexts when the label for the concept was not immediately accessible or current. As we saw in our discussion about the presence of republicanism in the era of the founding of the United States, a hypothesis may be entered in which it is claimed that the putative concept was captured by or contained in *other words* current at the time.[31]

---

[31] See Chapter 7, Introduction.

In other words, we need to inspect other words; words which capture or convey the concept of commercial society without using the two candidate terms in conjunction. Accepting this understanding of concepts – that they might, in historical corpora, be instantiated in language which is not exactly that which *names* a familiar concept as such – does not foreclose the issue of whether or not Smith did indeed use or have access to the concept Hont identifies as contained in the expression commercial society. But I want to conclude this chapter by arguing that the evidence above points towards a different observation: that the specific language used by Smith indicates that commercial society had no real valence in Smith's epistemic toolbox. And even if, as I shall demonstrate, another rather differently configured concept was active, this should not be conflated with what the reception history of Smith's works has assumed, namely that he was a pioneer in establishing the theoretical framework for one of, if not the key, economic concepts of late capitalism: commercial society.

We can get at this by noting that Smith used the phrase commercial system far more frequently than he used commercial society (a paltry two uses). This leads to the hypothesis that the underlying concept in Smith's thinking about the progress of society – what was doing the heaving lifting of ideational work – was not the concept of commercial society but of commercial system. This is the phrase that Smith really *does* use to name the fault line between the particularities of environment and a more general theory of commerce. In *The Wealth of Nations*, for example, uses of the phrase allow us to chart a progression in Smith's thinking from the commercial system as a particular, and also theoretical, concept:

Of the unreasonableness of those extraordinary restraints, the foregoing part of this Chapter have endeavoured to shew, even upon the principles of the *commercial system*, how unnecessary it is to lay extraordinary restraints upon the importation of goods from those countries with which the balance of trade is supposed to be disadvantageous.[32]

From here, we may survey other uses of the phrase that attest to a kind of transfer between the specific and the theoretical. At several points Smith seems to ascribe a kind of cognitive agency – a way of knowing and thinking – to a system which he sees as emerging organically from the history of humanity in its innumerable particular conditions:

THE two forts of restraints upon importation above-mentioned, together with these four encouragements to exportation, *constitute the six principal means by which the commercial system proposes to increase the quantity of gold and silver in any*

---

[32] Smith, *Wealth of Nations* (London, 1776), II, 29.

country by turning the balance of trade in its favour. I shall consider each of them in a particular chapter, and without taking much further notice of their supposed tendency to bring money into the country, I shall examine chiefly what are likely to be the effects of each of them upon the annual produce of its industry. (emphasis mine)[33]

The same kind of agency appears here:

TO lay extraordinary restraints upon the importation of goods of almost all kinds, from those particular countries with which the balance of trade is supposed to be disadvantageous, is the second expedient by which *the commercial system proposes to increase the quantity of gold and silver.* (emphasis mine)[34]

Or, again, in this example:

Every town and country, on the contrary, in proportion as they have opened their ports to all nations; instead of being ruined by this free trade, *as the principles of the commercial system would lead us to expect, have been enriched by it.* (emphasis mine)[35]

The *commercial system* proposes, and it has principles: for the concept to be theoretical or ideational, Smith ascribes agency to it. While it would be couching the case too emphatically to argue that he ascribes discretely human faculties to the system, there is the undeniable sense that Smith sees it as proceeding from the concrete, material and particularly the mineral to a kind of agential entity that can act.[36]

Returning one final time to the question of distinctiveness, we may compare what appears to be Smith's curious personification of a concept to instances of the phrase in the two larger corpora. On this occasion what we find is fascinating: the 171 uses across 'Scottish Enlightenment' and ECCO all appear to mirror what we find in Smith. The anonymous author of the *Glasgow Magazine and Review* of 1783 describes the legal impingement on a concrete system of commerce in the colonies:

It is the policy of France and Spain not to suffer foreign vessels to trade to their islands and colonies, and our own maxims have hitherto been the case, but the bill ... this most necessary restriction, to our whole commercial system.[37]

In William Robertson's celebrated 1778 *History of America* the historian describes a related issue after the treaty of Utrecht:

But though, on the cessation of the war, which was terminated by the treaty of Utrecht, Spain obtained relief from contraband one encroachment on her

---

[33] Ibid. 30.   [34] Ibid. 57.   [35] Ibid. 88.
[36] Note resonances between this argument about agency and that proposed in Chapter 7 on Smith and the concept of growth by de Bolla et al.
[37] *Glasgow Magazine and Review* (Glasgow: J. Mennons, publisher of the Glasgow Advertiser, 1783), 33.

commercial system, she was exposed to trade, another which she deemed hardly less pernicious.[38]

In 1794 Jedidiah Morse discusses the unification of American states in a commercial system.[39] These examples confirm what we found in Smith, namely that commercial system is used to refer to a set of procedures, rules or conventions that operate in a market.

Once more, and in conclusion, to return to the issue of distinctiveness and Smith's thinking as it has been represented in the history of ideas, it would be wrong to assert that the uses of commercial system noted above were hegemonic. In fact, the data indicate that not only in Smith but also in the other two corpora the phrase is used to refer to both a particularity – to the rules and conventions of a market – and to a more abstract conception. In Thomas Brydson's 1795 text *A Summary View of Heraldry in Reference to the Usages of Chivalry and the General Economy of the Feudal System*, we find a use of the phrase that taps into the extensive debate in the period about the nature of mixed government:

> THE several governments which Polybius describes as adopted in rotation, each with a view to correct the abuses of the foregoing, were alike hostile to those who had been thus thrust beyond the verge of society. NEITHER the feudal, nor the succeeding *commercial system* can be entirely acquitted of the same. (emphasis mine)[40]

This concept not only assumes some kind of moral content or knowledge in a *commercial system*; it also aligns something identified as 'the feudal', that is a type or kind of government, with a commercial system, here to be read as a *system of government*. We shall conclude with Mark Leavenworth's *Colony Commerce, or, Reflections on the Commercial System, as It Respects the West-India Islands* from 1790. The text as a whole is a salutary reminder of the geographical situatedness of so much 'commercial' discussion across 'Smith', 'Scottish Enlightenment' and ECCO. But the following passage demonstrates once again how *commercial system* rather than *commercial society* is the concept that is 'stretched' to become a theoretical object containing ideas, values, suppositions:

> THE principles of Commerce are so few, and simple, that they are perfectly understood by all, except Legislators and learned Politicians. Every other man knows, that he employs his time and capital best, when he does that business

---

[38] William Robertson, *The History of America*, II (Edinburgh: W. Strahan; T. Cadell; and J. Balfour, 1778), 408.

[39] Jedidiah Morse, *The American Geography, or, A View of the Present Situation of the United States of America* (London: John Stockdale, 1794), 197.

[40] Thomas Brydson, *A Summary View of Heraldry in Reference to the Usages of Chivalry and the General Economy of the Feudal System* (Edinburgh: Mundell & Son London, 1795), 228.

which will bring him the most valuable returns; and that he saves his profits best when he buys what he wants at the cheapest market. This rule is invariable and universal, nor can a case be even supposed, in which the commercial profit of a Country is not pursued in the best possible manner, if each individual does that business which produces the most value. Our present *commercial system* however supposes, that in some cases a man employs his time and his capital best, (at least for the public interest) not when he takes the cheapest and easiest method to obtain what he wants, but when he takes the most expensive and laborious method. (emphasis mine)[41]

And so it is here, in the lexical context of the commercial system that we most often find what Hont was looking for: 'invariable and universal' rules that 'every other man knows'.

---

[41] Mark Leavenworth, *Colony Commerce, or, Reflections on the Commercial System, as It Respects the West-India Islands* (London: R. Faulder, Bond-Street; sold also by W. and J. Stratford, 1790), 2.

9   The Age of Irritability

Ewan Jones and Natalie Roxburgh

The essays collected in this book have a good deal to say about both the means and ends of digital intellectual history. A variety of computational tools generate results that – such is our consecutive claim – differ from what more conventionally analogue methods produce. But where should intellectual history *begin*? Here, too, digital methods permit a qualitative shift. The accredited intellectual historian generally starts from a vantage that her peculiar expertise establishes: particular topics or texts appear worthy of discussion or investigation to the extent that they contribute to (or inflect or challenge) extant historiographic themes. Each discipline delimits a horizon of possibility. This form of expertise, so tacit that we seldom trouble to reflect explicitly upon it, facilitates much productive intellectual work. Like any method, it also brings drawbacks: these include confirmation bias (finding what we were all along looking for); or its converse, an over-heightened sensitivity to the unrepresentative utterance only because it runs against the grain of a received story.

Digital methods allow us to commence from a more agnostic position: by automating quantitative measurements, we can glimpse patterns to which our subjective preferences or disciplinary formations would otherwise have blinded us. Such, at least, is the claim of this chapter, which begins not from a pre-decided theme that is deemed to merit further computational analysis, but rather from a series of rudimentary comparative measures, to which greater complexity and granularity is gradually applied. This single case study thereby also offers a representative example of how to move from simple raw frequency to at least preliminary qualitative claims. As we shall see, these comparative measures open up conceptual histories that other chapters explore in more detail.

This book's methodological introduction established the construction of a bespoke measure of relative probability (*dpf*), which subsequently grounds more complex conceptual architectures. In the early phases of this essay, we wish to linger a little longer over the simpler numbers that inform this calculation, in order to show how it might open up research questions even for intellectual historians uninterested in more complex

computational procedures. Rather than choose a particular term or cluster of terms, we decided, as a preliminary step, simply to compare the
changing raw frequencies of *every* word in the corpus over the *longue durée*
of the eighteenth century. By dividing the summed raw frequency of
a term from 1770–1800 by the raw frequency of the same term 1700–
30, we gain a rough-and-ready sense of significant alterations in usage.[1]
Terms at the top of the list demonstrate the largest relative increase; those
at the bottom show the largest decline. (Or the smallest increase: given the
increase in publications across the century, the raw frequency of most
words rises.)

Eyeballing this automatically generated graph for the first time, several
results surprised us, despite – or because of – our common expertise in the
historical period in question. A small number of words (such as oxygen
and phlogiston) never occur across the first three decades, and hence
cannot be computed. Of the 24,496 remaining tokens, however, we
observe a few striking trends: patriotic is at the very top of the list,
occurring but once across 1700–30, before exploding into life in the
final three decades, where it registers 23,061 usages. Civilisation (9),
constitutional (25), commercial (42) all burst from nowhere into prominence. The emergence of despotism (15) and patriotism (89) suggests
a developing linguistic recourse to abstraction (the other -isms with which
we have since become familiar are, with the exception of atheism, conspicuous by their absence). Various prominent tokens (unnoticed (34),
unfeeling (86), uncommonly (119), inattention (187)) suggest a dawning
power of negation. The words at the very bottom of the list also deserve
notice. The massive increase in published material across the century
makes most declines relative rather than absolute. It is nonetheless striking that religious language predominates: God is 22,202 of all tokens;
Christendom 21,296; Christ 21,693; Christians 22,224; christen 24,292;
Christ's 24,303. (The one exception – predictably enough – is Christmas,
whose raw frequency increases steadily, placing it at 1,402 on the list.)

Several of the other chapters within the book trace the conceptual
consequences of such linguistic events: among other terms, Chapter 5
investigates atheism and despotism; Chapter 8 treats commercial society,
with the adjective registering the forty-second most rapid increase in
usage. This chapter investigates a different term whose shifting usage
offers a portal into a broader conceptual network, namely irritability,
whose rapid increase in raw frequency (from 6 occurrences in 1700–30
to 13,238 across 1771–1800) puts it in twelfth place on the aforemen-
tioned list. We began by suggesting that automated measures can

---

[1] Here, as throughout our analysis, we measure at a lexical distance of 10.

establish an intellectual inquiry with a more agnostic cast of mind. As soon as the decision arises over which result to pursue, however, interpretation and preference necessarily enter the stage. In the case to hand, irritability certainly did jump out at us given our shared interests and disciplinary expertise (we have both preciously written about medical culture in the eighteenth and nineteenth centuries). Yet the further statistical measures that we uncovered both deepened and unsettled what we thought we understood. As such, this case study offers a representative instance of how digital history affords the capacity to rethink what passes for established knowledge.

That irritability counts as an emergent concept across the eighteenth century hardly counts as news. In *De natura substantiae energetica* (1672), Francis Glisson established the term *irritabilitas* to describe a reactive yet vital power inherent to organic life.[2] While the word (as we have seen) remained rare in the early decades of the eighteenth century, the physician Thomas Fuller, in his *Pharmacopeia extemporanea* (1710), describes 'such Affects as arise from great Irritability of the Fibres and Nerves; and colliquation of the Blood and Humors'.[3] It was not until the Swiss anatomist and erstwhile poet Albrecht von Haller's pioneering work, however, that irritability entered the medical lexicon with consistency. His *Dissertation on the Sensible and Irritable Parts of Animals*, translated into English in 1753, split precisely what Fuller's account had lumped together: 'Fibres and Nerves'. The former, on Haller's dualistic account, exhibited irritability: it indicated reflexive and involuntary muscular contractions, which did not travel to the cerebellum, and which – as Haller proved with a series of grisly dissections – could continue even after decease. The latter, by contrast, exhibited sensibility: the nervous system of man, as distinct from the animals, proved both reactive and voluntary; it was connected both to the brain and to a broadly Cartesian conception of soul.

Despite Haller's cardinal significance for physiology, historians of science and medicine are divided regarding the broader significance of his cardinal terms. Hubert Steinke, who has written the definitive monograph on Haller's life and research, advances no large claims for irritability having travelled beyond the immediate applied context.[4] In a special edition of *Science in Context* dedicated to vitalism, meanwhile, Guido

[2] Francis Glisson, *De natura substantiae energetica* (London: Flesher, 1672).

[3] Thomas Fuller, *Pharmacopeia extemporanea, or, a body of prescripts. In which forms of select remedies, ... are propos'd ... Done into English out of Latin by the author Thomas Fuller, ... With large additions and emendations* (London: printed for Benjamin Walford, 1710).

[4] Hubert Steinke, *Irritating Experiments: Haller's Concept and the European Controversy on Irritability and Sensibility, 1750–1790* (Amsterdam, NY: Rodopi, 2005).

Giglioni claims that Haller's revised concept was of clinical use only to the extent that it drastically delimited Glisson's more dynamic monism: irritability, on this account, would be limited to reflexive actions, so as to make way for faith (sensibility).[5] While some historians of science and philosophy have considered the influence of this anatomical tradition upon the German idealism of Wolff, Kant and Herder, Haller's significance for anglophone thought is commonly thought to inhere only in a long and acrimonious squabble with the Scottish physician Robert Whytt.[6]

Yet the changing statistical profile of irritability suggests a more pivotal discursive role. The drastic increase in raw frequency offers only one metric; still more significant is the unusual force with which it binds and is bound by other terms, as a broader conceptual network rapidly coalesces over the final decades of the century. Taking the whole century into account, irritability stands out for both the extent and the strength of its bindings: 933 tokens occur prior to the bend in the curve; these have a median *dpf* of 2,122, rounded to the nearest even number. It should be pointed out that within the corpus as a whole, there is a tendency for concrete terms to feature larger and stronger binding-lists.[7] This is unsurprising, given the tendency for specific technical terms to occur often in close proximity to one another: the architecture formed from parallax, zenith, planet and related terms, for example, exhibits some of the highest values within ECCO as a whole. Of all the given abstract nouns, however, irritability binds with unusual force. (Compare its profile to the other words that we listed above, which emerged over the eighteenth century: civilisation features 777 words above the bend in the curve, with a mean *dpf* of 1,479; constitutional 619, with a mean *dpf* of 1,430; commercial 707, with a mean *dpf* of 1,528; despotism 710, with a mean *dpf* of 1,538; and patriotism 634, with a mean *dpf* of 1,354.)[8]

---

[5] Guido Giglioni, 'What Ever Happened to Francis Glisson? Albrecht Haller and the Fate of Eighteenth-Century Irritability', *Science in Context*, 21.4 (2008), 1–29. See also Dominique Boury's article in the same issue, 'Irritability and Sensibility: Key Concepts in Assessing the Medical Doctrines of Haller and Bordeu', *Science in Context*, 21.4 (2008), 521–35.

[6] For a magnificent account of Haller's influence in the Germanic tradition (and much besides), see John H. Zammito's *The Gestation of German Biology: Philosophy and Physiology from Stahl to Schelling* (Chicago: University of Chicago Press, 2018). Also relevant in this respect is Catherine J. Minter's 'The Concept of Irritability and the Critique of Sensibility in Eighteenth-Century Germany', *Modern Language Review*, 106.2 (2011), 463–76. For discussions of the Haller–Whytt argument, see Eugenio Frixione, 'Irritable Glue: The Haller–Whytt Controversy on the Mechanism of Muscle Contraction', in *Brain, Mind and Medicine: Essays in Eighteenth-Century Neuroscience*, ed. Harry A. Whitaker, C. U. M Smith and Stanley Finger (New York: Springer, 2007), 115–24.

[7] See Chapter 5, note 8.

[8] Here, as throughout our analysis, we measure at a lexical distance of 10.

Table 9.1 *The top ten terms having the highest* dpf *values for stimulus and nervous at a distance of 10 among all documents from 1780 to 1800. Total number of documents: 73,104. Source: ECCO.*

stimulus: distance 10 (top 10 of 880 total)				nervous: distance 10 (top 10 of 973 total)			
Bound token	*dpf*	*N* (total)	*N* (with focal)	Bound token	*dpf*	*N* (total)	*N* (with focal)
stimulus	98075	14639	288	nervous	40608	97591	2300
irritability	48528	14310	140	nerves	24362	187254	2294
fibre	30464	19750	113	irritability	19416	14310	246
irritation	24979	30489	130	muscular	19384	31992	460
debility	18948	26732	89	paralytic	13358	14500	171
accumulation	13600	22065	55	debility	13234	26732	273
contraction	13432	21899	54	palsy	12207	23667	229
secretion	12692	20247	48	fevers	12118	146458	942
fibres	12444	156532	232	fibres	11993	156532	982
muscular	11474	31992	62	nerve	10395	60981	408

Irritability, it might be objected, remains a particularly concrete kind of abstract word, which, while it names a property rather than a delimited entity, nonetheless operates in a precise technical context. Indeed, it does – yet in what follows, we develop the argument that the concept binds strongly and widely in large part through its ability to bring together a large amount of functional medical vocabulary (fibres, nerves, stomachs, etc.) with a variety of more abstract or evaluative ideas. This ability is inseparable from the concept's operation in a surprising variety of discursive contexts. To get to that point, however, we need first to scrutinise the binding lists in more detail. Two things jump out in this regard: the first is a pronounced tendency to *asymmetrical reciprocal binding*. The terms that appear on or towards the top of the binding list of irritability also feature irritability in equally or still more prominent positions in their own lists (see Table 9.1). Some examples: stimulus binds irritability second (after itself), system third (after system and systems), nervous third (after nerves and nervous), fibre second (after itself), temperament second (after itself), convulsions fifth (after three forms of the same lexeme and vomiting), sensibility first (above even itself). In short: a large variety of terms bind irritability more powerfully than any other token in the corpus.

The final instance of this asymmetrical reciprocal binding gives rise to a second, related observation: as irritability binds more powerfully to a variety of words it brings to them a dense network of associated terms.

Table 9.2 *The top ten terms on* dpf *lists for fibre and sensibility at a distance of 10 among all documents from 1780 to 1800. Total number of documents: 73,104. Source: ECCO.*

fibre: distance 10 (top 10 of 710 total)				sensibility: distance 10 (top 10 of 750 total)			
Bound token	*dpf*	*N* (total)	*N* (with focal)	Bound token	*dpf*	*N* (total)	*N* (with focal)
fibre	172460	19750	808	irritability	18102	14310	169
irritability	49945	14310	182	sensibility	18081	65974	556
stimulus	30464	14639	113	susceptible	7796	38969	159
fibres	24979	156532	705	feelings	7733	139737	427
cohesion	18948	15189	71	feeling	6854	181060	470
muscular	13600	31992	113	unfeeling	6056	19508	72
fibrous	13432	18077	66	nerves	5996	187254	416
muscle	12692	63081	145	sensations	5900	62528	174
contraction	12444	21899	62	nervous	5703	97591	238
elementary	11474	17845	52	delicacy	5653	126031	288

The developing link with sensibility (see Table 9.2) offers a case in point: unlike its sister term, this term already exists widely across the first half of the eighteenth century, with 2,245 separate occurrences across 1701–50. We find in this period, however, a very weak binding to a variety of more-or-less scattered words: connections, retributions, weaknesses, perceives and distilled figure at the top of the list.[9] It is hard to discern a coherent semantic field at this point. Across the second half of the eighteenth century, by contrast, the term increases significantly both in raw frequency (to 63,729 occurrences), and in the strength and consistency of its bindings: among the top twenty-five terms we find irritability, nerves, nervous, organs, temperament and sensation. Whether or not individuals directly read Haller's work, the nascent link with irritability established for sensibility a semantically coherent architecture.

What do such preliminary results suggest? For one thing, we might give rather more precision to what has long proven a contentious area for historians of ideas and literature alike: the somewhat vague notion of the 'culture of sensibility'. Even so sensitive and panoptic a critic as Northrop Frye could indicate this historical phenomenon with disarming generality:

The period of English literature which covers roughly the second half of the eighteenth century is one which has always suffered from not having a clear

[9] See Chapter 2 for corpus level baselines for binding values, Section 2.4.

historical or functional label applied to it. I call it here the age of sensibility, which is not intended to be anything but a label. This period has the 'Augustan' age on one side of it and the 'Romantic' movement on the other, and it is usually approached transitionally, as a period of reaction against Pope and anticipation of Wordsworth.[10]

Quantitative results enable us to delimit this period with more precision: sensibility does indeed permit the thinking of various affective states with which we commonly associate poets such as Wordsworth (feelings, emotions and sympathy also feature in the twenty-five most bound terms); yet such affectivity is clearly anchored in the somatic body. The objection that the same word simply operates in two distinct discursive contexts – that sensibility enables a consideration of the vascular system for surgeons, and a consideration of the affective system for aestheticians – cannot hold, when we consider that feelings and sympathy also bind nerves prominently.

All of the above would seem to lend credence to the argument that George S. Rousseau has been constructing for more than three decades: that sensibility is bound up overwhelmingly with the body. Indeed, it does: but these results enable us to make a series of finer discriminations, both with regard to the nature of this discursive matrix and to its varied effects within culture. In *Nervous Acts: Essays on Literature, Culture and Sensibility*, which collects the bulk of his significant contribution, Rousseau demonstrates the extent to which a contemporary and generally figurative understanding of words such as nervous anachronistically misreads what in the eighteenth century qualified as literal truth: when, for example, Marianne Dashwood complains, in *Sense and Sensibility*, that she suffers from 'nervous irritability', she does not mean that she is simply 'temperamental', in some vague psychological sense, but that her body is configured in a particular manner.[11]

Rousseau's historical recovery is all the more heroic for being conducted in a pre-digital age when many of its central texts and thinkers (such as Thomas Willis and George Cheyne) remained obscured. Yet the very scope of the tradition that he exhumes at times prevents him from drawing intellectual distinctions and casual inferences. Nerves and nervous systems are simply everywhere: across the medical tradition of Haller and Whytt, the philosophical tradition of Diderot and (the other) Rousseau, and the sentimental fictions of Smollett, Sterne and Austen. The issue of gender offers but one instance of where this textual surplus

---

[10] Northrop Frye, 'Towards Defining an Age of Sensibility', *English Literary History*, 23.2 (1956), 144–52; 144.

[11] *The Novels of Jane Austen*, I, *Sense and Sensibility*, ed. Robert W. Chapman (Oxford: Oxford University Press, 2015).

militates against conceptual discrimination: at one point, *Nervous Acts* makes the (fascinating) observation that 'nervous' is often identified as a salient and positive masculine trait, which connotes something like 'virility'; poets such as Byron are thus frequently dismissed as being both 'nerveless' and 'effeminate', adjectives that work as cognates.[12] Later, however, the same work makes the (just as fascinating) observation that women – particularly pregnant women – are often taken to be peculiarly 'nervous': as representative instance, Rousseau cites a sub-section from David Hartley's *Observations on Man*, entitled 'To Examine How Far the Longings of Pregnant Women Are Agreeable to the Doctrines of Vibrations and Associations'. Expectant mothers, Hartley claims, exist in 'a State of great Sensibility and Irritability'.[13] Like any rapidly evolving field, the discourse around the sensibility–irritability axis is indeed complex and frequently self-contradictory. Yet the binding profiles of these and related terms enable us to chart pertinent distinctions whose signal endures through the noise of culture.

Irritability, we contend, is the strongest such signal. While he directly quotes Hartley's use of the term, Rousseau seldom references it in a specific manner; despite adverting recurrently to the Haller–Whytt controversy, he does not venture into the substantive debate.[14] Yet at least some of its relevant distinctions do continue to operate, even in a suddenly nerve-saturated discourse that is frequently metaphorical or anatomically inaccurate. Haller, we may recall, localised irritability within muscle fibres, which proved subject to involuntary contractions (or con-vulsions); sensibility, by contrast, indicated those nerves that connected, via the medulla, to the brain, and as such involved higher cognitive powers (volition, apprehension). The respective *dpf* profiles bear out the enduring salience of this distinction. As can be seen in Table 9.2, fibre is one of several terms that exhibit a reciprocal binding, which in this case is symmetrical: the word occurs second on the list of irritability, and irrit-ability occurs second on its own list. With the case of nerve however, the specific link slackens: while irritability does occur above the bend in the curve, it is buried way down in the list.

Rousseau nonetheless treats (irritable) fibres and (sensible) nerves as if they are isomorphic terms. His 1975 essay 'Nerves, Spirits, and Fibres: Towards Defining the Origins of Sensibility' treats the former exclusively as a modality of the latter: he summarises rival theories of the composition

---

[12] George S. Rousseau, *Nervous Acts: Essays on Literature, Culture and Sensibility* (London: Palgrave Macmillan, 2004), 42.

[13] David Hartley, *Observations on Man* (London: J. Johnson, 1791), 164; quoted in Rousseau, *Nervous Acts*, 134.

[14] See Rousseau, *Nervous Acts*, 172, 233.

of the nerves as proposing either 'hollow tubes' or 'solid fibres'; at another point, he calls fibres a mere 'subsidiary' of nerves.[15] But this is to ignore Haller's cardinal distinction – a distinction that, as we shall show, holds large and previously unexplored consequences beyond specifically medical discourse. In order to demonstrate this wider significance, the remainder of our analysis will prosecute two separate modes of analysis (although in cultural practice both strands proved inseparable). The first conducts a more granular and qualitative reading of some of those texts that compose the statistical headlines that we have just outlined, and which cumulatively demonstrate the pertinence of the fibres–nerves distinction for questions of gender, colonialism and aesthetics. The second re-ascends from these individual texts so as to consider more distally two conceptual fields to which irritability attaches itself like a parasite, and whose composition it, like a parasite, changes.

9.1   Irritable Texts

Let us first move from statistical trends to the individual texts that they comprise. It is unsurprising that, in the sudden welter of medical textbooks and philosophical treatises that from the 1750s begin to harness the irritability–sensibility axis, many authors blur distinctions. All discourse suffers from conceptual fuzziness: eighteenth-century language users, schooled to avoid redundancy through what linguists now call 'elegant variation', armed with only a rudimentary understanding of developing anatomical research, frequently employ irritability and sensibility as mere synonyms.

There are, however, more philosophical reasons to resist Haller's dualism. Robert Whytt leads the way in this respect, conducting a lengthy quarrel with his Swiss counterpart over the latter's restriction of soul to those parts of the nervous system that connected directly to the brain. *An Essay on the Vital and Other Involuntary Motions of Animals* (1751) argued rather that a sentient principle operated in a far more distributed manner: soul acted routinely (if unconsciously) in even the reflexive spasm. Save for a couple of instances, which serve only to dismiss Haller's theories, Whytt drops the word irritability entirely: human beings are sensible all the way down.[16] As Nima Bassiri has observed, the net result is a curious animist–mechanist admixture.[17] Whytt himself never quite reconciled his

---

[15] Ibid. 167, 166.

[16] Robert Whytt, *An Essay on the Vital and Other Involuntary Motions of Animals* (Edinburgh: John Balfour, 1763), 280, 388.

[17] Nima Bassiri, 'The Brain and the Unconscious Soul in Eighteenth-Century Nervous Physiology: Robert Whytt's Sensorium Commune', *Journal of the History of Ideas*, 74.3 (2013), 425–48; 434.

extension of sentience to muscular contraction, on the one hand, with his experimental practice, on the other. When, for instance, the *Essay* enforces contractions in the muscles of a frog 'by pricking or tearing of their fibres', it is unclear on what grounds he denies soul to the reptile.[18]

Yet a series of less canonical thinkers and practitioners chose not to abandon Haller's distinction: they retained irritability, without either spiritualising it (as had Whytt), or restricting it merely to inert matter or mechanical reflex, as had Haller's 1732 work *De partibus corporis humani sensibilibus et irritabilibus*. It is these texts that drive the data patterns that we observed above; it is through them that a conceptual signal emerges amid linguistic noise and redundancy. Still more interestingly, the emergent concept of irritability often challenged its authors' stated intentions.

The first and perhaps most significant such discursive matrix concerns gender, where the delimited concept of irritability played an increasingly pivotal role. In his *Lectures on the materia medica* (1772), William Cullen retains and subtly reshapes Haller's distinction: 'irritability', he writes, 'is often connected with weakness of the nervous power; sensibility, more remarkably with its strength'.[19] This distinction helps to explain the cultural tendency that Rousseau uncovered but did not elucidate – why 'nervous' connoted virility until deep in the eighteenth century, while 'irritable' denoted the effeminate. The example from Hartley's *Observations*, to which we previously adverted, concerns pregnant women; Cullen's influential lectures similarly pave the ground for the several surgical texts that develop in the 1780s and 1790s, which drive home the association of irritability and femininity, particularly so far as it concerns the pregnant and/or hysterical woman. (Child bearing and pathology are often taken to come together.)

A few exempla suffice to represent the many.[20] Andrew Wilson's *Medical researches: being an inquiry into the nature and origin of hysterics*

---

[18] Whytt, *Vital and Other Involuntary Motions of Animals*, 413.

[19] William Cullen, *Lectures on the materia medica* (London: printed for T. Lowndes, 1772), 54.

[20] Many such medical texts and midwifery manuals make use of the concept. See for instance Edward Foster, *The Principles and Practice of Midwifery* (London: printed for R. Baldwin, 1781); Thomas Denman, *An Introduction to the Practice of Midwifery* (London: J. Johnson, 1794). This gendered association percolated into philosophical discourse: see Dugald Stewart's claim in the *Elements of the Philosophy of the Human Mind* that: 'In consequence of the greater nervous irritability of women, their muscular system seems to possess a greater degree of that mobility by which the principle of sympathetic imitation operates. Hence their proneness to hysteric affections, and to that species of religious enthusiasm which is propagated by contagion' *The Collected Work of Dugald Stewart*, ed. William Hamilton, 9 vols. (Edinburgh: Thomas Constable, 1854), IV, 240.

in the female constitution, and into the distinction between that disease and hypochondriac or nervous disorders (1776) devotes a whole chapter to irritability ('we are indebted to the truly learned and indefatigable physiologist, Dr. Haller, for this term').[21] The cognate sensibility is conspicuous by its absence: in its place, Wilson substitutes a comparable yet significantly distinct separation. On the one hand, we find '*insensible* Irritability', which occurs routinely in, for instance, the unperceived actions of the intestines; on the other, there is '*sensible* Irritability', in which the human 'frame' is 'easily shocked'.[22] This latter, Wilson asserts, lies at the root of hysterical distempers. Both terms offer instances of involuntary or reflexive action: there is no appeal to the soul, no mediation, via the medulla, to the cerebellum. Irritability extends diffusely through the material world: in addition to 'hysterical women', we observe it in the springs of watches, glass, musical chords and mounds of jelly; boiling and roasting meat can even restore this property.[23]

John Leake's *Practical Observations towards the Prevention and Cure of Chronic Diseases Peculiar to Women* (1792) similarly acknowledges its indebtedness 'to the celebrated Baron Haller for pointing out the essential difference between [irritability] and Sensibility, with which it had so often been confounded'; it too detects the former in material phenomena that encompass (and slide between) the liquid and solid:

EXPERIMENTS shew, that the degree of Irritability is in proportion to the firmness and consistence of that mucus or glue of which the whole bodily system is originally made up: Whatever, therefore, hardens this animal jelly, as cold, exercise, acids, and the link, diminish Irritability; and, on the contrary, the dissolving power of heat and moisture are found to increase it.[24]

Such extracts make clear to what extent the relatively sophisticated anatomical discourse of the eighteenth century absorbs the residues of early modern humoral theory. Indeed, a physician such as Hugh Smythson continues to speak, in *The Compleat Family Physician* (1781), of 'acrid humours' that congregate in the stomach: hysterical disorders, he claims,

have been supposed, as may be gathered from the name, to arise at first from a preternatural irritability of the womb; it is, however, undoubtedly produced by the irritation of the nerves, either general in the whole habit, or of the stomach, intestines, or some other particular part; and girls towards the approach of the

---

[21] Andrew Wilson, *Medical researches: being an inquiry into the nature and origin of hysterics in the female constitution, and into the distinction between that disease and hypochondriac or nervous disorders* (London: printed for S. Hooper, Ludgate-Hill; and Robson, 1776), 150.
[22] Ibid. 153.   [23] Ibid. 155.
[24] John Leake, *Practical Observations towards the Prevention and Cure of Chronic Diseases Peculiar to Women* (London: Baldwin, 1792), 229.

periodical discharge, and women of relaxed and tender habits, and who are in the first stages of pregnancy, are most liable to it.[25]

It might well seem difficult to extract much salutary worth from texts that routinely liken distempered women to tubs of jelly or reheated slabs of meat. The texts surveyed above, as with so many medical manuals across the last three decades of the eighteenth century, are indeed dismayingly if unsurprisingly misogynistic. Yet the very mechanism of their condescension – their materialist reduction – would inadvertently pave the way for suppler usages of the concept of irritability, which increasingly served to blur the lines between not only men and women but also human and non-human organic life. We catch a glimpse of this in several texts that prove no less culturally patronising, but which redirect their attention from the nervous system of women to that of indigenous populations. Take, for instance, the English translation of Guillaume Thomas Reynal's highly influential *Histoire philosophique et politique des établissements et du commerce des Européens dans les deux Indes* (1777). This text, a co-authored bricolage that featured eminent materialists such as the Baron d'Holbach, attempts to account for the purported resistance to pain in the native populations of modern-day Canada:

How shall we account for this insensibility? Is it owing to the climate, or to the manner of life? Colder blood, thicker humors, a constitution rendered more phlegmatic by the dampness of the air and the ground, may doubtless blunt the irritability of the nervous system in Canada. Men who are constantly exposed to all the inclemencies of the weather, the fatigues of hunting, and the perils of war, contract such a rigidity of fibres, such a habit of suffering, as makes them insensible to pain.[26]

If hysterical women are too irritable, indigenous persons suffer (or benefit) from a hardened insensitivity to the world.[27] Neither verdict essentialises any less than the other: yet such increasingly common judgements indicate a profound shift from Haller's absolute Cartesian dualism between (irritable) body and (sensible) mind to an exclusively materialist account of the human body as a dynamic equilibrium, whose balance can only emerge between two (pathological) extremes. Sensibility could and

---

[25] Hugh Smythson, *The Compleat Family Physician, or, Universal Medical Repository* (London: printed for Harrison and Co., 1781), 353.

[26] Abbé Reynal, *A Philosophical and Political History of the Settlements and Trade of the Europeans in the East and West Indies*, translated from French by J. Justamond, 5 vols. (London: printed for T. Cadell, 1777), IV, 462.

[27] Other texts made similar claims. James Hendy's *A treatise on the glandular disease of Barbadoes: proving it to be seated in the lymphatic system* (London: C. Dilly, 1784) also attributes glandular fever to 'a peculiar degree of irritability in the lymphatic system' occasioned by the hot climate (41).

did play a role in this system: we have seen from Cullen's definition how it was used to mark an excessive 'strength' of constitution. Yet its residual association with a spiritual or sentient principle helps to explain why irritability and fibres (rather than sensibility and nerves) more often do the work of accounting for the human constitution in physiological terms.

Such accounts are certainly materialist; yet they also evince an increasingly non-reductive dynamism. This emerges in two related ways: firstly, irritability involves the human subject in the immediate environment (the bad weather of Canada). Physical constitution both conditions and reflects habituated actions within that environment (hunting, waging war). Secondly, irritability manifests itself through and on anatomical parts that change: muscular fibres, which in infancy are 'smooth', can harden; one organ (the stomach) can affect another (the womb). Nerves too may be 'tight' or 'slack', but it is harder to imagine how they might be exercised; the entities that they communicate do not change the vessels of that communication. In short, this increasingly dynamic materialist conception of human physiology comes very close to the Brunonian critique of sensibility, which would come to prove so central to German romanticism, yet whose significance for anglophone discourse has generally been overlooked.[28] Brown's *Elementa Medicinae* (1780) system establishes 'excitability' as the ur principle 'on which the phaenomena of life depend': 'excitement', he writes, 'which affects the nerves and muscles, can prove excessive or insufficient; external as well as internal powers function in relation to each other'.[29] Brown's excitability displaces the irritability-sensibility distinction, yet clearly shares far more in common with the former.[30]

This more dynamic conception of the irritable physiological system, as embedded and enacted whole, would ultimately move beyond women or indigenous peoples, so as to designate not only the human organism but also vegetal life in its totality. To drive home this point, we turn now briefly to two works, both better known to scholarship than the motley of manuals and medical textbooks surveyed above, yet whose meanings and significance shift in light of the broader anatomical discourse in which they were embedded. Edmund Burke's *A Philosophical Inquiry into the Origin of Our Ideas of the Sublime and Beautiful* (1757) offers a case study in how we should read for irritability, when we more often read

---

[28] See Minter, 'Concept of Irritability', 463–76.

[29] John Brown, *The Elements of Medicine of John Brown, M.D.*, translated from Latin by the author (London: printed for J. Johnson, 1795), 127.

[30] In his introduction to the 1803 translation of Brown's treatise, Thomas Beddoes notes (and bewails) Brown's substitution of Haller's terms; *The Elements of Medicine of John Brown*, translated from Latin by the author (Portsmouth: Oracle Press, 1803), 84.

for sensibility. We remain prone, disfigured perhaps, by Kant's later example, to consider the capacity for sublime experience as a distinctively human cognitive accomplishment. For Burke, however, as Aris Sarafianos has brilliantly shown, sublimity occurs not in the head so much as in the fibres.[31] Sublime terror induces 'convulsions' in the subject, which leads the *Inquiry* to wonder, quite reasonably, why we should voluntarily procure such experiences. The answer is that human physiology is a dynamic equilibrium, threatened alike by over-excitation and over-relaxation. The latter 'takes away that vigour which is requisite towards the performing the natural and necessary secretions ... [and] in this languid inactive state, the nerves are more liable to the most horrid convulsions, than when they are sufficiently braced and strengthened'.[32]

Burke, here as elsewhere, mixes his terms rather loosely: convulsions and contractions really occur in muscles rather than nerves. Yet despite this slippage, the consistent stress upon 'exercise' ties the *Inquiry* to the broader conceptual network that we have traced, as Burke himself sometimes directly realises. 'I do not here enter into the question debated among physiologists', he observes in a footnote, 'whether pain be the effect of a contraction, or a tension of the nerves. Either will serve my purpose, for by tension, I mean no more than a violent pulling of the fibres, which compose any muscle or membrane, in whatever way this is done.'[33] The *Inquiry* is distinguished by its amazing and historically unusual sensitivity to putatively 'lower' forms of sense experience: touch, taste, smell. Burke may be interested in the darkness visible, but so too does he take pains to record the sensation of a glass marble in the palm of a child. In the section 'SWEETNESS relaxing', the fibres that elsewhere are casually interchanged with nerves come into their own: 'as smooth things are, as such, agreeable to the taste, and are found of a relaxing quality; so on the other hand, things which are found by experience to be of a strengthening quality, and fit to brace the fibres, are almost universally rough and pungent to the taste, and in many cases rough even to the touch'.[34] This enduring interest in an immediate tactile and gustatory experience, which 'custom, habit, the desire of novelty, and a thousand other causes' serve to blunt in us, serves notice of the remarkable inclusiveness of Burke's aesthetics.[35] Where previously 'sensible' men and 'irritable' women had been ranged (and valorised)

---

[31] Aris Sarafianos, 'The Contractility of Burke's Sublime and Heterodoxies in Medicine and Art', *Journal of the History of Ideas*, 69.1 (2008), 23–48.

[32] Edmund Burke, *A Philosophical Inquiry into the Origin of Our Ideas of the Sublime and Beautiful* (London: printed for R. and J. Dodsley, 1757), 127.

[33] Ibid. 123.   [34] Ibid. 157.   [35] Ibid.

along opposite ends of a physiognomic spectrum, now both alike strive to exercise into being a precarious balance.

Irritability is not restricted to human life, however. We have observed how its presence was imputed to watch springs, jelly and reheated meat. Cullen phrases the matter programmatically, in regard to plant life: 'somewhat analogous to it appears in vegetables, many of which are manifestly endowed with irritability. Perhaps it is common to all nature, and only under different modifications by certain conditions of other matter.'[36] Many of the greater and lesser authorities cited above were certainly very far from entertaining anything like a metaphysics of vitalism; rather, the putatively lesser or pathological subjects (women, children, colonial subjects) functioned mechanically.

Yet Erasmus Darwin appropriated the dense conceptual network around irritability, so as to produce the obverse effect: rather than mechanise human action, he spiritualises inert matter. Darwin's work often explicitly acknowledges its position in this now-familiar lineage. His *The Botanic Garden* states that

the irritability of plants is abundantly evinced by the absorption and pulmonary circulation of their juices; their sensibility is shewn by the approaches of the males to the females, and of the females to the males, in numerous instances; and, as the essential circumstance of sleep consists in the temporary abolition of voluntary power alone, the sleep of plants evinces that they possess voluntary power; which also indisputably appears in many of them, by closing their petals or their leaves during cold, or rain, or darkness, or from mechanic violence.[37]

On a first read, such a passage may appear to uphold Haller's old distinction: irritability is restricted to the unconscious circulation of 'juices' (we note once again the importance of liquidity to the concept), whereas sensibility denotes agency: the male plant that 'approaches' the female. Yet Darwin's pathetic fallacy should give us pause: we can scarcely imagine Haller extending en-souled volition to a plant (and certainly not through the negating of that agency through its 'sleep'!). We might well speculate that Darwin's retention of the distinction betrays a justifiable anxiety over the political and religious consequences of a collapsed monism: deism, revolutionary republicanism. Yet be this as it may, several of his other texts find it hard to hold the wavering line: if volition inheres not only in the most spiritual exercises of humans but also in the approach of a plant to its neighbour, how can we conclude such agency is absent from the (simpler?) nutritive acts? How can we conclude such agency is absent even from the sleeping plant?

---

[36] Ibid. 123 n.
[37] Erasmus Darwin, *The Botanic Garden*, 2 vols. (London: J. Johnson, 1791), i, 205 n.

The first volume of *Zoonomia* (1794) offers the richest trove in this respect. The work teems with references to the specific language of irritability, as distinct from sensibility: the work contains a full 206 usages of fibres (as opposed to 116 occurrences of nerves). Once again, he intermittently attempts to ground muscular action in the nervous or cognitive system: in the section marked 'Laws of Animal Causation', for instance, he writes that 'the spirit of animation is the immediate cause of the contraction of animal fibres, it resides in the brain and nerves, and is liable to general or partial diminution or accumulation'.[38] By the time that Darwin undertakes, only two sections later, to explain 'the four classes of Fibrous Motion', however, causal priority has been reversed. In place of a supervening cognitive or nervous impulse that 'animates' matter, we rather find that human sensation, however complex, derives ultimately from muscular irritability. 'Fibrous contractions', Darwin writes, 'were originally caused by the irritations excited by objects.' A sensible dialectic then enfolds: these contractions are frequently accompanied by sensations of pleasure and pain, until the moment when 'by habit these fibrous contractions become causable by the sensations'; it is only at this stage that human agency enters the arena, as 'by habit the fibrous contractions became causable by volition'.[39] Subjects only belatedly exert full cognitive control over embodied and sub-intentional reflexes (Darwin offers the memorable example of a subject straining to recite backwards an alphabet whose regular sequence has been automated). The four stages of 'fibrous motion' thereby provide a materialist dialectics *avant la lettre*: 'irritative motions' give rise to 'sensitive motions', which induce 'voluntary motions' and then 'associate motions'.[40] Darwin thereby gives us a drastically modified association-ism: the linkage between ideas and impressions does not, as for Locke, stem from the arbitrary fiat of custom or education, but rather the integration of sensorimotor activity, as the training of bodily habitus. Consciousness regulates a body that brought it into being, and whose traces convulsively endure.

Darwin's verse does not merely consolidate or distil his materialism; it raises it to a higher power, in large part through the widespread diffusion of the pathetic fallacy that we noted above. Here, for instance, is a passage upon the 'Reproduction of Life' from his final work, *The Temple of Nature*:

> Hence, ere Vitality, as time revolves,
> Leaves the cold organ, and the mass dissolves;

---

[38] Erasmus Darwin, *Zoonomia, or, The Laws of Organic Life*, 3 vols., 2nd ed. (London: J. Johnson, 1796), I, 30.
[39] Ibid. 34.   [40] Ibid. 35–6.

The Reproductions of the living Ens
From sires to sons, unknown to sex, commence.
New buds and bulbs the living fibre shoots
On lengthening branches, and protruding roots;
Or on the father's side, from bursting glands.
The adhering young its nascent form expands;
In branching lines the parent-trunk adorns,
And parts ere long like plumage, hairs, or horns.[41]

Darwin's heroic couplets always were workmanlike rather than spectacular; yet the enjambing personification of 'living fibre shoots / New buds', which inserts a wrinkle into the smoothly Popean, end-stopped rule, does all the work that could be expected of it. It demonstrates yet more fully, that is to say, that volition occurs through rather than upon fibrous contraction: even when, towards the apparent end of Darwin's reproductive parable, organic life expires before the inscrutable 'Will' of a tastefully shrouded deity, Darwin's enduring recourse to pathetic fallacy tells a different story: 'The goaded fibre ceases to obey / And sense deserts the uncontractile clay'.[42] This appointed end is not really the end; fibre mutinies against the death of one organism, so as to make new life, within a pantheism that dare not quite speak its name and yet is there all the same.

Darwin's work offers only the latest and most colourful and most positive example of a wide range of more-or-less-buried texts. Taken together, they suggest that anglophone thought was (in very different discursive contexts) conducting something like the sustained German philosophical engagement with irritability, which, as John H. Zammito has shown, turned Haller against himself. 'Our entire internal, excitable Self', as Johann Gottfried Herder put it, 'from that inexhaustible fount of excitation, the heart, down to the smallest fiber animated by *Reiz* [irritation], follows these simple laws.'[43]

9.2   Irritable Systems

Burke and Darwin offer exemplary instances of how irritability could be exported so as to perform real work in aesthetics. This shared emphasis enables two otherwise very different individuals to underscore common aspects of experience: it is not for nothing, for instance, that both Burke

---

[41] Erasmus Darwin, *The Temple of Nature, or, The Origin of Society: A Poem, with Philosophical Notes* (London: printed for J. Johnson, 1803), 61.
[42] Ibid. 184.
[43] Johann Gottfried Herder, *Vom Erkennen und Empfinden* (1775); quoted and translated in Zammito, *Gestation of German Biology*, 147.

and Darwin stress tactile experience to a degree highly unusual for their age. Yet their thinking in this regard did not spring *ex nihilo*. Their ability to develop an irritable aesthetics stemmed in large part from the prior establishment of a wide-ranging yet strikingly coherent conceptual architecture, whose broad dimensions the earliest part of this chapter traced. The cultural inflections and valuations of those terms changed (irritability, having previously indicated the merely mechanical or reflexive portion of human activity, now permitted a widespread animation of matter); yet the conceptual architecture itself remained substantially unchanged.

We hold that this partially submerged conceptual nexus offers something different from the more familiar strains of animism, vitalism or pantheism that developed across the eighteenth and early nineteenth centuries. To demonstrate this – to demonstrate the significance of irritability in other conceptual arenas – we re-ascend now from the codex to the corpus, from the strings of natural language to the patterns of data that they form. At the very beginning of this discussion, we conducted a simple comparison of raw frequencies across the first three decades and last three decades of the eighteenth century. We now undertake a more targeted form of vector space subtraction, which yields a more granular sense of the temporal transformation of conceptual architectures.

As our methodological introduction demonstrated, every focal term in the corpus generates a distinctive binding list for each year in the dataset, and at every lexical distance. Subtracting one of these binding lists from another provides a quick insight into significant differences in the binding profiles of two terms (or of the same term at different historical points). Table 9.3 applies this calculation to irritability: by subtracting the *dpf* values of 1700–50 from those of 1751–1800, it demonstrates which words enter its conceptual ambit. In keeping with the results observed above, a term such as fibre increases significantly in both *dpf* score (43,081) and in number of co-associations (182) relative to the first half of the century. The bottom of the list by contrast, demonstrates *dpf* bindings that weaken over time; here we find only miscellaneous, semantically dispersed terms (anecdote, vivid, receuil).

The remainder of our chapter conducts identical vector space subtractions upon two terms that have repeatedly emerged as part of the coalescing irritability architecture: habit and system. (For clarity of exposition, we now visualise some of the most significant such changes in the form of bar charts.) Unlike the pervasive anatomical lexis (fibre, stimulus, stomach, etc.), both terms figure in diverse discursive situations. Figure 9.1 demonstrates some of the most significant increases (and decreases) when we perform a vector space subtraction upon habit. The terms that drop out of frequent collocation generally refer to clothing: at the very

Table 9.3 *Vector subtraction:* dpf *profiles of irritability at distance 10, 1751–1800, minus* dpf *profiles of irritability at distance 10, 1700–51.*

irritability: distance 10 (top 15)

Bound token	*dpf* increase	*N* increase (with focal)
irritability	105543	446
fibre	43081	182
oxygen	15603	65
irritation	13684	95
sensibility	12444	169
debility	12085	80
fibres	11567	222
temperament	10560	44
opiates	9686	41
nervous	8877	244
muscular	8683	163
irritating	8610	32
torpid	8409	33
solids	8320	62
contraction	8241	40

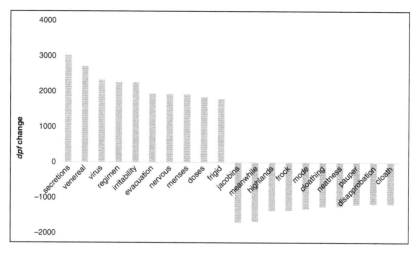

Figure 9.1 Vector subtraction: *dpf* profiles of habit at distance 10, 1751–1800, minus *dpf* profiles of habit at distance 10, 1700–51.

bottom of the list, we find, for instance, frock and the increasingly archaic cloathing and cloak. (The use of the word habit to connote attire became increasingly archaic.)

The terms that replace such associations demonstrate a familiar coherence: the top twenty-five terms include irritability and nervous; we also find gendered terminology such as menses and frigid; the prevalence of the latter indicates the recuperation of humoral theory for a more recognisably modern strain of misogyny. Habit, then, becomes irritable – which is to say that irritability becomes habitual. The chiasm matters, because this focus on embodied *habitus* differentiates this nascent discourse from more standard forms of animism. The latter imputes a vital property (be it electrical, galvanic or spiritual) intrinsic to matter. In the discourse on irritability that we have been tracing, however, this capacity also requires an external stimulus: irritability is the capacity to be irritated *by* something. A muscle contracts at a touch: one organ irritates another.

This more complex and dynamical conception of organic life also has a temporal dimension commonly absent from vitalism. Subjects, muscles and organs come to be irritated in familiar ways, over time, through habitual usage. It is for this reason that so much of the medical literature upon irritability focuses upon chronic rather than acute conditions, linked as the former are to diet or general bodily comportment: gout, venereal disease.[44] Habit plays a role here partly because it not only names recursive activity but also hints at (or sometimes more than hints at) moral conduct: hence the presence of relevant texts on gonorrhoea and masturbation.[45] Over the course of our earlier discussion, we have witnessed several such instances of this habitual employment of habit: Smythson talked of 'the whole habit, or of the stomach, intestines, or some other particular part' in pregnant women, who are themselves euphemistically referred to as possessing 'relaxed and tender habits'; the indigenous persons of Canada betrayed a 'habit of suffering'. Darwin once again took such patronising diagnoses and made a virtue of them: the conversion of 'fibrous contractions' into volition, which we just observed, takes place through the repeated specification 'by habit'.

This first vector subtraction thus gives a preliminary sense of the manner in which the delimited medical *concept* of irritability began to

---

[44] See William Nisbet, *First Lines of the Theory and Practice in Venereal Diseases* (Edinburgh: Charles Elliot, 1787); James Rymer, *A tract upon dyspepsy, or indigestion; and the hypochondriac disease; and upon the inflammatory or regular gout, and the atonic, irregular, or flying gout* (London: Thomas Evans, 1795).

[45] See Samuel Auguste David Tissot, *Onanism, or, A Treatise upon the Disorders Produced by Masturbation* (London: W. Wilkinson, 1767), which attributes 'lascivious dreams' to excessive irritability (164); Charles Armstrong, *An Essay, on the Symptoms and Cure of the Virulent Gonorrhoea, in Females* (London: Charles Dilly, 1783).

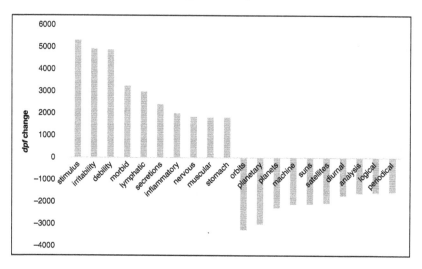

Figure 9.2 Vector subtraction: *dpf* profiles of system at distance 10, 1751–1800, minus *dpf* profiles of system at distance 10, 1700–51.

shape broader *ideas*, in keeping with the distinction outlined in Chapter 2. Such examples of embodied habitus contrast starkly with the more abstract Lockean model of association.[46] We can substantially develop such claims by turning to a further idea that the concept of irritability helps to establish. Figure 9.2 conducts the same comparison of *dpf* values across the former and latter halves of the eighteenth century; we now inspect the binding profiles for the focal token system. The results – in both quantitative and semantic terms – are yet more striking than they were for habit. Massively more powerful bindings arise for several of the terms that we have observed: stimulus, irritability, morbid and the rest.

Of equal interest, however, are the bound tokens that drop out of the ambit of system. Where habit lost only a narrow set of sartorial archaisms, we here find significant drops in several items from a coherent (and significant) semantic field: astronomy (orbits, planets, suns) and, to a lesser though still noticeable extent, mathematics (analysis, logical). Table 9.3 offers powerful support for the hypothesis that, as the eighteenth century wore on, irritability contributed decisively to – and was in turn shaped by – the replacement of one system by another. There is on

---

[46] The common-sense philosophy of Thomas Reid – who was much influenced by Whytt's surgical writings – would here stand as a case in point. For more on this connection, see Paul B. Wood, 'Thomas Reid's Critique of Joseph Priestley: Context and Chronology', *Man and Nature / L'homme et la nature*, 4 (1985), 29–45.

the face of it no necessary reason why the growing discourse on the nervous system should necessarily cause the comparative eclipse of another form of totality grounded in more exact measurement and periodicity. Yet such seems to be the case, indicating, perhaps, that conceptual binding is, at least to some extent, a zero-sum game: just as there are a limited number of words that can be deployed within a lexical window, so too can a subject retain a limited number of associations for a given concept.

It is tempting, when considering Figures 9.1 and 9.2, to call the displaced architecture 'Newtonian'. Yet this would be an over-simplification, to the extent that Newton himself inspired two divergent forms of systematicity: the differential calculus and exact measurement of the *Principia*, on the one hand; and the experimental method of the *Opticks*, on the other. The great anatomists (Boerhaave, Haller, Whytt) all advertised their Newtonianism, which they interpreted in this latter respect. In *System: The Shaping of Modern Knowledge*, Clifford Siskin uncovers the historical roots of the paranoiac tendency to blame 'the system' for whatever perceived modern ills the subject perceived.[47] Anti-systematicity has a similarly tenacious life within humanistic discourse, which likes for good reasons to defend singular particulars against what it takes to be rigid and top-down forms of knowing. Yet what if there never were only one form of system? 'The human body', Whytt wrote at the conclusion of his *Essay*, 'ought not be regarded (as it has too long been by many Physiologists) as a mechanical machine ... but as a system, framed with the greatest art and contrivance.'[48] Our data runs demonstrate that culture made good on such a claim. Whytt immediately and characteris-tically made appeal to the 'sentient principle' that unified this whole. Yet as we have seen, a new medical discourse could explore complex totalities without necessary recourse to souls or sentience, unencumbered by the residual associations and semantic fuzziness of sensibility. Perhaps we should supplement this more illustrious cognate: perhaps we should speak, also, of the age of irritability.

---

[47] Clifford Siskin, *System: The Shaping of Modern Knowledge* (Cambridge, MA: MIT Press, 2016).
[48] Whytt, *Vital and Other Involuntary Motions of Animals*, 360–1.

10 On Bubbles and Bubbling: The Idea of 'The South Sea Bubble'

Claire Wilkinson

There is no evidence that Jonathan Swift's 'The Bubble', published in early January 1721, was given this title by its author.[1] The poem, which is written in the style of popular broadside ballads, criticises the greed of the South Sea Company's directors following the catastrophic collapse of the firm's share price in the second half of 1720. The piece's textual history is complicated: it is likely that Charles Ford came up with the title for the unnamed manuscript Swift sent him in December 1720. Pope, editing the 1727 *Miscellanies*, published the substantially revised poem as 'The *South-Sea.* 1721', and Faulkner, in his 1735 edition of Swift's *Works*, called it 'Upon the South-Sea Project'.[2] There is a transcription in Stella's hand titled 'The Bubble. Printed in Ireland A.D. 1720', probably copied from the Dublin edition of the poem sent to Ford. Contrary to Ford's title's suggestion, at no point in the fifty-five verse poem does Swift refer to the South Sea Company's investment scheme as *the* Bubble. In fact, 'Bubble' does not appear at all until the closing line, where it is at last connected to the company and its failed scheme: 'South-Sea at best a mighty Bubble'. The difference in article between the title and the final line may seem insignificant but it betrays an epistemological fracture between an eighteenth-century and a present-day understanding of what financial bubbles might be: *a* bubble is a species of thing, whereas *the* bubble has a specific and singular referent. The certainty today with which we use the phrase 'South Sea Bubble' to describe the 1720 crisis means that Ford's 'The Bubble' is easily mistaken for an elided reference to 'The *South Sea* Bubble'. 'South Sea', however, is absent from Ford's title – the assumed reading a contemporary imposition on a phrase that gestures, like 'a mighty Bubble' in the poem's closing line, to a cheat or a trick.

[1] *The Poems of Jonathan Swift*, ed. Harold Williams, 3 vols. (Oxford: Clarendon, 1937), I, 248–59.
[2] Ibid. 248–9.

In fact, none of Swift's South Sea poems use the phrase South Sea Bubble, nor does it appear elsewhere in his writing.[3] When he mentions bubbles, which he does frequently in poetry and in prose, a sense of trickery is rarely far away. In the 'Ode to the Honourable Sir William Temple' (first printed in the 1745 *Miscellanies* but dated 1689 by Swift) and 'To Mr. Congreve' (first printed in 1789 but dated 1693), to be bubbled is to be cheated, as attested to by 'the bubbled Fools' of the 'Ode to William Temple' and 'the bubbl'd virtuoso' of 'To Mr. Congreve'.[4] These adjectival forms of 'bubble' are put to work in a similar way to the noun: in the light-hearted 'The First of April', which Harold Williams dates to between 1720 and 1724, a timely trick played by Apollo 'seems a Bubble'; in *Strephon and Chloe*, from 1734, 'mak[ing] yourself a Bubble' is a pun on flatulence and fraud, in reference to Strephon's recently disabused belief that Chloe's body functions differently from his own.[5] Where 'bubble' appears with a definite article, the sense of cheating continues. 'Apollo, to Dean Swift', which is roughly contemporary with the 1720 crisis, has an alchemical interest similar to that found in the Ford-titled 'The Bubble'. Swift makes further reference to a suite of words associated with the crisis – 'paper', 'trick' and 'stock' – all used here in close parallel to the author's wit. When 'the bubble' appears, it is as a trick that consumes its subject: 'And you like a Booby, the *Bubble* can swallow'.[6] 'An Essay on English Bubbles', which was prefixed to the first edition of *The Swearer's Bank* (1720), makes explicit reference to bubbles as financial schemes. The author 'Mr. Thomas Hope', addresses those 'who have suffered Depredation by the late Bubbles'. Bubbles, here, are discrete investment schemes run by different companies (the reference to the 11 June 1720 Bubble Act, which sought to protect joint-stock companies like the South Sea Company from competition, is implicit) and while the essay's logic frames the 'South-Sea' as one of the bubbles, it is

---

[3] Several of Swift's poems address the South Sea crisis directly. Others use South Sea as a point of reference. Of the poems that offer a response to the crisis, 'The Run upon the Bankers, and The South-Sea Detected' (1721) (usually published today as 'The Run upon the Bankers') names the 'South-Sea' only in the title (*Poems*, I, 238–41). 'The Bank Thrown Down' (1721) uses a similar set of metaphors to 'The Bubble' in its discussion of 'Those that dropt in the *South-Sea*' (*Poems*, I, 286–8; 288). Explicit references to the South Sea crisis include those in 'A Pastoral Dialogue' (1727), in which Henrietta Howard's house is apprised by 'some *South Sea* Broker from the City' (*Poems*, II, 407–11; 410) and 'On Poetry: A Rhapsody' (1733), where 'a South-Sea *Jobber*' appears in a list of dishonest figures (*Poems*, II, 639–59; 645).

[4] 'Ode to the Honourable Sir William Temple', *Poems*, I, 26–33; l. 10, p. 27. 'To Mr. Congreve', *Poems*, I, 43–50; l. 216, p. 50.

[5] 'The First of April', *Poems*, I, 320–2; l. 29, p. 322. *Strephon and Chloe*, *Poems*, II, 584–93; l. 311, p. 593.

[6] 'Apollo, to Dean Swift', *Poems*, I, 262–6; l. 89, 91, 95, p. 265.

one of many. These bubbles are as brittle as glass, 'only made to be broken' like an oath or promise, and they behave as vehicles for fraud.[7] This bringing together of the idea of 'bubble' as a cheat and 'bubble' as a financial scheme is evident in 'A Satirical Elegy on the Death of a late Famous General'. The poem was not printed until 1764, but it was likely written around the time of Marlborough's death in 1722. When Swift writes, 'Come hither, all ye empty things, / Ye bubbles rais'd by breath of Kings' (ll. 31–2), he positions the late duke's achievements as falsely inflated, while simultaneously criticising how the 1720 bubbles – Marlborough famously profited from his investment in the South Sea Company – proliferated thanks to the George I's endorsement.

The examples from Swift that describe financial schemes as bubbles were all published after the 1720 crash however, ample evidence exists to show that 'bubble' and 'bubbles' were commonly used to describe investment schemes before the crisis began. A broader commercial context informs the word too: a dialogue published in Tutchin's *Observator* on 22 February 1707, four years before the South Sea Company was founded, gives some sense of how 'bubble' (as a cheat or trick) and 'bubble' (as a financial scheme) would later collide. 'Solid Vertue', writes the author, 'is too weighty in it self to be blown up by Popular Breath; that's essential to the Nature of a Bubble.'[8] The bubble the *Observator* describes is not financial, but the idea that there is a crossover between a bubble as a trick 'blown up by Popular Breath' and an investment scheme becoming a bubble by virtue of popular interest is supported in a letter to Mist published in the *Weekly Journal* on 26 December 1719. The letter's author claims that it 'is easy for Men to raise a Subscription for a Million Sterling upon every *Bubble*', before asking if there is 'nothing to be found in England as good as a Missisippi *Bubble*?'[9] The ease with which money can be raised as part of a subscription (or investment scheme) shows how bubbles inflate thanks to popular interest, while the mention of the Mississippi Bubble in France gives a sense of how desirable the elevated prices are for investors (the foreign affairs section of the same edition talks at length about John Law's efforts to revive the price of Mississippi stock in Paris, which was beginning to crash).[10] Less than a month later, the *Daily Post*'s front-page article used 'Bubble' in a similar

---

[7] 'An Essay on English Bubbles', *The Works of the Rev. Jonathan Swift*, 19 vols. (London: Hansard, 1801), VIII, 433–8.
[8] John Tutchin, 'Master, what d'ye . . . ', *Observator*, no. 99, 22 February 1707.
[9] 'Mr.', letter to Mr. Mist, *Weekly Journal, or, Saturday's Post*, no. 56, 26 December 1719, p. 331.
[10] Ibid. 332–3.

way, to describe an attempt by the East India Company to recruit subscribers:

[The East India Company] have, it seems, set up a new Bubble by Way of Policy, to give the Purchaser the Refusal of the Stock at 2200 at half a Year, for which the People give 200 Livres Premium, and are ready to tread one another to Death to get to the Office to have them.[11]

This bubble is created *as* a bubble, with the East India Company offering futures contracts to drive up the price of their stock. A futures contract allows investors to purchase the right to buy stock at a fixed price on a fixed date in the future, regardless of the market price on that day. The public's expectation that the value of the stock will rise is reflected in their enthusiasm for the offer. As investors 'tread one another to Death', the speculative function of the scheme helps elevate the stock's price by attracting more investors. The sense of bubbles (as tricks) being 'blown up by Popular Breath', taken from the 1707 *Observator*, converges, even before the crisis, with the sense that financial bubbles might be inflated in this way too.

Swift's idea of a financial bubble depends very specifically upon the word's prior association with trickery and fraud; his use of it does not communicate the sense of a more broadly unstable financial market. Though there are examples of 'South Sea Bubble' in use from February 1721 onwards, the phrase bears little resemblance to the South Sea Bubble of the present-day historical imagination. This chapter traces the evolution of the South Sea Bubble, as a phrase and as an idea, and argues that the conceptual framework that underpins how we understand present-day financial crises has its origins in the latency of the words used, at the time, to describe the emerging and interlinked crises of 1720. In the preceding chapter, Natalie Roxburgh and Ewan Jones made an argument for the value of digital research methods in facilitating a relative agnosticism, particularly their ability to alert us to conceptual architectures that emerge over generations without recourse to a single fixed token. My work here takes an antithetical approach, using digital tools to answer some discrete questions that are as yet unresolved but that are nevertheless foundational to the increasingly interdisciplinary practice of South Sea criticism. I am interested in whether or not the concept of a bubble

---

[11] 'We are full here of . . . ', *Daily Post*, 15 January 1720. The edition also lists share prices for the day ('Yesterday South-Sea Stock was 135½. India 205½. Bank 154¼. African 26. Mississippi Stock 1900'). These figures accord with Castaing's in *The Course of the Exchange* for 15 January 1720; see Peter G. M. Dickson, *The Financial Revolution in England: A Study in the Development of Public Credit, 1688–1756* (Aldershot: Gregg Revivals, 1993; first published, 1967), 139.

market displaces older formulations that relate to economic instability, and also in what it might mean for financial modernity if the concept takes shape in response to an intrinsically new mode of market operation.

10.1   The Coining of a Phrase versus the Emergence of a Concept

The question of what South Sea Bubble meant in an eighteenth-century context is not new. Julian Hoppit made a compelling argument in 2002 for the phrase being coined several years after the 1720 crash. His claim that South Sea Bubble was first used in 1771 by the authors of the *Encyclopaedia Britannica* has since been proved incorrect; however, there is mileage in his argument that the setting of the crisis within a conceptual architecture describing unstable national and international financial markets happened substantially after 1720. Of 1771, he writes, 'What happened . . . was that a concept was invented to make sense of the confused events of 1720, but ever since this single label has suggested a unity to what were three different if interrelated events: the South Sea scheme, the 190 joint-stock bubbles and the crisis in international finance that began in Paris.'[12] Hoppit uses 'concept' and 'label' interchangeably here, which does not accord with the consensus in intellectual history that concepts are embedded in larger discursive formations and fields of meaning; though concepts leave traces in words, phrases and labels, their architectures are not synonymous with the language in which they reside. Even if Hoppit conflates 'label' and concept' and sees a concept as an 'invented' thing, his suggestion that there is a discernible point at which a particular way of thinking about the South Sea Bubble emerged is at the forefront of the following inquiry. The four separate phases that he demarcates in the evolution of South Sea Bubble give shape to his argument: he begins by describing references made to the incipient crisis in writing from 1720 to 1721; then he makes the claim about the 1771 *Encyclopaedia Britannica*; next, he notes the adoption and manipulation of South Sea Bubble as a point of comparison used by commentators on mid-nineteenth-century financial crises; and finally, he observes the phrase's eventual transmutation to metaphor, in which form it has become 'a particularly potent and apparently unambiguously negative exemplar in the cultural sphere'.[13]

---

[12] Julian Hoppit, 'The Myths of the South Sea Bubble', *Transactions of the Royal Historical Society*, 12 (2002), 141–65; 163.
[13] Ibid. 164.

Hoppit's scepticism about the suitability of literary writing to address the question of how contemporary actors in 1720 understood the crisis limits the parameters of his argument (he is particularly concerned about satire, which, he claims, 'makes no pretence to factual objectivity or principled subjectivity').[14] The validity of his scepticism has been questioned before: in a dismissal of Hoppit's broader argument, Pat Rogers is careful to emphasise how artistic accounts, including pamphlets, plays, etchings, playing cards and other ephemera, illustrate a cultural fallout that is not manifested in numerical data. Alongside his criticism of Hoppit's approach, Rogers finds 'at least a dozen' uses of the phrase South Sea Bubble from the 1750s to the 1760s, along with several mentions from substantially earlier.[15] The earliest reference he finds is not from the type of literary source that Hoppit fears, but from a journalistic account. An edition of Read's *Weekly Journal, or, British Gazetteer* published on 11 February 1721 compares the South Sea to John Law's Mississippi scheme in Paris, proposing 'that we receiv'd the Pattern of our South-Sea Bubble from the Resemblance of a mighty fine Lady in France'.[16] Rogers also points to 1725's *The Life of Jonathan Wild*, a criminal biography in which the semi-fictionalised Wild invents a new scheme to embezzle money from the public. Wild 'talk'd of a new Project; which was, for setting up a Policy, and opening an Office for taking in Subscriptions for insuring against Robbery ... bragging that it was no *South-Sea Bubble*'.[17] The narrator's reference to the '*South-Sea Bubble*' here is as apophatic archetype, a model for Wild's 'new Project' and its distinctive 'Subscriptions'. Rogers's examples present the 'South-Sea Bubble' as something copied and copied from, and they sustain the inference of cheating that is also found in Swift's contemporary references to bubbles. In *Twenty-Eight Sermons*, printed in 1723, Thomas Bradbury describes a pattern of imitation very similar to that described by the author of the *Weekly Journal* article from February 1721: 'You saw the *French Folly* [in the *Mississippi* Whim] before you begun your own [the *South-Sea* Bubble].'[18] Bradbury's '*Folly*' and 'Whim' indirectly modify his use of 'Bubble', such that it adopts their characteristics in being

---

[14] Ibid. 160.
[15] Pat Rogers, 'Credit These Accounts: Have We Really Burst the Bubble Myths?', *Times Literary Supplement*, 11 April 2014, 14–15.
[16] Ibid. 14.
[17] H. D., *The Life of Jonathan Wild, from His Birth to His Death* (London: printed for T. Warner, 1725), 62–63. *Jonathan Wild* is often attributed to Defoe, though Rogers suspects incorrectly.
[18] Thomas Bradbury, *Twenty-Eight Sermons Concerning Offences, Reveilings, and a Confession of the Faith; Preach'd at Pinners-Hall* (London: printed for John and Barham Clark, 1723), 171; brackets Bradbury's own.

derived from them. The sermon is addressed to the directors of the South Sea Company and the comparison of 'the *South-Sea* Bubble' to John Law's Mississippi scheme makes clear that both former and latter are scams.

It is striking how few times South Sea Bubble appears in writing from the first half of the eighteenth century. Though it is easy to point to several examples of the words in use together from before 1771 (thanks to the greater number of corpora that have become available since 2002, as well as their expansion, ease of access, improved optical character recognition and refined search tools), there is a middle ground to be taken between Hoppit's and Rogers's arguments. Rogers summons his evidence to argue that 'the notion of a South Sea Bubble, *eo nomine,* was already implanted in the public imagination' in the 1720s. This is partially true, at least in as much as the words appearing in sequence point to the eighteenth-century reading public being able to parse the phrase; however, the statement does not allow for the *notion* as a malleable one. What if the South Sea Bubble of the immediately post-crisis public imagination was substantially different from the South Sea Bubble as we recognise it today? My argument is that we are witnessing the emergence of a new conceptual framework that accommodates imaginatively the rise of the financialised nation in northern Europe. Arriving here by way of Hoppit and Rogers necessitates separating the coinage of a phrase (or label), and the emergence of a concept, from one another. Though the first use of the phrase can be traced to just months after the crisis began in the late summer of 1720, the concept in relation to the idea of unstable markets and their operation takes a discernible shape much later (albeit not as late as 1771). South Sea Bubble as we understand it today has a set of affordances that did not exist – and could not have existed – in 1720, meaning that the phrase as a label stands intact but as a token related to a broader architecture, it has a latency not developed until it solidified as a conceptual back-formation substantially after the crash.

To what extent is it possible to isolate the point at which this back formation took shape? Digital tools facilitate the sort of distant corpus study that allows us to discern changing patterns in the co-associations between sets of words. Figure 10.1 shows the results of searching the ECCO corpus (1701–1800) at distance 5 for 'south-sea' and 'bubble'.[19] The graph plots the original and duplicate instances of co-association

---

[19] Shared lexis recognises 'south-sea' as one term but 'south' and 'sea' as two. Data from 'south' + 'sea' and bubble has been included manually. The data has been cleaned to remove errors that arise from imprecise OCR (e.g. '1000' is commonly misread as 'iooo'). Data points generated by these errors have been excluded from the graphs included in the chapter.

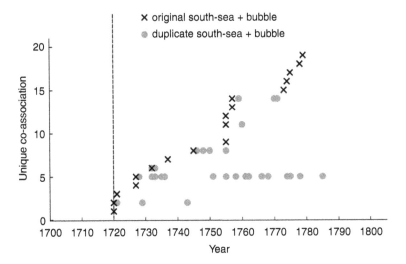

Figure 10.1 South-sea and bubble, distance 5, 1701–1800. Source: ECCO.

between the terms within the corpus by year. The first appearance of a particular co-association is marked with a black cross relative to its year (*x*-axis) and sequence within the corpus (*y*-axis); where the instance appears again in ECCO thanks to the re-issuing of a text in a subsequent year, the data point is logged as a grey dot parallel on the *y*-axis to the original reference, and placed on the *x*-axis in the year the re-issued text was printed. Multiple dots parallel (on the *y*-axis) with a cross indicates a single co-association reprinted many times.

There is no co-association between south-sea and bubble prior to 1720; the first occurrences are directly contemporary with the crisis in 1720. The relationship between original co-associations (black crosses) and repeated instances of the same reference (grey dots parallel with an original cross on the *y*-axis) is not significant. We can see that some co-associations appeared in texts re-issued frequently between 1720 and 1800; other instances of co-association appear only once in the corpus. Of the co-associations that appear after 1770, none appear in texts that were re-issued before the end of the century, whereas the majority of co-associations from before 1760 appear in texts that were issued again at least once. While a simple explanation may account for this (those texts printed earlier in the century have more time to be published again; the volume of material published in the second half of the century is substantially larger than in the first half, meaning an individual text may be less likely to be re-issued), the fact that the later references are found only once in the corpus may suggest that the co-associations are occurring in different contexts to those earlier in the century. It is possible to discern patterns in the occurrences of original co-associations. There are observable concentrations in 1720 (though the very low number, two, corroborates the idea that the South Sea Company's investment bubble in the 1720s is distinguishable from the more unified concept of a South Sea Bubble), in the 1750s and then another more gradual cluster of co-association between 1775 and 1782. These data support a thesis that is similar to Hoppit's but which, in place of the coining of a label in 1771, proposes that the emergence of a concept relating to the long reach of the Financial Revolution and the development of the fiscally interested state occurred in the mid-1750s. Co-associations at distance 5 between south-sea and bubble prior to 1755 are intermittent, which makes the cluster around 1755 particularly marked. Original co-associations that appear in the corpus from this moment onwards are different in character to those from between 1720 and 1755: they point to the availability of a metaphorical capacity, which in turn suggests that the South Sea Bubble has acquired a more fixed imaginative shape, making it suitable for comparison to other events within and without the financial market.

The earliest example of a distance-5 co-association between south-sea and bubble in the ECCO corpus is from Ned Ward's *The Delights of the Bottle*: 'When Disappointment gives us trouble, / In *South-Sea*, or some other Bubble'.[20] Though Ward doesn't directly call the South Sea a bubble, the logic of the syntax makes the assertion clear. The longer poem was printed with a shorter lyric, '*A South-Sea Ballad, or, Merry Remarks upon Exchange-Alley Bubbles*', appended. Both '*South-Sea*' and 'Bubble' appear independently of one another elsewhere in the original poem's four cantos (in which there is a particular focus on the South Sea Company over any other firm running an investment scheme) and in the second piece. Several other examples from the years immediately after the crisis feature a similarly suspended implication, wherein the South Sea Company's scheme is described as a bubble without being called the 'South-Sea Bubble'. A letter attributed to John Trenchard, reprinted in *A Collection of All the Humorous Letters in The London Journal* (1721), imagines the rise and fall of the South Sea Company's stock price as a bubble, without using the phrase itself. In the letter, which was later printed in *The Humourist* with the title 'Of South-Sea *Directors*',

---

[20] Edward Ward, *The Delights of the Bottle, or, The Compleat Vintner* (London: printed for Sam. Briscor, 1720), 4.

Trenchard argues that 'there is scarce a Director either of the *South* or *North* Bubble who possesses one great or good Quality'.[21] Though the piece is not one of Trenchard and Gordon's letters from Cato, which were originally published in the *London Journal* between 1720 and 1723 and subsequently collected as *Essays on Liberty, Civil and Religious* (1737), it is nevertheless consistent with these in its steadfast warning against corruption.[22] Likewise, *A Detection of the Whole Management of the South-Sea Company* (1721) sees the movement of South Sea stock as a form of bubble. Its author argues that they would 'distinguish between Men of former real Substance, and Men of imaginary Millions since the first coming of the South Sea Stock (as a Bubble) into *Exchange Alley*'.[23] These early examples do not show the *eo nomine* implantation of a concept that Rogers argues for, but they do demonstrate a clear sense of the South Sea Company's investment scheme being imagined and described as a variety of bubble from immediately after the crisis.

This pattern of use continues through the 1720s. In *An Essay on the Trade and Improvement of Ireland* (1729), Arthur Dobbs writes about the influence of the South Sea Company's investment scheme on British trade in 1721:

The succeeding Disturbances by the Rebellion in *Great-Britain*, the Confusions in *France* upon calling in and new coining their Money, and raising their Coin, the *Mississipi* Bubble in France, and *South* Sea in *England* were plainly the Reasons of the considerable Fall in our Exports to 1722, by the breaking of Merchants, and Fall of Markets every where upon it.[24]

As is the case in the examples encountered thus far, the 'South Sea' being a bubble is implied by the structure of the sentence, while the precise formulation is suspended. The connection is slightly less secure here given that '*South* Sea' stands alone without imaginary or rhetorical

---

[21] John Trenchard, 'Numb. VII', in *A Collection of All the Humorous Letters in* The London Journal (London: printed and sold by J. Roberts, 1721), 25–29; 29. This collected volume contains six other uses of bubble, including 'the great bubble', which refers to the South Sea Company (p. 19). The '*North* Bubble' is either in jest or in reference to Robert Lowther (Governor of Barbados) and Francis Cawood's 'North-Sea Bubble', for which Cawood was tried and found guilty in July 1721. See *Weekly Journal, or, British Gazetteer*, 3 June 1721, and *Daily Post*, 18 July 1721.

[22] These 144 letters have since been collected as *Cato's Letters*. Bubble and bubbled are used throughout the collection to describe cheating and fraudulent actions. See John Trenchard and Thomas Gordon, *Cato's Letters, or, Essays on Liberty, Civil and Religious, and Other Important Subjects*, ed. by Ronald Hamowy, 2 vols. (Indianapolis: Liberty Fund, 1995).

[23] *A Detection of the Whole Management of the South-Sea Company, from the First Rise of Their Stock to Its Present Declension* (London: printed for J. Roberts, 1721), 27.

[24] Arthur Dobbs, *An Essay on the Trade and Improvement of Ireland* (Dublin: printed by A. Rhames, 1729), 10.

recourse to bubble; however, the reference is all the more important for Dobbs's early conceptualisation of the '*South* Sea' as a definable event with a consequence as significant as the 1715 Jacobite rising, the issue of a new tender in France, and the specifically named '*Mississipi* Bubble'. He recognises the significance of the international movement of money for the British domestic market, but also points to the '*South* Sea' in a resolutely more abstract sense than the authors from 1720 to 1721 are able to. There is a gap here between the sense of a bubble being something and the South Sea's investment scheme being an example of this thing, and the South Sea taking on a demonstrative set of associations of its own. By 1749, this separation is better established. In *A Summary, History and Political, of the First Planting, Progressive Improvements, and Present State of the British Settlements in North-America*, William Douglass both names the South Sea Bubble and describes its formation separately from the South Sea Company: 'As Mr. *Law* borrowed his sham Name of *Mississippi Company*, from our cant Name of *South Sea Company*; so we copied our South Sea Bubble from his *Mississippi* Bubble.'[25]

While the imputation is very similar to Bradbury's in the 1723 *Twenty-Eight Sermons*, the resolute separation of '*South Sea Company*' from 'South Sea Bubble' makes clear that the bubble has different parameters from the company, and also that the 'South Sea Bubble' is more consistently distinguished from the more general earlier references to investment schemes as bubbles. Around this time there is a demonstrable shift in the way that south-sea is co-associated with bubble and bubbles. South Sea Bubble begins to cohere as a freestanding idea, which entails at once a shift towards metaphor and – seemingly paradoxically – a shift towards the concrete. In its pre-financial form as a cheat or a trick, a bubble's proximity to speciousness was particularly important: a bubble is inflated with air, ethereal and easily burst. These senses carry over into the early sense of a financial bubble; however, what happens around 1755 is that South Sea Bubble begins to cohere as a freestanding idea and acquire a set of metaphorical associations of its own. It maintains the connections to a physical bubble's characteristics, but also it becomes a point of reference for other financial schemes and, eventually, for a speculative financial market that has the potential to crash.

Comparing Figure 10.1 (which gives a graphical presentation of distance-5 co-associations between south-sea and bubble between 1701

---

[25] William Douglass, *A Summary, Historical and Political, of the First Planting, Progressive Improvements, and Present State of the British Settlements in North-America*, 2 vols. (Boston: printed and sold by Rogers and Fowle, 1749), I, 85. Douglass refers to the 'South Sea Bubble' and the 'Mississippi Bubble' eight times. He is not consistent with hyphenation in these examples.

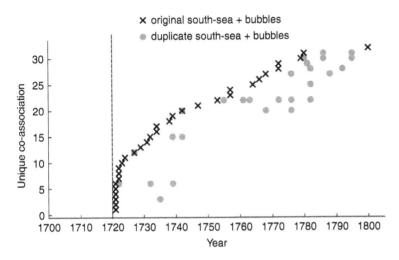

Figure 10.2 South-sea and bubbles, distance 5, 1701–1800. Source: ECCO.

and 1800) to Figure 10.2 shows a clear difference in how south-sea and bubbles were co-associated between 1701 and 1800 relative to south-sea and bubble. Figure 10.2 presents the co-associations between south-sea and bubbles using the same methodology.

Like south-sea and bubble, there is no co-association of the terms between 1701 and 1720; however, unlike south-sea and bubble, there is a particularly dense concentration of distance-5 co-associations between south-sea and bubbles immediately at the point the 1720 crisis happened. There is no significant relationship between original co-associations and repeated occurrences of the same co-association in ECCO, of which there are fewer compared to south-sea and bubble (broadly, if a text containing a reference is re-issued at all, it is within thirty years of the original publication date, whereas some of the Figure 10.1 items appear repeatedly throughout the remainder of the century). The smooth line of the plots shows that after the high volume of co-associations that occurred between south-sea and bubbles in the 1720s, subsequent new co-associations were relatively evenly spaced between 1730 and 1780. There is then an almost total absence of new co-associations in the twenty years between 1780 and 1800. The absence of co-associations in the final twenty years of the century makes it likely that the concept of the South Sea Bubble had displaced the more granular discussions of the contemporary financial market from earlier in the century. As we might expect, this suggests that south-sea and bubbles in close proximity to one another is not indicative of an emerging conceptual architecture, in the way that south-sea and bubble is. The two terms are nevertheless still subject to the same turn towards metaphor as bubble in its singular form.

Just as the earliest distance-5 co-associations of south-sea and bubble differentiated between the South Sea Company and other 'bubble' stocks sold in Exchange Alley, distance-5 co-associations of south-sea and bubbles maintain the same separation. Early examples of this sort of demarcation are found in Anthony Hammond's *A Modest Apology* (1721) and in *The Historical Register* for 1721. Hammond describes the 'great Distress among the several Traders in *South-Sea* Stock and Bubbles', envisioning the South Sea as similar to, but different from, a bubble. Slightly later, he reiterates this view: 'it is more fashionable to own one is ruin'd by the *South-Sea* than by a Bubble; as if there was something more brave in being wounded, or almost kill'd, by a great Bear, than by a ridiculous Mouse.'[26] Similarly, the author of *The Historical Register* sees the relationship between the South Sea Company and other bubbles as antagonistic:

Tho' the Treasury were provided with Ways and Means for the Supply to the Civil List ... those Projects, and others, had taken such deep Root in the House of Commons, and elsewhere, as made it impossible to oppose them; and they had that Consequence which the Directors of the *South-Sea* Company foretold and which every Body might foresee, viz. to encrease the Flame, by adding this unnecessary fuel to it.

And as the *South-Sea* Scheme might give Birth to the Bubbles so the Bubbles contributed to raise the *South-Sea* to that Height which brought us into this Condition.[27]

Hammond maintains the separation between '*South-Sea*' and the bubbles, whereas the author of *The Historical Register* describes the South Sea Company's investment scheme as being of the same genus as the multiple other bubbles. The final sentence cited above indicates that the piece's author understood a kind of auto-inflation as a feature of a speculative market, emphasising a pattern of specious but reciprocal inflation (both metaphorical and literal) as the '*South-Sea* Scheme' and the other 'Bubbles' rise in height. This sort of metaphor from relatively recently after 1720 is very different in character to an example crafted by Adam Fitz-Adam in issue 123 of *The World* (8 May 1755). In a whimsical account that has nothing to do with finance, Fitz-Adam recalls being served turtle soup at a dinner party. After praising the dish, he is issued

[26] Anthony Hammond, *A Modest Apology, Occasion'd by the Late Unhappy Turn of Affairs, with Relation to Publick Credit* (London: printed and sold by J. Peele, 1721), 6, 15.

[27] *The Historical Register, Containing an Impartial Relation of All Transactions, Foreign and Domestick* (London: printed by H. M., 1721), VI, 319.

with 'no less than twelve invitations to turtle for the ensuing summer'. Continuing, he writes:

Besides the honour herein designed me, I consider these invitations as having more real value than so many shares in any of the bubbles in the famous South-sea year; and I make no doubt but that, by the time they become due, they will be marketable in Change-alley.[28]

The financial crisis of 'the famous South-sea year' provides a metaphor for Fitz-Adam's dinner invitations. Within his description, numerous 'bubbles' are made subordinate to the 'South-sea year'. This does not represent a conflation of 'bubbles' and 'South-sea'; however, 'South-sea' is adopted as a label for all of 1720, meaning that, counter-intuitively, the South Sea Company's subscription scheme is one of the plural bubbles (investment schemes) that are encompassed by the broader 'South-sea year'. 'South-sea' here stands apart from South Sea Company, and in its shorter form begins to describe more widespread turbulence in the financial market. This shifting association allows the metaphorical qualities of bubble to be turned towards the South Sea, which is markedly different from the earlier examples. What is particularly significant about these metaphorical qualities is that they are not invoked in this way in earlier writing with strong co-associations between south-sea and bubble(s): *The Historical Register*'s (1721) 'Bubbles' rise, which is a metaphorical application of a property associated with a physical bubble, but here the metaphor plays upon what *financial* bubbles do, suggesting the embedding of the South Sea Bubble as a concept that describes more than the South Sea Company's moving stock price in 1720. This seems to be the moment at which South Sea Bubble starts to mean something separate from the South Sea as a Bubble. The metaphor that relates general market turbulence or uncertainty to the South Sea Bubble only becomes available once the idea of the South Sea Bubble is sufficiently established, with these ideas encompassed within.

When the author of an early edition of *The European Magazine and London Review* from 1782 writes that 'once the stocks [are] high they remind you of the South Sea which burst like a bubble', they are making use of the South Sea Bubble as metaphor in the same way as Fitz-Adam, despite the explicitly financial context.[29] What seems to be bubble's return to its bubble-*like* origins is in fact a deviation away from its origins in cheating and trickery; instead, it is a relocation within the language for

---

[28] Adam Fitz-Adam, *The World*, no. 123, 8 May 1755, printed in *The World* (London: printed for R. Dodsley, 1756), 737–42; 742.

[29] James Perry, ed., *The European Magazine, and London Review; Containing the Literature, History, Politics, Arts, Manners, and Amusements of the Age*, 8 (1782), 1–22.

which a conceptual latency always exists. While bubbles always have the potential to burst (as Allan Ramsay notes in 1720's 'The Rise and Fall of Stocks', in which a bubble, 'the shining beau-thing ... in a twinkling bursts to nothing'), the bursting described in *The European Magazine* is epistemic, relating to the function of a system that is liable to collapse when manipulated but that nevertheless depends upon its participants trusting that their exposure to risk is less substantial than their likelihood of gain.[30]

10.2   From Cheating to Bursting

This chapter began by arguing that Swift's idea of a bubble has an explicit connection to cheating and trickery. Though this is borne out by looking at examples of his use of the word in context, it leaves open the question of why eighteenth-century investors were so eager to invest in schemes already known as 'bubbles' when the sense of the word as 'cheating' was so available, and when bubbles in the material world were commonly understood to be things that burst. Few present-day investors would be 'ready to tread one another to Death', as the author of the *Daily Post*'s front-page article described on 15 January 1720, to get hold of stock in a known bubble.

To this day there is still no precise consensus on what a financial bubble is, although most economists agree that one occurs when asset price movement cannot be explained by analysis of a share's fundamentals. Larry Neal and Peter Garber have both argued that there were rational characteristics to the movement of South Sea stock prices in 1720 (a rational bubble occurs when 'asset prices continue to rise because investors believe that they will be able to sell the overvalued asset at a higher price in the future'),[31] which offers a way of reading contemporary enthusiasm for the 1720 bubble companies; however, to think of the 1720 crisis in these terms is to impose a modern vocabulary upon a period that had no recourse to it.[32] Today, we conceive of speculative markets as having a shape and a structure, with one of the most salient features of this understanding being that financial bubbles become overinflated and eventually burst. The language associated with this idea

---

[30] Allan Ramsay, 'The Rise and Fall of Stocks, 1720: An Epistle to the Right Honourable My Lord Ramsay' (London: printed for the author, 1720), ll. 29–30.

[31] Richard S. Dale, Johnnie E. V. Johnson and Leila Tang, 'Financial Markets Can Go Mad: Evidence of Irrational Behaviour during the South Sea Bubble', *Economic History Review*, 58 (2005), 233–71; 236–7.

[32] See Peter Garber, *Famous First Bubbles: The Fundamentals of Early Manias* (Cambridge, MA: MIT Press, 2000), 125; and Larry Neal, 'The First Rational Bubbles: A New Look at the Mississippi and South Sea Schemes', unpublished working paper, 1985, 4–5.

appears in all studies of the South Sea Bubble: describing the economic consequences of the South Sea Company's collapsed share price, John Carswell writes that 'the bubble had burst, with a consequent evaporation of surplus credit and the ruin of a group of speculators';[33] Peter G. M. Dickson writes at length about the months 'before the Bubble burst';[34] Helen J. Paul describes how 'London's own bubble inflated and burst';[35] and even Hoppit, despite his uncertainty about how contemporary actors would have perceived the crisis, writes that the Bubble 'was blown and burst in 1720'.[36] These descriptions are at odds with how financial bubbles behave, given that they splutter and struggle rather than bursting in a puff of air. Robert Shiller (who suggests that the English 'bubble' is a translation of 'boule', used in Paris to describe the Mississippi Bubble in the months before the South Sea Company's stock price began to rise) claims that the word implies 'something that is factually wrong, which is that they end in a crash, a one-day event, but that's not historically accurate'.[37] It seems improbable to suggest that early uses of bubble to describe speculative investment schemes might not have carried this weight of association, particularly when the very association between 'cheat' and 'bubble' exists because of a mutual speciousness; however, the relationship between bubbles and bursting in writing contemporary with the South Sea Bubble does not point to the collapse of integrated speculative markets, but rather to the collapse in the prices of particular stocks. What happened in the wake of the South Sea Company's investment scheme's failure is that that the idea of a bubble began to communicate a speculative market that has the ability to crash. This form of understanding emerged in response to the 1720 crisis, and it is integral to the emergence of the financialised nation.

If we take the finding from the previous section that shows South Sea Bubble beginning to adopt the meaning it has today around 1755, and use this date as a provisional dividing line, it becomes possible to isolate broader patterns of change relating to the evolving concept of the financial marketplace within the ECCO corpus. Comparing the persistent lexical company for bubble for the thirty-five years between 1720 and 1755 and for the thirty-five years between 1756 and 1791 shows how the relative strength of the words' co-associations change over the specified

---

[33] John Carswell, *The South Sea Bubble*, revised 2nd ed. (Stroud: Sutton, 2001; first published, 1960), 159.
[34] Dickson, Financial Revolution, 33.
[35] Helen J. Paul, *The South Sea Bubble* (Abingdon: Routledge, 2011), 47.
[36] Hoppit, 'Myths', 141.
[37] Robert Shiller, interview by John Authers, 'Fads, Bugs, Bubbles and Bitcoin', *Points of Return*, 9 June 2021.

Table 10.1 *Top twenty terms after vector subtraction. Source: ECCO.*

A. 1720–55 (bubble, persistent lexical company 1720–55 minus 1765–91)			B. 1765–91 (bubble, persistent lexical company 1756–91 minus 1720–55)		
Rank	Word	Relative abstraction (+ve concrete; −ve abstract)	Rank	Word	Relative abstraction (+ve concrete; −ve abstract)
1	tube	1.653	1	bubble	0.377
2	expanded	0.577	2	unwillingly	−1.111
3	vane	0.669	3	atoms	0.209
4	occupies	0.405	4	pard	1.095
5	vial	1.468	5	gull	1.099
6	cylindrical	2.010	6	toil	0.126
7	gilds	0.237	7	sparrow	1.004
8	equilibrium	−0.169	8	screw	1.529
9	stem	0.991	9	cheat	−0.587
10	glides	0.765	10	bubbles	0.712
11	cavity	1.446	11	polar	0.631
12	varying	0.089	12	helping	−0.201
13	pressure	0.133	13	cheated	−0.570
14	atmosphere	0.327	14	deceives	−1.277
15	subside	−0.761	15	barbarously	−0.404
16	blasts	0.369	16	hoop	2.206
17	buoy	1.257	17	snail	1.900
18	particle	−0.232	18	dissipated	−1.070
19	blown	1.037	19	adjust	−0.687
20	glass	1.473	20	trouble	−0.720

seventy-year period.[38] Performing vector subtractions (after data normalisation) in both directions allows us to see which terms are powerfully associated with bubble during the two periods.[39] Table 10.1 lists the twenty most highly ranked words from performing vector subtractions in both directions.

When the complete 1756–91 persistent lexical company is subtracted from the 1720 to the 1755 persistent lexical company (Table 10.1, A), the

---

[38] Persistent lexical company, as used here, is a vector (complete list) formed of the combined distance 5, 10, 40, 70, 100 co-associations for a given term.

[39] Shared lexis allows users to add, subtract, multiply or divide different vectors. In this instance, the vectors representing persistent lexical company between 1720 and 1755 and between 1756 and 1791 have been subtracted from one another to see which terms are more strongly associated with which period. The data normalisation involved accounting for the expanding rate of publication over the course of the century (the two datasets have been weighted to make their sizes directly comparable) and removing terms it is not possible to assess in terms of relative concreteness.

remaining terms with high bubble co-associations are almost exclusively scientific, with the most highly ranked terms very clearly pertaining to experimentation and natural philosophy rather than to economics and finance. Reversing the exercise (Table 10.1, B) demonstrates how much more clearly bubble is associated with manipulation of the market after the emergence of the conceptual structure underlying South Sea Bubble around half way through the century. The terms relating to experimentation fall away when the 1720–55 persistent lexical company is subtracted from the 1756 to the 1791 persistent lexical company, and in their place appears more abstract language describing bubble in the context of a system. Of the top 200 terms in the 1720–55 minus 1756–91 vector subtraction (Table 10.1, A), 140 (70%) are relatively concrete and 60 (30%) relatively abstract. The number of relatively concrete terms in the top 20 co-associations decreases considerably, when the opposite vector subtraction is performed (Table 10.1, B), to 104 (52%), with relatively abstract words accounting for 96 (48%) of the 200 strongest co-associations. Cylindrical, tube, glass and vial are among the top 20 co-associations when the 1756–91 persistent lexical company is subtracted from the 1720–55 (Table 10.1, A) persistent lexical company, compared to, for example, deceives, cheat, unwillingly, dissipated and trouble when the exercise is performed in reverse (Table 10.1, B). The appearance of bubble at the head of the 1756–91 minus 1720–56 subtraction (Table 10.1, B) and bubbles at point 10 shows that bubble and bubbles are considerably more firmly associated with bubble in the later period. The increased prevalence of abstract terms, particularly abstract terms that have no contiguousness with experimentation, shows the embedding of a bubble as an idea related to post-Financial Revolution market innovation, rather than as a discernible thing (whether material or metaphorical).

All of this serves to answer the overarching question of whether or not the emergence of a conceptual architecture to describe unstable national and international financial markets displaced a preceding way of thinking about crisis. There are particular consequences for how we understand financial modernity here. The broad argument that John G. A. Pocock makes in *The Machiavellian Moment* posits the financial innovations of the late seventeenth and early eighteenth centuries as crucial for the conceptual reconfiguration of time during the early modern period. This transformation – from the cyclic and Aristotelian model that dominated medieval and early Renaissance thought to an understanding of time as a secular and linear sequence bound by finitude – was the consequence of events that arose from and within discrete moments in history.[40] The growth of public credit, which saw private investors purchase a stake in the state's political, military and financial endeavours via firms like the South Sea Company, not only created a class of investors with a particular interest in the country's economic success but also tied futurity to discrete dates on which payments or repayments were due.[41] This imaginative reorganisation sees speculative financial markets become intrinsic to the operation of the state and, further, modifies the concept of instability such that it can be a necessary or even a desirable function of the market. That 'to bubble' appears to gain its earliest weight of reference from tricks played upon one individual by another, before taking this sense of small-scale manipulation to the institutions and companies that pursued investment schemes in Britain in 1720, suggests that prior to the crash there was little need for a mode of thinking about financial crisis in a way that integrates the actions of individual investors with the systemic properties of the market. The episode we now recognise as the 'South Sea Bubble' changed this: over the remaining eighty years of the century, bubble became more tangibly linked to the intangible as it started to represent the critical idea that instability is a fundamental feature of the financial market. The South Sea Company's bubble is therefore very different from the South Sea Bubble.

[40] John G. A. Pocock, *The Machiavellian Moment: Florentine Political Thought and the Atlantic Republican Tradition* (Princeton, NJ: Princeton University Press, 1975), 213.
[41] Pocock, *Machiavellian Moment*, 425–6.

11   Embedded Ideas: Revolutionary Theory and Political Science in the Eighteenth Century

Mark Algee-Hewitt

Amid the discussion of the revolutionary fervour of the French Revolution and its possible consequences for the British polity, Edmund Burke, in his *Reflections on the Revolution in France*, singles out a sermon delivered by Richard Price for what he feels is Price's inappropriately pro-revolutionary take on the divine rights of the monarchy:

> His doctrines affect our constitutions in vital parts. He tells the Revolution Society, in this political sermon, that his Majesty [George III] 'is almost the *only* lawful king in the world, because the *only* one who owes his crown to the *choice of the people*'.[1]

In addition to the content of the sermon itself, 'of which the Revolution in France is the grand ingredient in the cauldron', one of Burke's chief points of contention lies in the genre of the address: the *political sermon*.[2] In the intersection between the pulpit and politics, Burke finds not only a misappropriation of the platform afforded to Price but also a category error that combines political sentiment with theology in a way that, for Burke, undermines them both. It is this point that Mary Wollstonecraft seizes upon in her rebuttal to Burke in *A Vindications of the Rights of Men*, arguing that the mitigating term once again lies in an intersection between the social and the political:

> I agree with you, Sir, that the pulpit is not the place for *political discussions*, though it might be more excusable to enter on such a subject, when the day was set apart merely to commemorate a *political revolution*, and no stated duty was encroached upon.[3]

---

[1] Edmund Burke, *Reflections on the Revolution in France* (London: printed for J. Dodsley, 1790), 16; emphasis in original.
[2] Burke, *Reflections*, 12.
[3] Mary Wollstonecraft, *A Vindication of the Rights of Men, in a Letter to the Right Honourable Edmund Burke* (London: printed for J. Johnson, 1790), 33; emphasis mine.

Although the terms of their debate might be lifted directly from Kant's essay 'An Answer to the Question: What Is Enlightenment?' (in which the private, or professional, use of public reason is one of the few intellectual acts decried by Kant),[4] it is the work of the term political and the conceptual stakes that it carries that emerges as a key point of their disagreement. Political sermon, political discussion and political revolution: each phrase demonstrates the degree to which the adjective political gives not just a new meaning but a different valence to each object, particularly in the context of this debate. While the ideas of political sermons and political discussion suggest, on the surface, a mediating relationship (politics as the content of a sermon or discussion), the particular emphasis that Burke places on '*this* political sermon' suggests an evolution of both terms: a combination of political and sermon that is fully neither, but an amalgamation of both that is more than the sum of its parts.

Nowhere is this more evident, however, than in Wollstonecraft's use of 'political revolution'. Unlike the other two combinations, which suggest a fitting together of topic and mediation, the political revolution has no immediate cognates. Once again, the combination of the constituent elements, 'political' and 'revolution', points beyond the meaning that either term carries alone, towards a *compound* idea whose work is substantively different. In choosing this particular mixture of words, Wollstonecraft indicates that something profound is taking place.[5] With 'political revolution', she is at once downplaying the event, marking it as a 'mere' commemoration of a bounded event in the history of Europe, and, at the same time, characterising that event as historically unique (and therefore worthy of commemoration). By confining the revolution to the political sphere, Wollstonecraft is able to downplay the social ramifications of the political upheaval in France (and the violence that had already taken place), providing an implicit answer to Burke's concerns in the *Reflections*, while, as we will see, making a strong claim for the necessity of the revolution in the process of political history. In the debate over the

---

[4] Immanuel Kant, 'An Answer to the Question: What Is Enlightenment?', in *What Is Enlightenment? Eighteenth-Century Answers and Twentieth-Century Questions*, ed. James Schmidt (Berkeley: University of California Press, 1996), 58–64.

[5] While Wollstonecraft might be the best-known author to use this phrase in relation to the French Revolution, the formulation is not unique to her, nor to her political stance. John Courtenay, for example, in his own reflections on the revolution and its meaning for political dissent in England uses it to contrast the supposedly 'happy' lives of the French peasants prior to the revolution: 'I am confirmed in the justice of these sentiments by the philosophical observations of Mr. Necker, who describes, with sympathetic delight, the happiness of the French peasantry before the late political revolution.' John Courtenay, *Philosophical Reflections on the Late Revolution in France, and the Conduct of the Dissenters in England* (London: printed for T. Beckett, 1790), 46.

French Revolution, in other words, revolution gains a new sphere of action, while the political gains an underlying system through which it can work.

In this chapter, I explore the ways in which the idea of a political revolution emerged during the British eighteenth century and what differentiated its use by Wollstonecraft to refer to the French Revolution from how the term was applied to the Glorious Revolution of a century before. How did the concept of the political become attached to revolution and what did this compound idea offer to the century that was not available before? My central focus will be on the transformation of political revolution, an oft-overlooked compound concept that emerged in the anglophone eighteenth century, but I shall also explore ways in which computational methods can enable us to understand how concepts intersect, combine and evolve over time.

11.1   From Concepts to Vectors

It might be argued that the eighteenth century was particularly attuned to the generation and use of compound concepts – writers such as Locke, for example, were interested in understanding how ideas can be combined to make larger units of thinking –[6] and that the period developed theories of language and meaning that can be easily compared to, even overlaid upon our own contemporary accounts. In particular, the reliance on 'combination' for meaning that is evident in Locke's work, can be easily mapped onto contemporary linguistics in its deployment of the distributional hypothesis.[7] According to this hypothesis, words with similar meanings will appear in similar distributions, or, more simply, meaning can be better inferred by shared context than by definition.[8] Drawing on

---

[6] See John Locke, *An Essay Concerning Human Understanding* (Oxford: University of Oxford Press, 2013), 289: 'every *mixed Mode* consisting of many distinct simple *Ideas*, it seems reasonable to enquire, *when it has its Unity*; and since such a precise multitude comes to make but one *Idea*, since that Combination does not always exist together in Nature. To which I answer it is plain, it has its Unity from an Action of the Mind combining those several simple *Ideas* together, and considering them as one complex one, consisting of those parts; and the mark of the Unions, or that which is looked on generally to compleat it, is one name given to that Combination.'

[7] See Chapters 2 and 3.

[8] This strong version of the distributional hypothesis follows, I argue, from Locke's theory. Distributional semantics has been a key theoretical component of contemporary computational linguistics and builds on a rich tradition of twentieth-century language theory. For overviews of its contemporary significance, see Alessandro Lenci, 'Distributional Semantics in Linguistic and Cognitive Research', *Italian journal of linguistics*, 20.1 (2008), 1–31; Gemma Boleda, 'Distributional Semantics and Linguistic Theory', *Annual Review of Linguistics*, 6 (2020), 213–34; Alessandro Lenci, 'Distributional Models of Word Meaning', *Annual Review of Linguistics*, 4 (2018), 151–71.

language theory from, among others, Wittgenstein (theory, which we can already see taking shape in Locke's writing), current computational approaches to word meaning rely largely on similarities described by vector spaces, *embedding* each word into a higher dimensional representation wherein two words are more similar if they inhabit the same region of the embedding space.[9]

To the *combination* of complex concepts in eighteenth-century language philosophy, word embeddings add the logic of *substitution*. Whereas collocations describe the syntagmatic relationships between words, in the dense vector representations of an embedding space, shared context becomes equally as important. Two words that never appear together but often appear with the same words as each other are more similar within the model.[10] For example, in the series of embedding models that I use throughout the chapter, the closest word to political between 1715 and 1720 is polity, even though the two words never occur within five words of each other during this period in the ECCO corpus.[11] The association between the two terms is conceptually clear (the polity provides the field on which the political operates), but their close association in the language model lies not in their co-occurrence but in their shared adjacency to the same words – a set of relationships surfaced by the embedding model.

While the collocation analysis described in the previous chapters can give a high degree of specificity to the kinds of adjacency that may produce

---

[9] Wittgenstein, for example, works through word meaning as a function of relationships within a system, or game, for which speakers understand the rules, rather than pointers that reference an external reality. See Ludwig Wittgenstein, *Philosophical Investigations* (Oxford: Blackwell, 2009), 20–1. For the background theory of word embeddings, particularly word2vec, see Tomas Mikolov, Kai Chen, Greg Corrado and Jeffrey Dean, 'Efficient Estimation of Word Representations in Vector Space' (2013), arXiv: 1301.3781; Yoav Goldberg and Omer Levy, 'word2vec Explained: Deriving Mikolov et al.'s Negative-Sampling Word-Embedding Method' (2014), *CoRR*, abs/1402.3722. Turney and Pantel theorised many of the developments, in using contextual similarity to relate words, that have been made over the last decade in their 2010 article, Peter D. Turney and Patrick Pantel, 'From Frequency to Meaning: Vector Space Models of Semantics', *Journal of Artificial Intelligence Research*, 37 (2010), 141–88.

[10] In methods based on probabilistic modelling (still the most frequently used), this vector is either calculated from training neural networks on the immediate context of each word in the model (as in word2vec) or from a log bi-linear model of a co-occurrence table (as in GloVe); Mikolov, Chen, Corrado and Dean, 'Efficient Estimation'; Jeffery Pennington, Richard Socher and Christopher Manning, 'GloVe: Global Vectors for Word Representation', in *Proceedings of the 2014 Conference on Empirical Methods in Natural Language Processing (EMNLP)*, ed. Alessandro Moschitti, Bo Pang and Walter Daelemans (Doha: Association for Computational Linguistics, 2014), 1532–43.

[11] The vector models I use are initially based on an adjacency of PMI within a five-word window.

complex ideas, if we focus an analysis through a single word, as required by collocations, we risk missing the multidimensional many-to-many relationships between words. For the problem at hand, for example, the full work of political revolution is not reducible to either just the attachments of political or revolution. Instead, the emergent idea is something different from either and its analysis requires careful attention to not just words that attach to both terms *but the system of relationships between those regions of the model*. The promise of this multidimensionality is what word embedding methods offer to the history of ideas, should there be some way to account for the importance of *combination* (which is described better by collocation methods) rather than the *substitution* on which most word embedding models rely.[12]

Beyond the multidimensional relationships modelled by word embeddings, time is also a critical factor in understanding the evolution of compound ideas. A key weakness in embedding methods, however, lies in their difficulty in describing historical change. While serial word2vec or GloVe models can account for broad changes in discourse, the signal of the individual relationship between two terms is overwhelmed by the noise generated by the probabilistic models used to create the embeddings. When models are created independently and set next to each other without being aligned, it is impossible to differentiate actual changes in relationships between a given set of terms from the noise created by each model.[13] Although standard probabilistic word embedding models can be aligned, the method is complex, and it still leaves the first question – the need for associations based on syntagma rather than substitution – unanswered. There is, however, a solution that answers both of these needs: rather than build vectors based on probabilistic models, given a large enough corpus we can use collocations to produce a series of dense vector representations of a corpus by using a singular value decomposition to reduce a co-occurrence table of shared PMI scores between words (as

---

[12] While word embedding models have played a large role in computational linguistics and artificial intelligence research over the past decade, they have only recently been applied to literary textual corpora. See, for example, Michael Gavin, Collin Jennings, Lauren Kersey and Brad Pasanek, 'Spaces of Meaning: Computational History, Vector Semantics, and Close Reading', *Debates in the Digital Humanities*, ed. Matthew Gold and Lauren Klein (Minneapolis, MN: University of Minnesota Press, 2019), 243–67.

[13] Hellrich and Hahn have estimated the variation in word embedding models and suggest that although GloVe is slightly more stable than word2vec, neither can easily account for historical change; Johannes Hellrich and Udo Hahn, 'Bad Company – Neighborhoods in Neural Embedding Spaces Considered Harmful', in *Proceedings on COLING 2016, the 26th International Conference on Computational Linguistics: Technical Papers*, ed. Yuji Matsumoto and Rashmi Prasad (Osaka: The COLING 2016 Organizing Committee, 2016), 2785–96.

described in Chapters 2 and 3) into a dense multidimensional representation of words as vectors.[14]

Using the ECCO corpus from Gale, I created a series of embedding models for the same set of terms at five-year increments.[15] Each model describes the relationship between all of the words based on their co-occurrence with each other: two words are closer together if they share more information – which, in this case, indicates a higher likelihood of appearing together – and farther apart if they are rarely paired (within five words before or after).[16] For a single model, we can calculate the distance between any two words based on the cosine similarity: this gives us a single measurement of the similarity between any two terms in one of the models. By repeatedly taking this measurement across the aligned models, we can track the ways in which two words interacted across the century, within the ECCO corpus.[17] More importantly, we can calculate the relationship between not just the terms themselves but between the larger embedding space of the two words. In a compound formulation such as political revolution, each component, political and revolution, comes embedded within its own context and its own cluster of related

---

[14] This method was described by Levy et al., and it was used by Hamilton et al. to create diachronic word embeddings that describe historical changes in word use; Omer Levy, Yoav Goldberg and Ido Dagan, 'Improving Distributional Similarity with Lessons Learned from Word Embeddings', *Transactions of the Association for Computational Linguistics*, III, ed. Michael Collins and Lillian Lee (Cambridge, MA: MIT Press, 2015), 211–25; Omer Levy and Yoav Goldberg, 'Neural Word Embedding as Implicit Matrix Factorization', in *Advances in Neural Information Processing Systems 27*, ed. Zoubin Ghahramani, Max Welling, Corrina Cortes, Neil D. Lawrence and Kilian Q. Weinberger (New York: Curran Associates, 2014), 2177–85; William L. Hamilton, Jure Leskovec and Dan Jurafsky, 'Diachronic Word Embeddings Reveal Statistical Laws of Semantic Change', in *Proceedings of the 54th Annual Meeting of the Association for Computational Linguistics*, ed. Katrin Erk and Noah A. Smith (Stroudsburg, PA: Association for Computational Linguistics, 2016), 1489–1501. Here I follow Hamilton et al.'s method, noting that the resulting vectors must still be aligned, as the solution to a singular value decomposition involves a square root that must be resolved to the positive or negative solution across the models.

[15] The complexity of these embedding models scale exponentially with vocabulary size. To reduce computational time, I restricted the vocabulary of the models I created to words that appeared more than 9,999 times in the ECCO corpus – or the top 19,211 terms (excluding commonly used function words).

[16] Although, as previously described, this predicates similarity within the embedding space on co-occurrence, the size of the corpus and the use of mutual information also reveal similarity based on substitution (if two words always occur together – for example 'King George' – they can be substituted for each other without losing information: 'King' gives the same information as 'George'). In this way, the model reveals a deeper relationship between co-occurrence and substitution.

[17] See Chapter 2 for a full discussion of the ECCO corpus, including its method of selection and potential biases. For the purpose of this chapter, then, when I refer to the eighteenth century, it is only the limited facet of the eighteenth century represented by the ECCO corpus.

terms. We can imagine the evolution of the idea as a gradual approach between these two clusters in the discourse of the corpus: as the two central terms are drawn closer together based on their shared usage, their respective contexts begin to intersect, with some terms drawn into the orbit of the central paired words, linking them closer together, while others remain on the periphery, pulling the two back towards their initial clusters. In this way, the evolution of an idea can be represented as a set of interacting forces, with shared contexts attracting the terms together into a compound idea, while disparate contexts pull them apart.[18] The word embedding models allow us access to this complex system at discrete moments of its evolution: by aligning these models over time, we can witness the mechanisms behind the emergence of these ideas.

Word embedding models, particularly when they are employed for exploratory, rather than classification tasks, are often studied through visualisations. For example, while we can calculate that the distance between political and revolution is 0.99 in 1700–5 and increases to 0.44 in 1795–9, these figures neither help to contextualise what this distance means nor the contours of the greater regions of the model in which these terms are embedded.[19] It appears that across the century, the two terms approach each other (a fact we already know from their appearance as a united idea in the 1790s), but the raw numbers alone give us no insight into how this took place.

What we require, then, is a visualisation that can project both axes that pertain to the evolution of the idea simultaneously: semantic change and time. On the semantic change axis, the visualisation should offer information about the relationship between the two terms in question, situating them both in relationship to each other, as well as within the wider language context of the conceptual milieu that they inhabit. On the time axis, we need information about the change in relationship between the two terms with respect to each other and their wider contexts: are they moving in tandem, or are they approaching towards or diverging from each other? And in the holistic process of their movement over time, what forces are acting to bring them together or pull them apart? Figure 11.1 uses the information stored in the embedding model described earlier to

---

[18] This way of modelling the relationships between clusters of terms is similar to the interpretation of the network graphs in previous chapters, especially in Chapter 5 where despotism is understood to exert both binding and repelling forces on a cluster of terms around government.

[19] These distances are the inversions of the cosine similarities calculated between political and revolution in the 1700–4 and 1795–9 models respectively. A cosine similarity of 1 indicates that the terms occupy the same space in the multidimensional embedding space, while a cosine similarity of 0 indicates that they are on opposite 'sides' of the embedding space.

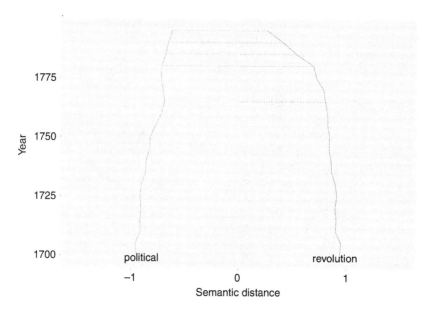

Figure 11.1 Graph of the semantic difference between political and revolution within the embedding spaces over time. Source: ECCO.

visualise the relationship between political and revolution in exactly this way. Time is represented on the y-axis, moving from bottom (1700–4) to top (1795–9), while semantic distance is visualised on the x-axis, which is oriented around 0, showing the relative position of both terms, political and revolution, on the left and right respectively: the two lines therefore (each one representing one of the terms) trace the movement of the anchoring terms towards or away from each other over time.[20] The distance between the two lines is based on the cosine similarity between the terms that they represent: as they mark out the changing relationship between the terms over the century, they give a visual account of how close or far away from each other they are, or, given that the embedding space is based on PMI scores, how much meaning or information they share.

The dotted lines mark points at which the two principal terms enter into the close orbit of each other: a dotted line drawn from one of the two

[20] Although the lines give the impression of continuous movement (which enables us to better understand the relative change), they are a projection of the relationship between the terms at each five-year time slice as continuous movement along the century. The lines themselves have been smoothed by a 3-period rolling average.

lines into the centre indicates a point at which, for example, revolution becomes one of the closest terms to political (as happens in 1760). Their lack of symmetry (e.g. in 1760 revolution is a top term of political but not vice versa) suggests the ways in which the movement of these concepts is not equivalent. Although by the end of the century each was a top term of the other (this is true for any period after 1780), in this earlier period, revolution had moved far enough outside of its embedding space to enter into the orbit of the political, which itself was too tightly bound to the rest of its conceptual cluster to admit revolution into its top terms. This asymmetry is reflected in the lines themselves. As the cosine similarity between two words in an embedding space is symmetrical, the distances in Figure 11.1 should mirror each other across the 0; instead I have scaled each distance between the two terms by the degree to which each is connected to its immediate neighbouring words in the embedding space. Each distance is scaled by the difference between the mean distance between each term and set of words that they share in common among their respective top 100 closest terms in the embedding space.[21] This gives critical information about the direction of movement, not of the individual words but of the system that the words and their respective companies co-create. In Figure 11.1 we can see that revolution makes a significant turn towards the political after 1780. The distance between the two words grows smaller for the rest of the century, but it is revolution that is leaving its cluster of terms and joining with the political, rather than the reverse (although there is a slight covalent movement of political towards revolution in the final years of the century).[22] Between the changing scaled semantic distances between words represented by the vertical lines and the degree to which they incorporate each other among their closest terms, shown by the dotted horizontal lines, this diagram gives a surprisingly robust set of information about this changing nature of this proto-idea political revolution, allowing us to watch the political approach and eventually merge with revolution.

[21] This is calculated by finding the set of words in the embedding space that are in *both* the top 100 terms of political and revolution and calculating the mean distance from each word (political and revolution) to all of the others. The two means are then subtracted to indicate whether political is moving towards revolution with respect to its surrounding cluster of words, or if revolution is moving towards political (as is in the case in the graph here).

[22] Given that these calculations are ultimately based on PMI scores, we can interpret the asymmetry in terms of the directionality of the shared information between the two terms. As the entire system shifts towards political (it remains relatively steady, while revolution moves sharply towards it), we can say that revolution carries more information of political than political carries of revolution. At the end of the eighteenth century, talking about revolution implies something political, while talking about politics could imply any number of topics, revolution only being one of them.

Although the graph gives the impression that the terms are isolated, moving relative only to each other, nothing could be further from the truth. The forces acting upon the words, pulling them closer together or pushing them apart, are a function of the clusters of associated terms in which each word is embedded. The graph simplifies the complex combination of terms working against and for the eventual merger of political and revolution by summarising their effects within the embedding space through the semantic distance. To better understand the mechanisms that lie behind the movement of the terms over time, it is crucial that we return to this complexity and explore the composition of the clusters acting upon the terms in our model.

Table 11.1 shows a portion of the words working within the embedding space to shape the relationship between pollical and revolution. For each five-year incremental model, the two central columns (political: binding and revolution: binding) show the terms common to the immediate (100 words) contexts of both terms.[23] These binding terms show what parts of the respective clusters of terms surrounding both political and revolution are becoming part of the new compound political revolution. The choice of which column a word shared by both terms appears in is a function of which term that word is closer to. For example, in 1795 in Table 11.1, both national and administration are among the top 100 terms closest to both political and revolution. As national is closer to political while administration is closer to revolution, they appear in each term's respective column of binding words. The outside columns (political: non-binding and revolution: non-binding) show the opposite set of forces. These columns contain words connected to political or revolution that are not shared by the other term. Not only do they offer important information on the respective semantic neighbourhood of each term independent of the other; they also suggest what clusters of words are actively working to keep the terms separate.

Again in 1795, we can see that moral (the closest word to political not shared by revolution) and reform (the closest word to revolution not shared by political) represent the forces both binding and repelling the terms that are compounded in the idea of political revolution.

The relationship between the two central concepts in Figure 11.1 as mediated by the terms exerting both binding and repelling forces on their historical trajectories points at something far deeper within the embedding space. A key advantage of representing a discursive system within

---

[23] Note that this table, like the graph in Figure 11.1, reads bottom to top in terms of date, with the latest models from 1795 at the top and the earliest at the bottom.

Table 11.1 *Binding and opposing terms of political and revolution at five-year intervals between 1700 and 1795. Source: ECCO.*

Year	political: non-binding	political: binding	revolution: binding	revolution: non-binding
1795	moral; religious; society; religion; mankind; human; genius; laws	political; national; civil; politics; principles; popular; government; constitution	revolution; administration; republican; monarchy; europe; tyranny; events; france	revolutions; reform; convention; measures; rebellion; anarchy; reformation; event
1790	moral; religious; human; religion; laws; genius; mankind; private	political; popular; civil; national; principles; politics; government; constitution	revolution; monarchy; administration; republic; republican; tyranny; parliament; parliamentary	reformation; revolutions; burke; convention; reform; measures; anarchy; commons
1785	politics; national; government; policy; moral; civil; system; principles	political; popular; administration	revolution; monarchy	revolutions; restoration; reformation; revolving; rotation; diurnal; downfall; revolve
1780	national; principles; civil; moral; commercial; policy; religious; interests	political; politics; government; system; constitution; popular	revolution; monarchy; administration; parliamentary; kingdoms; period; commons; whig	revolutions; restoration; reformation; diurnal; revolve; alteration; ministry; establishment
1775	political; politics; civil; national; policy; system; principles; popular	constitution; commonwealth; republican; empire; slavery	reformation; monarchy; administration; measures; popery; tyranny	revolution; revolutions; restoration; revolve; revolving; diurnal; accession; rebellion
1770	political; politics; national; moral; policy; civil; interests; popular	system; whig	reformation; popery; monarchy; administration; commonwealth	revolution; revolutions; restoration; diurnal; rotation; revolve; revolving; moons
1765	political; politics; national; policy; civil; republic; popular; domestic	system; monarchy; administration; whig	revolution; popery	revolutions; restoration; planet; eclipses; comet; ecliptic; satellite; revolve

Table 11.1 (*cont.*)

Year	political: non-binding	political: binding	revolution: binding	revolution: non-binding
1760	political; politics; national; policy; morality; moral; politic; interests	system; republican; faction	reformation; administration; whigs; monarchy; whig	revolution; revolutions; diurnal; revolve; restoration; comets; rotation; satellite
1755	political; politics; policy; civil; national; system; popular; commercial		administration; monarchy	revolution; revolutions; revolve; restoration; revolving; diurnal; rotation; reformation
1750	political; politics; policy; polity; morality; national; utility; commercial	establishment; republican	monarchy	revolution; revolutions; planet; revolving; ecliptic; rotation; axis; restoration
1745	political; national; policy; politics; politic; civil; system; moral		monarchy; whig; scheme	revolution; reformation; rotation; revolutions; diurnal; projected; restoration; moons
1740	political; politics; national; politic; critical; commercial; philosophical; policy		parliamentary; republican; scheme	revolution; restoration; revolutions; revolve; rotation; solar; diurnal; moons
1735	political; politic; politics; policy; polity; popular; moral; purely	monarchy	establishment; administration	revolution; revolutions; rotation; diurnal; restoration; revolving; planet; revolve
1730	political; politics; politic; philosophical; policy; purely; national; maxims	commonwealth; arbitrary	administration; republican	revolution; revolutions; restoration; monarchy; diurnal; planet; protestant; revolving
1725	political; politics; politic; polity; commonwealth; governments; institutions; monarchical		monarchy	revolution; revolutions; diurnal; rotation; revolve; orbits; comet; moons

Year				
1720	political; politics; politic; polity; purely; governments; morality; philosophical	establishment; arbitrary; economy	monarchy	revolution; revolutions; restoration; rotation; episcopacy; eclipse; rebellion; disc
1715	political; polity; purely; national; social; morality; religions; politics	arbitrary; legislature; hierarchy	episcopacy; monarchy; establishment	revolution; succession; popery; whigs; dissenters; revolutions; protestant; tories
1710	political; calculated; societies; economy; regulated; prudential; politic; moral	governments	scheme	revolution; pretender; popery; doctor; presbyterian; toleration; protestant; resistance
1705	political; polity; politic; societies; ceremonial; economy; national; magistracy	monarchy; system; arbitrary	administration	revolution; revolutions; restoration; alteration; rotation; diurnal; presbyterians; alterations
1700	political; polity; politic; societies; governments; institutions; civil; politics	popular; preservation		revolution; revolutions; restoration; popery; conversion; calculation; diurnal; planets

a series of vectors lies in the possibility of using the relationality of all terms in the system to approximate meaning shifts through vector maths. As they are represented by vectors of numbers, individual words can be added together and subtracted from each other such that the resulting vector will describe a portion of the embedding space that is the sum of both constituent vectors, or the difference between them (depending on the operation). If the location of words within an embedding space tells us about their conceptual neighbourhoods, then adding or subtracting these vectors from each other allows us to explore the relationships of these words to each other based on their place within the model. By moving us around the embedding space, such operations not only establish the relationship between two terms as endpoints, but they also describe the specific changes in multidimensional contexts, or neighbourhoods of words, that one has to go through to become the other.

The words in the rows of Table 11.1 work in fundamentally the same way. The terms in the centre columns, binding the individual words together, are additive; the ones at the edges, pulling the words apart, are subtractive. By substituting the mathematical operations for their positionality on the graph, we can actually use the visualisation as a proxy for the vector maths of the model. For example, in 1725, we can see that politics pulls political away from revolution, while diurnal and rotation pull revolution in the opposite direction: the two are connected only by monarchy. To get from political to revolution during this period, therefore, we can use the formula 'political – politics + diurnal + rotational + monarchy' to arrive at a word set that includes revolution among its closest associated words. The length of the formula speaks to the relatively large distance, within the embedding space, between revolution and political at this point in their shared history: political must go through four transformations to reach revolution. At the end of the century, however, when the two terms converge, political is pulled away from revolution by moral and bound to it through civil. This allows us to calculate 'political – moral + civil', which results in a vector whose closest ten associated terms include revolution. As only two transformations are necessary to reach revolution from political, therefore, we can infer that the contexts of the two terms within the model are much more similar at the end of the century. The use of vector maths is therefore crucial to our understanding of the relationship between the terms in Figure 11.1 in two ways. First, it describes a possible set of intermediary transformations that can take us from one term to the other, giving us valuable information about the nature of their relationship. Secondly, the complexity of the formula itself speaks to the degree of separation between the two terms within the embedding space.

11.2   Rebels, Revolutionaries and the Science of Revolution

Between the path traced by the terms in Figure 11.1 and the underlying language of Table 11.1, we can see that the history of political revolution marks a clear course across the eighteenth century. While the two terms are markedly separate at the beginning (sharing only popular and preservation among their respective top 100 terms), they trace a general convergence over the course of the century, slowly approaching each other between 1700 and 1780, before revolution turns sharply towards political in the last two decades. At first glance, then, the idea of political revolution seems to mark out a clear historical trajectory that corresponds with an easy story about the eighteenth century and the French Revolution: one that transports us back to where we began in the work of Burke, Wollstonecraft and Price's speech. But a closer inspection of Figure 11.1 raises more questions than this naive interpretation can answer. If, for example, the French Revolution was the *precipitating* event in the history of political revolution as a cohesive idea, why does the convergence happen nearly a decade before the official advent of the French Revolution in 1789? Or, conversely, if it was the American Revolution that served as the historical manifestation for the approach of the two terms, why does their convergence begin a decade too late? And, given the civil unrest surrounding the Jacobite rebellions of 1715 and 1745, why does the term revolution in the middle of century move away from the restoration and reformation of the early decades towards the Newtonian mechanical contexts of diurnal, rotation, orbit and planet during this key period? The graph reveals contours of ideas that both complicate the simple reading of the history of political revolution in the eighteenth century that the writing around the French Revolution suggests and open up new lines of inquiry that can help us think about the evolution of these concepts and their union through a more detailed history of the events of the period.

These questions, centred on the history of revolution, are particularly computationally tractable: the eighteenth-century history of revolution has already been the locus of a critical exploration using computational methods. Keith Baker's 'Revolution 1.0' uses collocations of revolution in the ECCO-TCP corpus to trace the transformation by which 'the notion of revolution as fact gave way to the conception of revolution as an ongoing act'.[24] Baker's work lays important groundwork for the questions that I raised earlier, as his collocations indicate a changing temporality of revolutions across the eighteenth century, from the use of revolution as a descriptor of something that had happened (a settled fact in the history of

---

[24] Keith Baker, 'Revolution 1.0', *Journal of Modern European History*, 11.2 (2013), 189.

a country) to an ongoing action that is possible and necessary to purpose-fully undertake.[25] The model that I employ here builds on Baker's conclusion in two key ways. First, the increased size of the corpus and the complexity of the embedding model shows a multivalent set of transformations in revolution across the century. The description of revolution that Baker offers for the majority of the eighteenth century pushes back explicitly on Hannah Arendt's argument that, until the French Revolution, the term not only referred primarily to the movement of celestial bodies but that this type of motion, when applied to governmental change, metaphorised a cyclical history of political power: 'if used for the affairs of men on earth, it could only signify that the few known forms of government revolve among the mortals in eternal recurrence with the same irresistible force which makes the stars follow their preordained paths in the skies'.[26]

The terms in Table 11.1 seem to suggest an important convergence by which the term was applied in political contexts associated with both the Glorious Revolution and the exclusion crisis at the beginning of the century, before moving back to Newtonian mechanics by the mid-century. The models that I use here indicate that the idea of revolution passed back through its scientific usage on the way to becoming a *political* category of action. Secondly, whereas the use of collocations are unidirectional (allowing Baker to explore the semantics of revolution insofar as they are centred on the word itself), the embedding model allows us to witness the co-evolution of political *and* revolution, *and the discourse that they are embedded within* as a multivalent transformation. The key, in other words, to understanding both the questions that I posed earlier, as well as the underlying logic to the evolution of revolution that both Baker and Arendt trace, lies in its relationship to the political.

In describing the evolution of political revolution, Figure 11.1 tells two histories that converge into a single idea. To understand the historical transformations that result in the final idea, it is critical to explore both parts of the composite idea, political *and* revolution. Of the two, the history of political in the eighteenth century tells a more straightforward story. Across the century, political moves primarily within its cluster of associated terms, accumulating new associated concepts and gaining new traction

---

[25] Baker, 'Revolution', 194. For a description of the ECCO-TCP corpus, see 'About ECCO-TCP', Eighteenth Century Collections Online (ECCO) TCP, Text Creation Partnership, https://textcreationpartnership.org/tcp-texts/ecco-tcp-eighteenth-century-collections-online/. Although much more accurate in its optical character recognition, this small sample of ECCO is even more highly canonical and selected than the corpus as a whole.

[26] Hannah Arendt, *On Revolution* (London: Penguin, 1990), 42. Compare to Baker: '"revolution" did not, *pace* Hannah Arendt, necessarily imply a return to an original state or position, as in the astronomical sense'; 'Revolution', 192.

within discussions of governmental administration such that it becomes central to a number of different ideas that emerge across the century, including, for example, Godwin's idea of political justice. Much like the convergence of political revolution, however, Godwin's work does not initiate a wholesale transformation of the political. Rather than sparking the union of the concepts into the idea, Godwin's work brings the evolution of the idea of political justice into focus by making explicit a convergence that was already taking place.[27] The fact that revolution moves towards a relatively stable political in Figure 11.1 suggests that the more volatile concepts moved towards the political as an effect of its slow but robust transformation across the century. It also suggests that it is necessary to first understand the political in order to explain revolution's attraction to it.

As opposed to its limited sense at the beginning of the century, bound, as it was, with civil institutions and societies, the breadth of the context of the political grew across the eighteenth century as enlightenment thinkers continued to put increasing pressure on all forms of government.[28] Within the embedding model, political expands in both its valence and its significance in eighteenth-century discourse by the end of the period. Two aspects of the evolution in political in the eighteenth century are immediately apparent in the change in its associated terms at the beginning and end of the century. First, between the beginning and the end of the century political, as a concept, became more central to the regions in which it was embedded – the distances between it and its surrounding clusters of words shrink over the period. This describes the way that political moves from the periphery of discussions about government and civics to the centre. Secondly, the specific words that attach to political reveal the details of this transformation. In the early five-year segments of the century, political was largely attached to polity, society and governments; by the last fifteen years, a wealth of new terms had entered its immediate context, including constitution, principles, moral and system. What these terms suggest, I argue, is a *generalisation* of the political: where the term political had, earlier in the century, been attached to specific instantiations of governmental or social institutions (the British government, or European society), by the 1790s it finds company with terms associated with philosophical discourse (principles, moral and system) or with objects which express these principles (constitution), thereby

---

[27] Mark Philip, in *Godwin's Political Justice*, reads Godwin's book as an extension (and transformation) of a current of moral and political thought that, far from merely responding to the French Revolution, draws on ideas that had been developing in radical circles and their pamphlet literature for much of the previous century; Mark Philip, *Godwin's Political Justice* (London: Duckworth, 1986), 73–5.

[28] See Chapter 5.

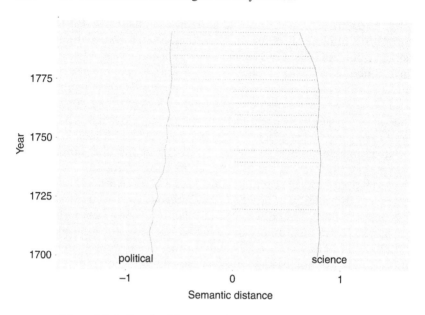

Figure 11.2 Graph of the semantic space of political and science within the embedding spaces over time. Source: ECCO.

locating the idea of the political within a body of theoretical knowledge.[29] Over the course of the eighteenth century, therefore, political moves from politics, as a practical description of a government, to political theory, a sociological account of government in general.

This reordering of the embedding space helps account for the growing attachment of political to a wealth of new contexts at the end of the eighteenth century. In each of these cases, the theorisation of the political brings its attached terms (revolution, justice) into a generalisable theory of government that the political, in turn, assumes. This is nowhere more evident than in the relationship between political and science itself (Figure 11.2). Here, much like political revolution and political justice, the graph of political and science shows a clear convergence between the two terms across the eighteenth century, with, once again, a more volatile science moving towards the more stable political. Like the previous graph in Figure 11.1, we can once again witness a significant turn in the last quarter of the century towards a heightened convergence. Again, this suggests that the movement of revolution at the end of the century

---

[29] The kind of generalisation that I describe here is similar to the kinds of movement from particularities to abstractions in political ideas that are described in Chapters 5, 6 and 7.

towards political was not an *effect* of the French Revolution (as I noted earlier it actually begins before the historical revolution itself), but instead was the culmination of an already emergent transformation in the attachments of the political. Here, the convergence of the terms suggests the ways in which political explicitly takes on the contours of science towards the end of the century. As we can see from a table of their underlying language (Table 11.2), they not only share system, civil, moral and principles, but science gains philosophy, learning and knowledge among its own top terms. The convergence between political and science helps us to understand the shifts in the region of political in Figure 11.2: politics becomes political theory in the service of a nascent science of politics that emerges out of the Enlightenment. The concentration of the embedding space, which represents the growing importance of the word political to the contexts in which it was used (as can be seen in the greater number of closely attached terms to political towards the end of the century), was due to the new use of political in a compound – political science – that expressed the idea of a *theory* of government or society. As such, it opened up the possibility of articulating many different *theories*, such as Godwin's, thereby establishing a general science of politics.[30]

If the transformation of political in the eighteenth century can be explained, at least in part, by the growing tendency of political to share the discursive contexts and conceptual architecture of science then what happens to revolution, whose transformations are somewhat less clear? Again, in Figure 11.1, the changes undergone by revolution are far more volatile than those of political. At the beginning of the century, the repelling forces on revolution (those terms pulling it away from the context of political) reflect the aftermath of the Glorious Revolution of 1688, and the restoration and exclusion crisis that preceded it. Terms such as restoration and popery (in 1700–4) and especially pretender (in 1710–14) suggest that the term was primarily used to describe the political events of the recent English past (the usurpation of the throne by

---

[30] It is not the case, however, that political moves closer to all terms across the eighteenth century. As it gains these new capacities, it sheds previous associations that no longer function effectively in the new ideational constellation that political finds itself in by the end of the century. Although tangential to the argument that I make here, the idea of 'political arithmetic', very much in vogue at the beginning of the eighteenth century, shows a sharp divergence across the ECCO corpus, effectively providing a mirror image to the convergence of 'political science'. The shifts in quantitative thinking about the government's role in demographics, which led to the decreasing viability of political arithmetic as a method for thinking through political theory, is well described by Peter Buck in 'People Who Counted' – Buck also describes the non-universality of the statistics informing political arithmetic as fundamental to its transformation in the eighteenth century; Peter Buck, 'People Who Counted: Political Arithmetic in the Eighteenth Century', *Isis*, 73.1 (1982), 28–45; 44.

Table 11.2 *Binding and opposing terms of political and science at five-year intervals between 1700 and 1795. Source: ECCO.*

Year	political: non-binding	political: binding	science: binding	science: non-binding
1795	national; popular; government; revolution; constitution; republic; military; opinions	political; civil; politics; principles; moral; religious; system; society	science; philosophy; learning; genius; knowledge; literature; education; philosophical	sciences; arts; study; mathematical; logic; mathematics; chemistry; understanding
1790	popular; civil; national; politics; government; revolution; constitution; religious	political; principles; moral; system; opinions; society; human; religion	science; philosophy; learning; arts; knowledge; genius; literature; philosophical	sciences; study; theology; geometry; logic; physics; physic; mathematics
1785	national; popular; government; policy; civil; interests; constitution; military	political; politics; moral; system; principles; religion; human; morality	science; philosophy; learning; literature; genius; education; literary; talents	sciences; arts; knowledge; study; mathematics; logic; metaphysics; astronomy
1780	national; government; civil; constitution; commercial; popular; policy; religious	political; politics; principles; system; moral; human; religion; mankind	science; philosophy; learning; knowledge; genius; wisdom; education; commerce	sciences; arts; mathematics; geometry; literature; metaphysics; study; logic
1775	civil; national; policy; system; popular; government; politic; religious	political; politics; principles; morality; mankind	science; philosophy; genius; moral; philosophical; commerce; ideas; religion	sciences; learning; mathematics; arts; knowledge; literature; geometry; physics
1770	political; national; policy; civil; interests; popular; government; politic	politics; moral; modern; system; morality; literary; principles; religion	science; sciences; philosophy; literature; genius; philosophical; commerce; ignorance	learning; arts; metaphysics; mathematics; logic; knowledge; study; theology
1765	political; national; policy; civil; republic; popular; monarchy; domestic	politics; system; moral; principles	science; philosophy; philosophical; genius; morality; education; poetry; theological	sciences; learning; physics; geometry; literature; mathematics; metaphysics; study

	political	politics	science	sciences
1760	political; national; policy; politic; interests; administration; republican; civil	politics; system; morality; moral	science; philosophy; literature; theology; philosophical; genius; mechanical; physical	sciences; learning; mathematics; metaphysics; logic; physics; geometry; arts
1755	policy; civil; national; system; popular; commercial; military; interests	political; politics; moral	science; sciences; philosophy; mathematical; study; metaphysics; philosophical; physic	mathematics; learning; literature; knowledge; geometry; logic; physics; arts
1750	political; policy; polity; national; utility; commercial; politic; institutions	politics; morality; moral	philosophy; literature; theory; philosophical; speculative; practical; speculation; notions	science; sciences; learning; mathematics; logic; metaphysics; physics; knowledge
1745	political; national; policy; politic; civil; system; essay; polity	politics; moral; theological	science; philosophy; logic; philosophical; study; theology; morality; genius	sciences; mathematics; geometry; physics; astronomy; learning; metaphysics; physic
1740	political; national; politic; critical; commercial; policy; historical; polity	politics; maxims; moral	science; philosophy; mathematics; metaphysics; ethics; speculative; mathematical; practical	sciences; learning; physics; literature; studies; geometry; study; physic
1735	political; politic; policy; polity; popular; purely; national; regulation	politics; moral	philosophy; theology; practical; philosophical; morality; theological; mechanical; profound	science; sciences; mathematics; geometry; logic; learning; mathematical; metaphysics
1730	political; politic; policy; purely; national; maxims; polity; historical	politics; morality; theological; system	sciences; philosophy; mathematics; mathematical; physic; speculative; theology; philosophical	science; logic; metaphysics; learning; geometry; physics; astronomy; study
1725	political; politics; politic; polity; commonwealth; governments; institutions; monarchical		speculative; theology; speculation; philosophical; speculations; practical; morality; theological	science; sciences; philosophy; mathematics; geometry; metaphysics; literature; learning

Table 11.2 (*cont.*)

Year	political: non-binding	political: binding	science: binding	science: non-binding
1720	political; politic; polity; purely; governments; prudential; policy; judicial	politics; moral	science; sciences; philosophy; mathematics; theology; physics; philosophical; mathematical	geometry; astronomy; literature; logic; learning; physic; knowledge; skilled
1715	political; polity; purely; national; social; religions; politics; politic	morality	mathematics; mathematical; theology; speculative; philosophical; academy; theological; mechanical	science; sciences; philosophy; geometry; logic; physic; astronomy; divinity
1710	political; calculated; societies; economy; regulated; prudential; politic; social	moral; theological	philosophy; sciences; physic; theory; skilled; morality; grammar; politics	science; mathematics; theology; metaphysics; logic; divinity; physics; geometry
1705	political; polity; politic; societies; ceremonial; economy; national; magistracy	maxims	theology; philosophic; morality; politics; system	science; sciences; philosophy; mathematics; geometry; astronomy; mathematical; literature
1700	political; polity; politic; societies; governments; institutions; civil; commonwealths	politics; academy; theological; ethics	sciences; philosophy; geometry; physics; mathematical; astronomy; metaphysics; speculative	science; mathematics; logic; theory; physic; literature; study; knowledge

William III and Mary and the flight to France of James II). And yet, the discourse changes sharply after the first quarter century: from the periods 1725–9 to 1760–4 the words most closely associated with revolution are not governmental or sociological in nature but mechanistic. Terms such as diurnal, rotation, revolving and planet are most often associated with Newtonian mechanics and astronomical study: their close proximity to revolution in the embedding space suggests that it too shares this association. As revolution binds with political towards the end of the century, terms such as reformation, administration, parliamentary, system, and, of course, political become more closely associated with revolution in the embedding space (as seen in the binding terms between political and revolution in Table 11.1) even as the words associating revolution with Newtonian mechanics continue to exert their force, pulling political and revolution apart well into the 1790s. Is there, however, something behind the forces that pull revolution into the contexts of Newtonian mechanics throughout the century that may help us explain the eventual convergence of political and revolution and the ways in which political revolution came to have such import for both political and revolutionary theory?

In the history of revolution in the eighteenth century described by Figure 11.1 and Table 11.1, there is a notable absence. The Jacobite rebellion of 1745 seems to be largely missing from the contexts of revolution, replaced by revolution's turn into Newtonian mechanics. Traces still remain, particularly around the first set of conflicts in 1715 and 1719, with the appearance of pretender among the words most associated with revolution; however, the periods surrounding the 1745 conflict show a marked absence of political terms closely attached to revolution. Part of the difference is terminological. The Jacobite uprising was referred to primarily as a rebellion. Most of the co-occurrences of Jacobite and revolution in the literature of the period do not refer to the attempts to restore the Stuart monarchy but rather speak to the politically sanctioned Glorious Revolution as a root cause of the uprising.[31] The revolution described in these instances invariably refers to the events of 1688: 'they were mostly Episcopals in Religion, and Jacobites in Politicks, Enemies to the Revolution, the present Establishment of the Church of *Scotland*, and the Protestant Succession'.[32] Instead, revolution is sharply pulled towards the neighbourhood of Newtonian mechanics within the embedding space both immediately before and during the aftermath of the 1745

---

[31] This description of the Glorious Revolution conforms with Baker's theory that revolutions pre-1789 were mostly described only as historical fact – that which had occurred instead of that which is occurring; 'Revolution', 195.

[32] Robert Campbell, *The Life of the Most Illustrious Prince John, Duke of Argyle and Greenwich* (London: printed for the author, 1745), 94.

rebellion. Although revolution and rebellion do inhabit different regions, they remain relatively constant at a distance of 0.35 on average – well within each other's most associated terms. In fact, the embedding models show both terms as members of the other's most closely associated terms through most of the periods. In both cases, the clusters of associated words are much closer to their respective anchoring terms (rebellion and revolution). Clearly the events of the rebellion itself exerted sufficient pressure on the language to cause a small ripple effect in the usage of both terms, but not enough to pull revolution away from the discourse of mechanics within which it was embedded (and, by 1750, the relative position of both words in each other's lists had declined to 1735 levels).

From the standpoint of political history, the lack of a significant or meaningful impact of the 1745 uprising on the embedding space of revolution is a reflection of the way in which the Jacobite rebellion was understood. In British accounts of the conflict, it was named a rebellion, not a revolution, and understood at the time to be an interruption in the natural course of political history.[33] The primary difference in the representation of the Jacobite conflict and the Glorious Revolution lies in the way that the revolution was described, and understood, as a necessary event. Faced with a dangerous backsliding into Catholicism with the exclusion crisis, the Glorious Revolution served as a corrective to the teleology of Britain as a modern, Protestant nation. The Jacobite cause, therefore, represents the possibility of sliding backwards into history, of undoing the critical work that the revolution of the previous century accomplished.[34] The terms closest to rebellion in the model (and which remain present across the century) include words such as treason, sedition and conspiracy. The connection between rebellion and criminality reinforces its place as an aberration within an otherwise progressive history of the eighteenth century. Like the Jacobite rebellion before it, the American Revolution was not named a revolution in England, except by the radical factions who supported the American cause.[35] In both instances, designating the conflicts as revolutions introduces

---

[33] Murray Pittock links the historical dismissal of the Jacobite Rebellion of 1745 to the rise of 'Whig History': 'Whig history is essentially a history that conditions its interpretation of the past by regarding it primarily as an explanatory prelude to the present'; Murray Pittock, *Myth of the Jacobite Clans: The Jacobite Army in 1745* (Edinburgh: Edinburgh University Press, 2019), 8–9.

[34] 'As the movement itself [Jacobitism] was regarded as an atavistic and despotic sideshow, there hardly seemed to be any need to take its politics seriously' (Pittock, *Myth*, 141). This also suggests that the model of revolution as return that Arendt describes was not the model understood by the opponents of the uprising.

[35] 'In Britain, the war that broke out in 1775 between Britain and the Whigs of British America was called "the American War"; it was condemned as a "rebellion"; or lamented as a tragic civil or "brother's war." After the war was over, it was dubbed "the

a problematic deviation into the arrow of progress that characterised Whig history, particularly given their proximity to the earlier revolution on which so much was a stake.

The investment of British history in naming the Jacobite uprising a rebellion, and the American Revolution the 'American War' can help explain why the history of revolution, in relation to its embedding spaces, does not move radically closer to the language of government and polity in the mid-century, and why its sharp turn towards the political corresponds more closely with the debates around the French Revolution rather than the American conflict a decade earlier. But neither does revolution move away from the political at any point during the period. If this history provides a schematic for why revolution was embedded in other contexts than the language of reformation and polity in the middle of the eighteenth century, it is still not yet able to explain where it travelled to and why. Nor, given the unique history of the contexts of political that we have witnessed, can it explain why it makes such an abrupt turn in the 1780s, accelerating its convergence with the political in an unprecedented shift in its movement. The nature of the turn towards orbital mechanics in the mid-century, I want to argue, is not arbitrary, nor is it merely a function of the official desire to decouple the Jacobite rebellion from any trace of revolutionary energy. Rather, to understand both the nature of its change and its sudden convergence with the political at the end of the century, it is crucial to first know where revolution went and, more importantly, *how it returned*.

The role that revolution played in the discourse of Newtonian mechanics in the mid-eighteenth century seems clear. Articulated through words such as revolve, orbit, planets, moons, satellite and diurnal, revolution is a crucial concept for understanding the orbital mechanics of the solar system and, by extension, the physical world. Revolution describes the periodic nature of much of Newton's theory and the mechanical theory of the eighteenth century that was built upon his work. Planets depart in their orbits and then return: the cyclical nature of revolution promises repetition and recurrence. It is also *science*. It is no coincidence, I argue, that when revolution loosens its connection to reformation and government in the middle of the century (partly, as we have seen in response to the Jacobite uprising), the cluster of polity terms is replaced by scientific concepts (at least insofar as we currently understand mechanics as part of

American War for Independence," as if that protracted struggle was always motivated by its outcome'; William Warner, 'Transmitting Liberty: The Boston Committee of Correspondence's Revolutionary Experiments in Enlightenment Mediation', in *This Is Enlightenment*, ed. Cliff Siskin and William Warner (Chicago: University of Chicago Press, 2010), 102–119; 104.

science). Revolution becomes entangled with science, not just through its
connection to Newtonian mechanics of orbital motion but in the ways
that it brings the Newtonian terms into contact with the political as it
returns to the region of government and constitution at the end of the
century. The return of revolution to the political sphere in the 1780s only
sharpens this focus. Whereas in the early century, revolution shared an
embedding space with politics through their shared connection to terms
related to governmental administration, its return to this space at the end
of the century did not require it to jettison the scientific attachments that
it had picked up in the middle of the century, as evidenced by the new
connections that revolution has formed to words such as system and
principles. Revolution does not abandon its attachments to political for
a brief detour through mechanics only to reattach itself later in the
century. Instead, it moves *through* science back to political: the mechanical terms persist as part of revolution even as the word retains its connections to Newtonian science within a new shared embedding space.

Figure 11.3 offers a striking visualisation of this process. While revolution and the eighteenth-century concept of science remain at a distinct

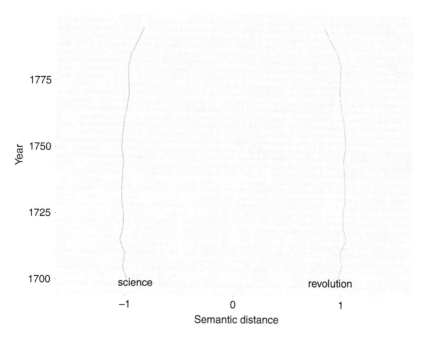

Figure 11.3 Graph of the semantic space of revolution and science
within the embedding spaces over time, 1700–1800. Source: ECCO.

remove throughout the century, they experience a sudden, mutual convergence in the last decade of the eighteenth century. Returning to the ways in which these graphs represent vector maths, the sudden turn towards convergence at the end of the century can be supplemented by looking at the binding language of the terms in the last few periods captured by the graph (see Table 11.3). Using the same principles outlined earlier, we can add philosophy to revolution (revolution + philosophy) and the very first term that appears in the resulting word list is science. This convergence, in terms of both the movement of the two terms and the time period when the convergence takes place, replicates the same convergence between political and revolution that we witnessed in Figure 11.1. Like that convergence, the two terms are so close by the end of the century that only a single mathematical operation is necessary to move revolution into the region of science in the embedding model. It is not a coincidence that political and revolution independently approach the contexts of science, even while they converge with each other, so as to create the compound idea of political revolution. From these results, it appears as though political revolution involves the convergence and eventual binding of political and revolution *as they are mediated by science*. The technical and theoretical terms that become associated with revolution (principles, system and constitution) are the terms that bind revolution with political into a new complex compound idea, political revolution, that draws on each component and yet is more capacious than either. If, as we have seen, political is transformed by its association with science, thereby shedding its association with governmental administration, and, in the process, becomes generalisable and attached to theory (as political science), then revolution must undergo a similar transformation (although, given its sojourn with Newtonian science in the mid-century, this is in many ways easier to trace). While revolution at the beginning of the century, like political, was tied to the specific institutions of governance (administration, monarchy and establishment), by the end of the century it has carried its association with rotation and planetary motion into the science of political revolution in the immediate historical context of the French Revolution, giving rise to something new: political revolutionary theory.

Drawing on its attachments to the language of mechanics, revolution imports science into revolutionary theory. In this way, political revolution becomes something both naturalised and inevitable, subject to the same immutable laws that govern orbital motion. It describes cyclical events in the history of politics: a cycle of revolution, growth, stagnation and then revolution that follows the natural order of things. This helps to shed light on the particular status of the Glorious revolution as a *necessary* event, one

Table 11.3 *Binding and opposing terms of science and revolution at five-year intervals between 1700 and 1795. Source: ECCO.*

Year	science: non-binding	science: binding	revolution: binding	revolution: non-binding
1795	science; sciences; philosophy; learning; arts; genius; knowledge; literature	nations	political; system; principles; politics; civil; universal	revolution; revolutions; national; administration; reform; constitution; popular; convention
1790	science; philosophy; sciences; learning; arts; knowledge; genius; literature	principles; society; universal	political; system; plan; opinions	revolution; constitution; reformation; monarchy; popular; revolutions; burke; national
1785	science; sciences; philosophy; learning; arts; knowledge; literature; study	political		revolution; revolutions; restoration; reformation; revolving; rotation; diurnal; monarchy
1780	science; sciences; philosophy; learning; arts; knowledge; genius; mathematics	politics	political; system	revolution; revolutions; restoration; reformation; diurnal; monarchy; administration; revolve
1775	science; sciences; philosophy; learning; mathematics; arts; knowledge; literature			revolution; revolutions; reformation; restoration; revolve; revolving; diurnal; monarchy
1770	science; sciences; philosophy; learning; arts; metaphysics; mathematics; literature	system		revolution; revolutions; reformation; restoration; diurnal; rotation; revolve; revolving
1765	science; sciences; philosophy; learning; physics; geometry; literature; mathematics	system		revolution; revolutions; restoration; planet; eclipses; comet; ecliptic; satellite
1760	science; sciences; philosophy; learning; mathematics; metaphysics; logic; literature	astronomy; system		revolution; revolutions; diurnal; revolve; reformation; restoration; comets; rotation

Year			
1755	science; sciences; philosophy; mathematics; learning; mathematical; literature; study		revolution; revolutions; revolve; restoration; revolving; diurnal; rotation; reformation
1750	science; sciences; philosophy; learning; mathematics; logic; metaphysics; physics	astronomy	revolution; revolutions; planet; revolving; ecliptic; rotation; axis; restoration
1745	science; sciences; philosophy; mathematics; geometry; physics; astronomy; learning		revolution; reformation; rotation; revolutions; diurnal; projected; restoration; moons
1740	science; sciences; philosophy; mathematics; learning; physics; literature; studies		revolution; restoration; revolutions; revolve; rotation; solar; diurnal; moons
1735	science; sciences; philosophy; mathematics; geometry; logic; learning; mathematical		revolution; revolutions; rotation; diurnal; restoration; revolving; planet; revolve
1730	science; sciences; philosophy; mathematics; logic; mathematical; metaphysics; learning		revolution; revolutions; restoration; monarchy; diurnal; planet; protestant; revolving
1725	science; sciences; philosophy; mathematics; geometry; metaphysics; speculative; literature		revolution; revolutions; diurnal; rotation; revolve; orbits; comet; moons
1720	science; sciences; philosophy; mathematics; theology; geometry; astronomy; literature		revolution; revolutions; restoration; rotation; episcopacy; eclipse; rebellion; disc
1715	science; sciences; philosophy; mathematics; geometry; mathematical; theology; logic		revolution; succession; popery; whigs; dissenters; revolutions; protestant; tories
1710	science; philosophy; sciences; mathematics; theology; metaphysics; logic; divinity		revolution; pretender; popery; doctor; presbyterian; toleration; protestant; resistance
1705	science; sciences; philosophy; mathematics; geometry; astronomy; mathematical; theology	system	revolution; revolutions; restoration; alteration; rotation; diurnal; presbyterians; alterations
1700	science; sciences; philosophy; mathematics; geometry; physics; mathematical; logic		revolution; revolutions; restoration; popery; conversion; calculation; diurnal; planets

that was unavoidable were Britain to continue to advance as a society.[36]
These intuitions, derived from the quantitative models, are confirmed by
the language surrounding the French Revolution itself. The radical
thinkers who welcomed the French Revolution as yet another cyclical
and necessary event in the progress of liberty (or the advancement of
enlightenment) spoke in detail about the inevitability of the revolution,
often linking it with millenarian theology, as here in Catherine
Macaulay's response to Burke:

> Has Mr Burke never heard of any millennium, but that fanciful one which is
> supposed to exist in the Kingdom of Saints? If that be the case, I would recom-
> mend him to read *Newton on the Prophecies* ... some passages in the Revelations
> point out a period of time when the *iron* sceptre of *arbitrary* sway shall be broken;
> when *righteousness shall prevail* over the whole earth, and a *correct* system of equity
> takes place in the conduct of man.[37]

Much of what we have already witnessed in the graphs is evident in this
passage: Macaulay speaks explicitly about Newton, albeit in a theological,
or even mystical, context. By connecting the political theory of revolution
that had emerged at the end of the century to the theology of the book of
Revelation in the Bible, Macaulay reveals the connection between revolution as a natural and necessary phenomenon within a world history that
is teleologically oriented towards continual improvement. In fact, her
response to Burke himself inverts the terms of the debate as she draws
on theological reference and a faith in progress to argue that the success of
the French Revolution will result in progress on many social, ethical and
political fronts. A member of the radical London Revolution Society
(LRS), Macaulay's views were shared widely with the supporters of the
revolution. In fact, the LRS itself was founded in the 1780s, not necessarily in anticipation of the French Revolution but rather as a way to cele-
brate the Glorious Revolution, marking out a century of progress even
while they agitated for further revolutions (along the lines of the French
Revolution itself, once it began in earnest).[38] Understanding this world-
view, wherein revolutions are a natural, even cyclical, consequence of the
progress towards liberty, requires us to come to terms with the ways that
revolution carried with it its scientific attachments into the nascent political theory of the period. As the idea of political revolution emerged, it
became contextualised, embedded, within the rapidly emerging scientific

---

[36] This builds on Arendt's theory of revolutions in the early eighteenth century (through
their attachment to celestial mechanics) as inevitable processes (*Revolution*, 42–3).

[37] From Catherine Macaulay's *Observations on the Reflections by the Rt Hon Edmond Burke*,
quoted in Philip, Godwin's Political Justice, 61.

[38] Philip Anthony Brown, *The French Revolution in English History* (London: Frank Cass and
Co., 1965), 26.

explanations of the natural and human world. Members of the LRS included prominent scientists, notably Dr Richard Price himself, who helped usher a political revolution that was aware of the scientific attachments embedded in the idea of revolution itself.

Price, of course, returns us to where we began; however, through the quantitative models that we have developed, we can now better understand the stakes involved in the debate between Burke and Wollstonecraft over Price's sermon. Burke's use, for example, of 'political sermon' is not simply a statement on the inappropriateness of addressing politics through the medium of the sermon: media is simply not at issue here. Rather Burke points at something much more profound. Given the connection between political and science (and the ability that it gives thinkers to generalise about political theory in ways that they were unable to before), Burke's complaint speaks directly to his concern for Price's desire to mix theology with the kinds of generalisations that become possible through political science. In addition to being a category error (scientific knowledge expressed through the medium of theology), Burke is concerned about the ability of political theory to give a scientific imprimatur to Price's revolutionary theory. Wollstonecraft's use of 'political revolution', in the same way, is no longer simply a descriptor of the French Revolution. Instead, it invokes the larger schema of political revolutionary science to suggest to her readers, Burke most of all, that the French Revolution, like all true revolutions, are necessary stages in the kind of advancement of society that both she and Burke share a belief in.

12 Computing Koselleck: Modelling Semantic Revolutions, 1720–1960

Ryan Heuser

12.1 Introduction

This book introduces a range of computational methods to the history of ideas. It also applies them in a series of case studies drawn from eighteenth-century intellectual history in particular. On the one hand, this book remains focused on that period in order to offer a sustained rather than a scattershot example of digital intellectual historiography, and the framework itself might as usefully find application in other periods, regions and languages.[1] On the other hand, perhaps there is a certain resonance or felicity between the digital and the eighteenth-century history of ideas. New linguistic conditions in that period – increased nominalisation, abstraction, singularisation, the rise of 'isms' and other trends – may particularly invite lexical analysis by giving rise to the singular, nominal, lexical focus (the 'keyword') on which digital, corpus-based methodologies depend.[2]

At the same time, though digital methods begin with keywords and lexical data, they do not end there, but extend their analysis of words into the inter- and supra-lexical relations composing the larger history of an idea. In this book's chapters on liberty (Chapter 4), government (Chapter 5), republicanism (Chapter 6), growth and improvement (Chapter 7), irritability and sensibility (Chapter 9), digital analysis begins

---

[1] Or at least those fortunate enough to have large-scale corpora of texts available to them in digital form. Admittedly, this is a large exception, one which particularly disadvantages the digital analysis of non-English, and especially non-European languages. For a discussion of the colonial origins and continued impact of this so-called digital divide within digital forms of humanistic study, see Maya Dodd and Nidhi Kalra, *Exploring Digital Humanities in India* (London: Taylor & Francis, 2020), 17–39.

[2] For a digital investigation of this rise of the 'ism', see Chapter 5, Section 5. On the rise of the 'ism' and the abstract singular noun, see Reinhart Koselleck, 'Introduction and Prefaces to the *Geschichtliche Grundbegriffe*', trans. Michaela Richter, *Contributions to the History of Concepts*, 6 (2011), 1–37; 10–15. For a discussion of the long-standing dependence of 'traditional' research on keyword searches in library-owned digital corpora, see Ted Underwood, 'Theorizing Research Practices We Forgot to Theorize Twenty Years Ago', *Representations*, 127 (2014), 64–72.

with an abstract singular noun but soon transforms it into a loose, complex set of shifting relationships with other words and concepts. This transformation helps to bridge the lexical to the conceptual, words to an idea. In the case of republicanism, for instance, as the author of Chapter 6 shows, the concept first arrived in adjectival phrases like republican principles long before nominalising into the strong form of republicanism that now names the idea.

However, because all digital methods must rely on and begin with lexical data from digitalised corpora, studies of words like republicanism and improvement cannot but get swept up and entangled with the powerful new linguistic currents accelerating in the eighteenth century. Obtaining within these chapters and methods is therefore a complex relationship between word and concept, the history of language and the history of ideas. Though a similar tension would seem to play out across intellectual historiographies, from Arthur O. Lovejoy through Quentin Skinner and Reinhart Koselleck, it may be particularly acute in those projects which rely most heavily on lexicographical information. These include not only computational-linguistic methods, whose basis in text mining and large-scale digital corpora compels such reliance, as we have seen. Importantly, they also include other intellectual histories rooted in lexical data, and perhaps above all those mimicking the lexical structure of a dictionary. Raymond Williams's *Keywords: A Vocabulary of Culture and Society* (1976), for example, and the monumental *Geschichtliche Grundbegriffe* (1972–97), edited by Otto Brunner, Werner Conze and Reinhart Koselleck, arrange their histories alphabetically, each on the centuries-long history of a specific word.[3] They do so, however, precisely on the methodological gambit that such individual histories of words, when properly analysed under the semantic-historical method of a *Keywords* or *Begriffsgeschichte*, tease out larger conceptual and semantic patterns that themselves disclose the sociopolitical forces that 'concentrate' in their 'semantic contents'.[4] 'A concept may be attached to a word, but it is simultaneously more than that word', writes Reinhart Koselleck rather unhelpfully in the introductory article to the *Geschichtliche Grundbegriffe*, before offering his 'pragmatic' definition – one constructed by the needs of a methodology no less technical and self-conscious as the

---

[3] For Williams, in English; for Koselleck, in German, but with a wide scope of reference to related linguistic developments in English, French and other European languages. Their primary lexicographical work is found in Raymond Williams, *Keywords: A Vocabulary of Culture and Society*, 2nd ed. (London: Oxford University Press, 2015); and *Geschichtliche Grundbegriffe* [Basic concepts in history], ed. Otto Brunner, Werner Conze and Reinhart Koselleck (Stuttgart: Klett-Cotta, 1972–97).

[4] Koselleck, 'Introduction', 20.

digital one of this book.[5] 'In terms of our method, a word becomes a concept when a single word is needed that contains – and is indispensable for articulating – the full range of meanings derived from a sociopolitical context.'[6] Greater than the sum of its lexical parts, new concepts nevertheless require words for their emergence, thinking, expression and social force.

The historiographical projects of *Keywords* and *Begriffsgeschichte* are therefore in many respects similar to those in this book. In each case, lexical data on a word's usage is studied and decoded as an index to its changing conceptual forms – changes that themselves imprint the sociopolitical forces driving and demanding their transformation. For all its novelty, the digital history of ideas in fact follows in an older analogue tradition of semantic-historical method, taking on both its affordances and tensions – both peculiarly mired in, and peculiarly attuned to, the linguistic substrate of conceptual change.

12.1.1 Sattelzeit

In that case, what does it mean that both Williams's and Koselleck's analogue semantic histories also orbit the eighteenth century? In carrying out their projects' plans, following the historical trail of words like history and culture back to their convergence point with their modern conceptual forms, both historians find themselves again and again somewhere in the long eighteenth century. Indeed, both authors point to this period, and particularly the revolutionary decades surrounding the turn of the nineteenth century, as a kind of semantic crucible for many of modernity's key social and political concepts, which either first emerged (organisation, feudalism) or underwent a revolutionary transformation in meaning (honour, liberty, progress). 'At this critical period', as Williams writes, these lexical-semantic shifts 'bear witness to a general change in our characteristic ways of thinking about our common life', a change for him owing ultimately to the unprecedented social and material changes wrought by industrialisation's revolutionary triumph in this period.[7]

---

[5] For a discussion of the origins of *Begriffsgeschichte* as a conceptual-historical method, see Niklas Olsen, *History in the Plural: An Introduction to the Work of Reinhart Koselleck*, (New York: Berghan Boooks, 2014). As Olson there writes, 'To probe the relation between social history and language was one of the fundamental ambitions of the *Geschichtliche Grundbegriffe*', but 'in this endeavour it departed from the tradition of German academic philosophy, in which the analysis of semantic developments was aimed at a systematic clarification of the essential meanings of philosophical concepts.'

[6] Koselleck, 'Introduction', 19.

[7] Raymond Williams, *Culture and Society, 1780–1950* (Garden City, NY: Anchor Books, 1960), xi.

'Words are witnesses which often speak louder than documents', writes Eric Hobsbawm, in a bout of semantic history opening his *Age of Revolution*, whose characteristic clarity and forcefulness deserves quotation at length:

Let us consider a few English words which were invented, or gained their modern meanings, substantially in the period of sixty years [1789–1848] with which this volume deals. They are such words as 'industry', 'industrialist', 'factory', 'middle class', 'working class', 'capitalism' and 'socialism'. They include 'aristocracy' as well as 'railway', 'liberal' and 'conservative' as political terms, 'nationality', 'scientist' and 'engineer', 'proletariat' and (economic) 'crisis'. 'Utilitarian' and 'statistics', 'sociology' and several other names of modern sciences, 'journalism' and 'ideology', are all coinages or adaptations of this period. So is 'strike' and 'pauperism'. To imagine the modern world without these words (i.e. without the things and concepts for which they provide names) is to measure the profundity of the revolution which broke out between 1789 and 1848, and forms the greatest transformation in human history since the remote times when men invented agriculture and metallurgy, writing, the city and the state.[8]

Tall words – yet echoed in various ways by historians and intellectual historians since without serious opposition. Usefully for our purposes here, Koselleck goes still further, explicitly naming and theorising this period of conceptual transformation.[9] The *Sattelzeit*, the 'saddle time' or pivot period into conceptual modernity, is presented as the major historical hypothesis of the *Geschichtliche Grundbegriffe*. To trace changes in meaning of words across this threshold is therefore to trace the 'process of transformation into modernity': a mode of history that 'seeks to comprehend the process by which experiences came to be registered in concepts'.[10]

For both the essays in this volume as well as for Williams and Koselleck, lexical analysis ends up revealing a set of conceptual and social forces gathering across the eighteenth century and concentrating in a pivotal period of transformation at its end. If not a coincidence, then, that such semantic histories gravitate towards the eighteenth century, it may reflect this turning point, this *Sattelzeit*, in the linguistic conditions of modern sociopolitical concepts themselves. That such terms and concepts increasingly nominalised into abstract forms, bringing the lexical and the conceptual into an especially tight relationship, has both intellectual-historical as well as historiographic consequences. In tracing the history of

---

[8] Eric Hobsbawm, *The Age of Revolution: Europe 1789–1848* (London: Abacus, 2014; orig. 1962), 1.

[9] For criticism of the *Sattelzeit* concept and its overemphasis on discontinuity, see Gabriel Motzkin, 'On the Notion of Historical (Dis)continuity: Reinhart Koselleck's Construction of the Sattelzeit', *Contributions to the History of Concepts*, 1 (2005), 145–58.

[10] Koselleck, 'Introduction', 16.

abstract singular nouns like liberty and improvement, both analogue and digital semantic histories rely on the very linguistic and conceptual processes that they historicise.

12.2   Modern Abstractions

This self-reflexivity to their project, however, is no disadvantage. In fact, it may be uniquely appropriate as a framework through which to examine the semantic conditions of abstraction and singularisation that shape their conditions of possibility. Williams's entry in *Keywords* on labour demonstrates how semantic histories engage with these abstracting linguistic conditions rumbling beneath their feet.[11] If labour initially emphasised the pain, physical toil and ardour of work, a sense which survives only in the labour of giving birth, it developed meanings 'with a more distinct sense of abstraction': labour as a 'general social activity' or 'all productive work'. When for example in Locke's infamous defence of private property – that once someone 'hath mixed his Labour with' the natural world he henceforth owns it – labour is not a particular task, nor a particularly painful one, but encompasses and refers to 'all productive work'. Abstracting still further, in the eighteenth century the term developed, in its 'most important change' in its history, a general law or abstract force of political economy, signifying 'that element of production which in combination with capital and materials produced commodities'. Finally, by metaphorical extension through a kind of personification, in the early nineteenth century its additional sense as a social abstraction of that class of people who performed 'labour' came through.[12] In tracing, then, the semantic history of labour from its earliest to its modern uses, Williams does in fact uncover a semantic history that 'bears witness' to real changes in social organisation. Concentrated in its increasingly abstract semantic contents is not only a cultural history of labour and changing attitudes towards work but a material history of labour's social reorganisation into industrial capitalist production and of the forms of agency, explanation, collectivity it demanded and provoked.

That profound changes in social organisation are encoded not only in words but in specific aspects of their semantic form, like their abstractness or generality, is a theme that runs throughout Williams's and Koselleck's work, developing into a core of their vision of the new semantic conditions

---

[11] Williams, *Keywords*, 127–30.
[12] Largely by way of the political pamphlets of that period's reform movements: in *Labour Defended against the Claims of Capital* (1825), for instance, 'one "component" [of political economy] was set against the other but in terms which identified both as social classes'; Williams, *Keywords*, 129.

of modernity. Its basic insight, however, may derive from Marx's own semantic history of the word labour. 'It was an immense step forward for Adam Smith', as he writes in the *Grundrisse*, 'to throw out every limiting specification of wealth-creating activity: not only manufacturing, or commercial or agricultural labour, but one as well as the others, labour in general.'[13] Unlike the sixteenth- and seventeenth-century mercantilists, who located value in money, or the eighteenth-century Physiocrats, who found it in agricultural production, Smith performed an historically unprecedented feat of abstraction when he located value in labour as such, irrespective of its contents or qualities. Marx's crucial insight is that it is precisely the abstract simplicity of Smith's 'labour in general' that makes it an accurate representation of labour's concretely complex social organisation under capitalism: 'Indifference towards any specific kind of labour presupposes a very developed totality of real kinds of labour, of which no single one is any longer predominant.'[14] On this view of its semantic history, (the word) labour's semantic realignments along higher scales of abstraction and generality arise from and mediate the newly abstract, fungible, dislocated organisation of (the practice of) labour in early capitalist society. That the abstract simplicity of a word depends on and mediates the concrete complexity of its practice even suggests to Marx a useful principle of semantic historiography: 'As a rule, the most general abstractions arise only in the midst of the richest possible concrete development.'[15]

Although this strong dialectical take on abstraction and modernity is perhaps peculiar to Marx and Marxian intellectual histories, it underscores a complex relationship between them which is developed by Williams and made explicit and systematised in Koselleck. Williams, for example, runs again and again in the *Keywords* into these pivotal moments of abstraction: 'industry' transforms from a 'particular human attribute' (industriousness) to a 'collective word for our manufacturing and productive institutions'; 'art', from a term for individual skill to a 'kind of institution . . . a set body of activities of a certain kind'; 'culture' from the 'tending of natural growth' to the 'general state of intellectual development, in a society as a whole'; and so on.[16] Although he does not explicitly name this 'general pattern of change in these words', the semantic trajectory they typify, from the concrete domain of an individual life to the abstract one of a social collective, implicitly and repeatedly invokes the semantics of abstraction in articulating these concepts' pivotal turns into

[13] Karl Marx, *Grundrisse: Foundations of the Critique of Political Economy*, trans. Martin Nicolaus (Harmondsworth: Penguin, 1993), 104.
[14] Ibid.   [15] Ibid.   [16] Williams, *Culture and Society*, xi–xv.

their modern form.[17] Similarly, for Koselleck, because a 'defining experience of the modern world is the loss of those specific and particularistic terms which once designated social conditions' – like the specific duties, freedoms and obligations enjoyed by and enjoining the various classes and estates of the *ancien regime* – then 'many older concepts, increasingly overtaken by events or changes in social structures that they could no longer either articulate or explain, became more and more abstract'.[18] Somewhere in the semantic crucible of the *Sattelzeit*, under pressure from its seismic revolutions and transformations into the modern industrial world, this older, particularistic mode of organising sociopolitical language gives way to a modern, abstract and nominalised one.

However, what makes Koselleck's approach to semantic history particularly useful to a computational analysis of lexical change is the extent to which it specifies the linguistic mechanisms that enable these semantic realignments. 'History, pure and simple'; 'labour as such': these new, compressed, abstract singular nouns Koselleck calls the 'collective singular', a syntactic-semantic compound for him distinctive of the *Sattelzeit* and lying behind many of its changes. 'History', for example, is for Koselleck the collective singular *par excellence* and central to his later work on the temporality of historical concepts. 'Histories', he shows, give way in this period to 'history' as the former's plural, 'concrete usages such as stories or histories (*Geschichten*) were replaced by a singular abstract term, history (*Geschichte an sich*)'; similarly, 'separate advances in one or another field now were lumped together as *progress*'.[19] Calling this process one through which words became 'more and more abstract', Koselleck more importantly helps to localise this abstraction in a set of semantic and syntactic processes: a broadening of semantic range to the collective through a contraction of grammatical number to the singular. As a singular noun, history carries a new potential for syntactic agency, becoming an independent entity capable of acting, judging or taking sides in the course of human events. Temporally, the new singularity of history also registers a new uncertainty over whether, following the period's unprecedented political and industrial revolutions, history's plural, repeatable, edifying stories (or 'histories') drawn from antiquity and early modern life could any longer predict the horizon of future experience. Indeed, the 'step from a plurality of specific histories to a general and singular history is a semantic indicator of a new space of experience and a new horizon of expectation' distinctive of modern social life.[20]

---

[17] Ibid. xii.   [18] Koselleck, 'Introduction', 13.   [19] Ibid.
[20] Reinhart Koselleck, *Futures Past: On the Semantics of Historical Time*, trans. Keith Tribe (New York, NY: Columbia University Press, 2005), 195.

Newly abstracted, singularised and re-temporalised, history steps into its modern conceptual form through an interlocking series of semantic transformations. Again and again, not only Williams and Koselleck but corpus linguists and digital humanists, including the authors of this book's chapters, have unearthed similar patterns of semantic and syntactic change – many of which also centre on changes in abstractness, singularity and conceptual scale. Not only history and progress transform into a newly abstract, singular, re-temporalised form: as de Bolla et al. write in Chapter 7 of this book, humbler words like growth and improvement develop along broadly similar lines, becoming increasingly abstract in scope and anticipatory in time, with a verbal process taking on a substantive form.[21] Lying between and peeking through these individual histories of abstract singular words, then, histories of abstractness and singularisation themselves may remain to be told: histories focused less on specific words than on the abstracting and singularising processes that enable and shape them.

12.3   Computing Keywords

Within a digital, corpus-based framework of intellectual history, 'collective singulars' and *Sattelzeit* are neither untestable historical hypotheses nor regulative historiographic ideals, but concrete linguistic practices that leave behind identifiable and measurable traces within digitised historical archives. 'As yet no unambiguous answer can be given to the question of whether the rate of change in social and political terminology has accelerated since 1750', Koselleck writes.[22] This chapter sets out to explore the ways in which new computational methods of intellectual history can supply such an answer.

And yet, can digital methods really capture sufficient nuance and complexity of semantic information to reproduce the contours of Koselleck's and Williams's historical-semantic arguments? Consider again Williams's most key of keywords, culture, which he calls 'one of the two or three most complicated words in the English language'.[23] Williams tells a striking tale of its semantic history. Of humble semantic origins in the early fifteenth century, culture had originally meant, until its 'critical period' of change in the late eighteenth, land cultivation. Gradually extended by analogy to the cultivation of the mind, only in the nineteenth did the word shift phase into its modern form. No longer denoting an action or process of cultivating land

---

[21] See Chapter 7, Section 1.
[22] Reinhart Koselleck, 'Introduction and Prefaces to the *Geschichtliche Grundbegriffe*', trans. Michaela Richter, *Contributions to the History of Concepts*, 6 (2011), 10.
[23] Williams, *Keywords*, 49.

or the mind, it came to signify the products of cultivation: originally on an individual scale, as a 'habit of the mind', but later escalating into a society's 'general state of intellectual development', or 'general body of the arts', or finally its 'whole way of life, material, intellectual and spiritual'. A rags-to-riches semantic story if ever there were one: dramatic, sweeping, revealing and putting at stake an entire set of modern social and material relations.

Surely, then, such monumental changes in meaning ought to register in the semantic data collected here – if not, we might as well pack up our tools and head home. In fact, as will become clear, the changes Williams describes do indeed leave their traces in the digital historical archive. But first: in *which* archive?

12.3.1 Corpus: British Periodicals Online, 1680–1980

Because many of Williams's keyword histories, as well as Koselleck's hypothetical *Sattelzeit*, straddle the eighteenth and nineteenth centuries, the following data derive not from the more comprehensive ECCO, which supplies the data for most of the other chapters in this book, but the British Periodicals Online (BPO (ProQuest)), which extends well through the eighteenth and nineteenth centuries. Composed of around 480 journals active during the seventeenth through twentieth centuries, from *The Athenian Mercury* (1691–7) and *The Spectator* (1711–14) to *The Gentleman's Magazine* (1736–1833) and *Athenaeum* (1830–1921), BPO covers an impressive range of periodical history. Over 2 million distinct 'articles' or sections of the periodical, from advertisements and poems to review essays and serial fiction, make up over 3 billion words, divided unevenly but reasonably across its three centuries. Table A12.1 (in the Appendix) shows BPO's composition by number of texts, sentences and words, along with an estimate of their OCR accuracy.[24] Although far from ideal, the OCR accuracy rates of above 75% from 1700, above 80% from 1800 and 90% from 1875 are sufficient for word embedding models whose unsupervised learning of word vectors, which tends to cluster words near their alternative spellings, and frequent OCR errors is robust across text qualities.

The major difference between BPO and ECCO is not its size – they are both on the order of a few billions of words – but its generic composition.

---

[24] Accuracy of OCR is loosely calculated as the percentage of a text's words (tokens) present in one of several spelling dictionaries, from one specialising in early modern orthography, developed by Philip R. Burns of Northwestern University – see 'Spelling Standardizer', MorphAdorner V2.0, Northwestern University Information Technology, http://morpha dorner.northwestern.edu/morphadorner/spellingstandardizer/ – to a larger lists of words curated from data by linguists at Brigham Young University (see 'Word Frequency Data', www.wordfrequency.info/), as well as those commonly used by spell-checking software (see https://github.com/dwyl/english-words).

Full-length treatises, pamphlets, novels, poems, plays, trial transcripts are all included in ECCO – anything published in English or in the UK or its colonies between 1701 and 1800. The sole focus of BPO, however, is the print medium of the periodical: daily, weekly or monthly serial publications of miscellaneous content (essays, dialogues, poems, correspondence, reviews), which by all accounts emerged in the seventeenth century, a modern byproduct of a flourishing early print culture stuffed with pamphlets, sermons and broadside ballads.[25] If ECCO embodies the generic miscellany of this period through its sheer comprehensiveness, the periodical is itself one of its most miscellaneous media, including a variety of genres and discourses within it.[26] The curators of BPO have included genre annotations for just over half of its included sections of text.[27] The majority of texts are of unknown genre; the next most prevalent are review essays, advertisement, fiction and correspondence. Besides a marked decline in correspondence and a marked rise in fiction, the distribution of text among these genres remains relatively stable across the corpus. Though serious methodological questions present themselves here – which genres underwrite a computational-semantic model for 'conceptual change'? Should recipes be included along with book reviews, fiction alongside editorials? – they cannot concern us long here. For the time being, I take an agnostic approach and include all genres in the computational-semantic models, a decision to some extent justified theoretically on the principle that all discourse, of whatever scale or genre or medium, responds to and is constructed out of the semantic shape of any given word.

12.3.2   Computing Keyword Histories

From the available data in the BPO corpus, word embedding models were trained on texts published 1720–1960, before and after which data becomes too sparse and noisy for robust analysis.[28] How well do these

---

[25] For a history of the genre's formations, see Howard Cox and Simon Mowatt, *Revolutions from Grub Street* (London: Oxford University Press, 2014), 18ff.

[26] It remains an open question in the field whether specific corpus designs – broad or narrow, comprehensive or delimited – enable specific variants of semantic or conceptual history, whether taking place in 'discourse' or within certain genres and subject to their own internal discursive histories. Such questions are beyond the scope of the present study; here we must take a pragmatic approach and note that, although further work of comparison is needed, ECCO and BPO, both sizeable corpora well suited for large word embedding models, have produced largely similar semantic data.

[27] Table A12.2 in the Appendix shows the percentage of total words in a given period vertically across the genres, with 'Undefined' showing the lack of a genre annotation.

[28] Ten separate word embedding models (using the word2vec algorithm with default settings on its 'gensim' implementation) are trained on each historical period, either a five- or twenty-year segment from 1720 to 1960. Unless otherwise noted, subsequent

models perform? Do we in fact see abnormal changes across this hinge period? Do words like culture turn as hypothesised by Williams, or history as by Koselleck? Figure 12.1 shows, within word embedding models trained on each twenty-year period between 1720 and 1960, the words semantically most similar to (or most substitutable for) culture.

Taking the five most similar words to culture from each of the twelve periods produces a total of twenty-eight unique words, with each word's first appearance highlighted in grey. Words are shown as they rise and fall in the strength of their similarity with culture across the word embedding models. Some periods show more words than others in their column: words, chosen because in the top five for any given period, are still shown for any period in which they appear in the top twenty-five, so that periods showing more than five words in their column (whether highlighted or not) indicate times of semantic transition, when words formerly linked with culture continue to appear while words strengthening in their association begin to emerge.

Broad changes in the semantic history of culture are easily discernible in this figure. According to the data, cultivation is the longest reigning synonym for culture, consistently ranked its most substitutable word from 1760 to 1880. But beneath this stable top-level association, changes among the others words' similarity with culture reveals the changing nature of this cultivation.[29] Initially, senses related to the culture or cultivation of land (gardening, vegetation, tillage and irrigation) dominate the word's semantic environment; related agricultural terms continue to appear in its wider orbit well into the nineteenth century, though many of them (planting, sowing, soil) reach the end of their line as a most similar term to culture in 1820–1840. Around this time, the word begins to pivot into senses relating to the cultivation of minds (education, intellectual, learning), and eventually an entire society (enlightenment, sciences, civilisation). These data, in other words, sketch out a semantic process similar to that which, as we've seen, Williams emphasises in Keywords, with culture gradually sublimating the manual toil of land cultivation into the cognitive and social cultivations of learning, education, enlightenment and civilisation.

results in this chapter are reported as averaged across ten model runs in order better to ensure robustness. This step is discussed and recommended in Maria Antonia and David Mimno, 'Evaluating the Stability of Embedding-Based Word Similarities', in *Transactions of the Association for Computational Linguistics*, VI, ed. Lillian Lee, Mark Johnson, Kristina Toutanova and Brian Roark (Cambridge, MA: MIT Press, 2018), 107–19.

[29] See Chapter 3, Section 3, for a discussion of how these hypernymic relations (x is a subclass of y), which to some extent inhere in the culture–cultivation relationship, structure conceptual forms.

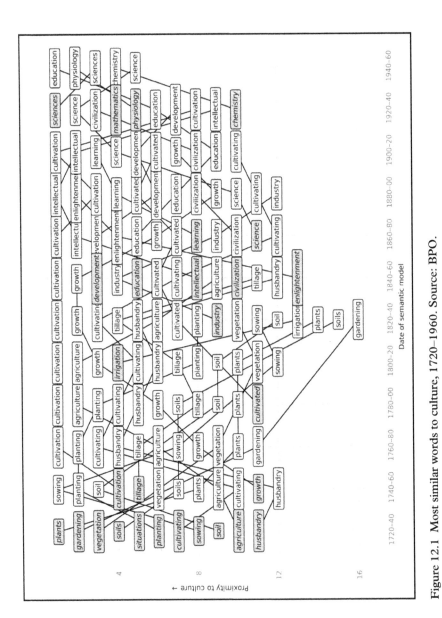

Figure 12.1 Most similar words to culture, 1720–1960. Source: BPO.

In this way Williams's compact semantic histories, complete with rough dates for specific pivots in words' meaning, already so rich in their own right for their insights into the cultural logic of semantic change, now bear new fruit as a storehouse of testable hypotheses for a computational historical semantics. Many of these pairings of decades-old genealogies and present-day data match well, as here with culture.[30] But the data do not always play so nicely with existing hypotheses, nor always uncover such dramatic shifts and transformations. Not liberal but liberty, for example, that great watchword of the Jacobin revolutions in late eighteenth century, appears in these data, which measure semantic change between the mid-eighteenth and mid-nineteenth centuries, as hardly more than a blip. For Koselleck, liberty is another 'collective singular', having singularised the plural liberties and privileges enjoyed by specific feudal classes into the singular, abstract political condition of freedom enjoyed (or theoretically enjoyable) by all rational individuals. And yet liberty seems to undergo no sizeable alterations of meaning whatever: digitally, a dud (see Figure A12.2). Following the same pro-cedure as outlined earlier, collecting every word which at any point was among the five most similar to liberty, yields just fourteen unique words – half as large a group as in liberal and culture. Liberty's associations with other words are simply too stable to generate a more diverse list of semantic neighbours over time. Those words which do appear alternate position only slightly, with freedom nearly always the most similar word, and liberties, rights and independence commonly second, third and fourth most similar respectively. The semantic core of liberty is remark-ably stable across two centuries of turbulent political and economic

---

[30] For another example, see the identical graph for liberal in Figure A12.1 – a term discussed by Koselleck as one of an emerging set of 'counter-concepts' like 'liberal'/'conservative'. Using the same parameter settings as in Figure 12.1, taking the five most similar words to liberal for each period yields a total of twenty-nine unique words that at any point occupied that position. As with culture, a broad pattern is manifest. Liberal in its oldest senses signified what befit a 'free' or noble man, as in the traditional contrast of 'liberal and mechanick arts', or in the social virtues of generosity and liberality proper to the noble classes; Williams, *Keywords*, 130–2. Both these traditional senses would seem to appear in the earlier decades of the figure, with words like education, learning and talents encoding its uses in the liberal arts and words like amiable, humane and generous indicating the social virtues of liberality. Transforming, according to Williams, by the end of the eighteenth century into a concept of open-mindedness, the word plunged in the mid-nineteenth century into a full-blown counter-concept of political identity. Again, in the data these changes appear: tolerant, indicative of this sense of open-mindedness, arrives in the 1820s, pursued by an army of political buzzwords (conservative, Whig, democratic, radical, etc.), which quickly take over the word's semantic core. Even this suddenness fits with Williams's and Koselleck's accounts of the word's history, both of which emphasise the word's rapid conscription into political-rhetorical warfare.

change: a remarkable finding, which lends yet more evidence to the argument developed by de Bolla et al. in Chapter 4 that, *pace* Quentin Skinner, liberty is both attracted to and repels semantic change from republicanism.[31]

Practically for our purposes here, the semantic stability of liberty provides an ideal contrast to a word not discussed by Williams or Koselleck, but which surfaces in the data presented in the next section as among the most violently changing words in the corpus: station. Redrawing the same neighbourhood plot as in Figure 12.1 for the word, we can immediately see why, here in Figure 12.2.

If station, like culture, shifts into its modern meaning in the 1840s and '50s, it does so not so much by pivoting as crashing into it. The sudden emergence in the 1840s of terminus as a top synonym for station indicates this technological upheaval: all at once in the mid-nineteenth century, station comes to signify a *railway* station.

What kind of change is this? Semantic? Technological? Economic? Political? Sociological? Some complex of these? Perhaps the new, iconic phase of industrial development of railway travel ushered in not only economic and social changes but also semantic ones, requiring newly adapted or re-invented vocabularies with which to articulate its profound changes in basic patterns of mobility and proximity. In doing so, even old and complex words like station seem to have been drawn into its orbit. In earliest uses a standing point for soldiers or a port for ships, the term developed in the sixteenth and seventeenth centuries the figurative senses of a 'priestly calling or vocation' (1574), a 'high position in a hierarchy' (1591) or a 'position in the social scale' (1603).[32] These earlier senses are also recorded in the data presented earlier: prior to the 1840s, the most similar word to station is rank, another frequent proto-class concept denoting one's position in a social hierarchy, and near it also appear profession, capacity and employments. Semantically, then, we find the most sudden of reversals: station plummets from a highly complex social abstraction of class relations – prior to the consolidation of class itself as a word and concept – into something as specific and concrete as a railway station.

---

[31] See Chapter 4, Section 5, which develops this critique of Quentin Skinner's classic claim of a subterranean republican discourse of liberty in light of a similar critique in Andreas Kalyvas and Ira Katznelson, *Liberal Beginnings: Making a Republic for the Moderns* (Cambridge: Cambridge University Press, 2008), 5–17.

[32] The first use of this latter sense in the Oxford English Dictionary is Hamlet's in 1603: 'For the apparrell oft proclaimes the man. / And they of France of the chiefe rancke and *station* / Are of a most select and generall chiefe in that' (emphasis mine). See Oxford University Press, 'Station, n', *Oxford English Dictionary Online*, accessed 1 June 2021.

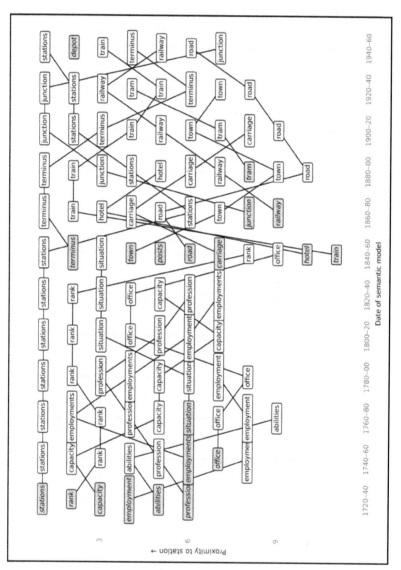

Figure 12.2 Most similar words to station, 1720–1960. Source: BPO.

The foregoing charts and data are offered primarily as a demonstration of the sensitivity of computational models to the kinds of semantic change and realignment that have long interested the lexical-semantic historians of 'keywords' or 'basic concepts'. The words so far considered, once analysed under a digital microscope, already exemplify a range of processes and forms of change: gradual and sudden; stable and dramatic; political, technological, metaphorical and conceptual. These forms of change interweave and return in a variety of ways throughout the following data and methods, which will seek to extend these incidental analyses of keywords into a more systematic analysis of the changes taking place over this pivotal period of semantic history.

12.4   Measuring Semantic Change

Digital methods of intellectual history offer more than the chance to re-examine particular keywords and their existing accounts of specific semantic change. Indeed, the foregoing remarks already begin to suggest ways in which digital methods open up new kinds of questions, frameworks and protocols for semantic history. The striking contrasts noted earlier, for instance – between the sweeping semantic transformations of culture and liberal and the remarkable stability of liberty; or the gradual change of culture versus the technological-semantic rupture in station – raise newly quantitative kinds of question about semantic change. How *much* did words change in meaning? How quickly? When, exactly? Which other words change in meaning to the same degree?

A sceptic might rightly ask whether such a complex phenomenon as changes in word meaning could ever be usefully quantified in simple units of magnitude. We've already seen that, over 240 years of usage, only fourteen unique words ever reached liberty's innermost core of five most similar terms, whereas for culture and liberal twice as many had. By themselves, these numbers cannot offer a suitable metric for the magnitude of semantic change. But they raise motivating questions: if the semantic neighbourhood of liberty undergoes less change than that of culture and liberal, which words undergo even *less* change than the former, or *more* change than the latter? Questions regarding the magnitude of semantic change, if seemingly reductive, help to move digital analysis onto new and powerful inductive perspectives on semantic history that are capable of discovering new shifts, turns and gaps in semantic change.

To answer these questions, however, requires that we reshape and realign the word embedding models to enable cross-historical comparisons. Because these models encode the semantic similarity of two words as their spatial proximity within a many-dimensional virtual space, in the typical case of 'vector space semantics' one measures the semantic distance between words in a single embedding.[33] But each such vector space expresses words' relative positions and distances in its own untranslatable units. Attempts to align separate matrices often result in bifurcated or misaligned models in which global patterns of difference – linguistic drift, register shifts, changes in vocabulary composition and so on – override the specifically cultural and conceptual logics of semantic change.

To overcome this difficulty in separating 'cultural shift' from 'linguistic drift', I turn to a measurement explicitly designed to bring out the former while dampening the latter. This 'local neighbourhood measure of semantic change' (LNM) obviates the need for bifurcated and noisy global alignments between word embedding models by modelling only the local changes in a word's 'neighbourhood' composition of words over time.[34] The data LNM considers are therefore comparable to the lists of most similar words visualised in Figures 12.1 and 12.2; it simply expands the net of considered words and adds a layer of statistical sophistication.[35] Moreover, in comparing the changing compositions of these neighbourhoods, LNM is also comparable to the correlation of *dpf* score neighbourhoods explored in Chapter 5, Section 1. Both there and in the following figures and data, measurements of semantic change turn on local changes in a word's changing semantic neighbourhood – that is the ins-and-outs of the *n* words closest to a given focal word in a semantic space.

Table A12.3 shows an example of this LNM calculation at work, comparing the mid-eighteenth- and mid-nineteenth-centuries' semantic neighbourhoods for the four words whose degrees of semantic change we've already seen to vary widely. Table A12.3 extends the analysis from a handful to a few thousand words in order to measure which words undergo the most change, and which the least, between their pre- and

---

[33] For more details on word embedding models, see Chapter 3, Section 1.

[34] The measure is introduced and evaluated in William L. Hamilton, Jure Leskovec and Dan Jurafsky, 'Cultural Shift or Linguistic Drift? Comparing Two Computational Measures of Semantic Change', in *Proceedings of the 2016 Conference on Empirical Methods in Natural Language Processing*, ed. Jian Su, Kevin Duh and Xavier Carreras (Association for Computational Linguistics, 2016), 2116–21.

[35] One can already eyeball these differences of 'neighbourhood' or most similar words in Figures 12.1 and 12.2, but LNM enables a more sophisticated measurement than is there apparent. It measures, first in one period's model and then in another's, the relative distances from a given focus word like culture to every word present in either model's neighbourhood. This process yields two sets of distances, which then themselves can be compared. Are these word-to-neighbour distances roughly similar over time (as with liberty), or does the focus word shift in its relative distance from the other words (as with culture)? A clever cross-model comparison of a word's within-model distances, LNM provides a simple and robust measure of historical-semantic change.

post-*Sattelzeit* neighbourhoods. Although this is not the occasion to examine in depth the results for individual words, scanning through them helps to underscore the kinds of semantic and historical changes caught up in the LNM measurement. Among adjectives, for instance, the word radical (like liberal) is drafted into a political concept; local becomes a political category of space (provincial, metropolitan), not the quality of space itself (physical, external). Among nouns, accommodation reifies into apartments and convenience, shifting from its interpersonal senses of negotiation and agreement; while drawback, originally a tax or levy, becomes a metaphor for any 'obstacle' or 'inconvenience' to forward progress. Among verbs, recalling psychologises into a mental concept of memory, while embracing dilutes into a synonym for 'includes' or 'comprised'. Politicisation, abstraction, psychologisation, commodification: these are just some of the semantic forces we find while rummaging through these lists of words with the greatest magnitudes of semantic change between the mid-eighteenth and mid-nineteenth centuries.

And yet this chapter also aims to dilate and complicate this simple, before-after analysis of semantic change. Such measurements depend on a (unfortunately) binary historiography, a simple juxtaposition of pre- and post-*Sattelzeit* corpora. By refining and rescaling the measurements already introduced, we can tune in more closely to the contours of the data, to the finer historical shapes as well as the grosser magnitudes of semantic change. Identifying these contours allows us to specify semantic changes in new ways, dating their points of transition while visualising them within periods of semantic stability and consolidation. To discover, through measurement, that culture changes more than liberty across the *Sattelzeit* helps us to compare those words; to learn that culture changes more between 1810 and 1850 than it does between 1850 and 1890 tells us something about the course of that word's semantic development. But to measure a word's semantic difference across *all* possible pairs of the historical models of its usage elevates the framework of analysis beyond individual comparison into a wider and more holistic view of semantic history. Figure 12.3, for example, shows the distance in the semantic environments for culture across every pair of its half-decade semantic models from 1720 to 1960.

Separate models for each half-decade run up and down the x and y axes; the darker the square at their intersection, the greater the distance in their semantic environments. The distance between culture's 1850s semantic environment and its environment in every other period can be read by finding 1850 on the x-axis, and then scanning upward for differences in shading. By this method, one can indeed see that culture in the 1850s lies farther from its 1810s counterpart, indicated by the darker shading at this intersection, than any of those in the later nineteenth century.

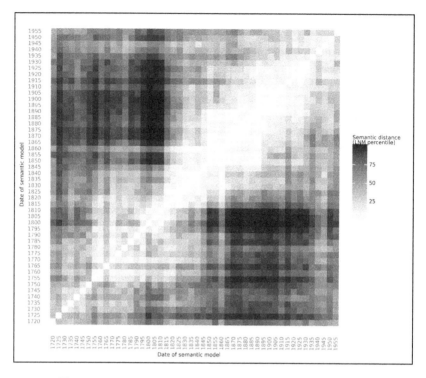

Figure 12.3 Historical-semantic distance matrix for culture, 1720–1900. Source: BPO.

Like an ultrasound for semantic change, such distance matrices show the shapes and contours of a word's semantic history. The light-coloured block in the upper right-hand corner of Figure 12.3, from roughly 1840–60, signifies a period of time in which the neighbour-hoods of culture remained relatively close to one another; likewise, the light-coloured block on the bottom left shows a period, roughly 1720–1820, in which the semantic neighbourhoods also particularly cohered. But the years of 1820 and 1840 mark a separation between these two clusters of meaning, showing the word's transformational passage from one relatively stable neighbourhood for another. And indeed, as we've seen, in exactly these decades the word shifts in meaning from horticultural to mental and societal cultivation. Figure 12.3 visually decodes this historical-semantic process, showing a word's periods of semantic stability as well as its crucial pivotal moments of transformation.

A comparison with station – whose sense as a railway station arrives on the linguistic scene quite suddenly in the mid-nineteenth century – is again instructive. Figure A12.3 shows just how precise a moment of revolutionary transformation this was. As expected from the results of Figure 12.2, the new semantic regime of station as a railway station crashes, if you will pardon the pun, headlong into the word's older meanings in the 1840s. This precipitous semantic change, followed by a new and long-lasting stability of meaning, is visualised in Figure A12.3 in the near-total separation of the two bright rectangles at the bottom left and upper right of the figure. These discrete boundaries indicate a sharp rather than fuzzy threshold between two historical blocs of similar meaning: one stretching from the beginning of the data (1720) until roughly 1840, when another takes over and rules until the end of the data in 1960. The narrow passageway between these historical blocs, in the 1840s, dates a semantic revolution, if you will – which in the case of station directly reflects an industrial one.

12.4.1 Modelling Revolutions

Perhaps revolution, itself a complex keyword for both Williams and Koselleck, ought not to be used too lightly in this context. But if, as they argue, revolution abstracts from its physical senses of 'turning' a new political orientation towards the future centred on an idealised 'overturning' of an older system for a newer one, then in fact locating so-called semantic revolutions is no misuse of the term but helps to clarify how revolution operates in and through language. Besides, within this context and these data, revolution takes on a mathematical, even geometric meaning – one visible, as we've seen, in the narrow and wide, discrete and diffuse shapes in the semantic-historical distance matrices shown just above.

But these distinct shapes can also be measured and examined statistically: by applying a 'novelty' metric to the distance matrix of Figure 12.3, for instance, one can statistically identify its 'pivot-points' during which one historical bloc of similar meanings turns and face another, as in the 1840s for station.[36] The pivot-ness, as it were, of these moments can be

---

[36] I adopt the Foote novelty metric as an approximation of the speed of cultural change from Matthias Mauch, Robert M. MacCallum, Mark Levy and Armand M Leroi, 'The Evolution of Popular Music: USA 1960–2010', *Royal Society Open Science*, 2 (2015), https://doi.org/10.1098/rsos.150081. This study claims to identify three 'stylistic revolutions' in popular music (in 1964, '83 and '91) through a large-scale analysis of their changing harmonic and timbral properties. They identify these moments of accelerated musical change by applying, to an historical-acoustic distance matrix formally identical to the historical-semantic ones in Figures 12.3 and A12.3, a segmentation algorithm

estimated in a measurement of their novelty over time. Foote novelty, for instance, drags a moving historical window – in our case, of sixty years in length – diagonally across a larger distance matrix. Visually speaking, along the way it estimates the degree of contrast between the lightness of its bottom left and top right quadrants (i.e. those measuring within-period distances) and the darkness of the top left and bottom right quadrants (i.e. those measuring cross-period distances). For example, the sixty-year period from 1820 to 1880, centred on 1850, shows just such a contrast: its two within-period distances (i.e. those between the half-decades within 1820–50 and those within 1850–80) are bright with semantic similarity, while its two cross-period distances (1820–50 versus 1850–80) are dark with semantic distance. A test of statistical significance is then performed on these moving historical windows by re-calculating this contrast on the same window with its light and dark squares randomly permuted. Is the original, actual contrast stronger than that found in 95 of 100 such random permutations? If so, then the Foote novelty score for the given historical window (here, 1820–80) is considered statistically significant (p<.05). In this way, the sharpness or fuzziness of certain words' semantic change, already seen visually in the distance matrix, become historically measurable and statistically tractable.

Here, for instance, in Figure 12.4, measured along a sixty-year moving window, are the points of least and greatest novelty for four of the keywords discussed earlier.

Peaks in the graph represent pivot-points in these words' histories, moments of transformation between waxing and waning semantic regimes. Station, as we know, transforms in the middle of the nineteenth century from a concept of status or class into the concept of a railway terminus; and indeed at around this time in Figure 12.4, station's novelty score skyrockets, showing a marked acceleration in its semantic change, peaking in the 1850s but statistically significant from 1840 to 1865.[37] Comparatively, the turning point for liberal arrives later, shifting into its political meaning fairly quickly in 1870–5. Culture reaches its own pivot-point in 1825, but its arc is blunter, slower: although an historical

originally designed to detect the boundaries between verses in a song. By scrambling these distance matrices, 'Foote novelty' measures how likely one could arrive at the same discreteness and segmentation as in the original graph by chance. I adopt the refined measurement of statistical significance, one which controls for the normal drift of historical change, from Ted Underwood, Hoyt Long, Richard Jean So and Yuancheng Zhu, 'You Say You Found a Revolution', 7 February 2016, accessed 7 July 2021, https://ted underwood.com/2016/02/07/you-say-you-found-a-revolution/.

[37] See previous note. Foote novelty scores were considered statistically significant if their result was greater than 95 of 100 random permutations (i.e. p<=0.05) for a given sliding sixty-year moving window.

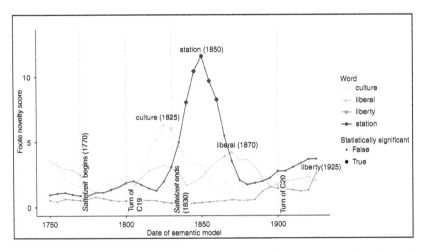

Figure 12.4 Novelty scores for keywords culture, station, liberal, liberty, 1750–1930. Source: BPO.

boundary between its past and future meanings is certainly discernible in the 1820s (Figure 12.3), one never appears quite as suddenly or sharply in the semantic history of culture as it does in station (Figure A12.3), and consequently the peak novelty score of the former is only about half the latter. Still, both are significant, whereas the novelty scores for liberty, a word whose semantic stability over this period has already been noted, in fact never rises to statistical significance: meaning that whatever semantic changes it underwent, the 'shape' they left behind cannot be reliably separated from background noise and chance in the data.

12.4.2 Hidden Pivots

Semantic regimes, semantic revolutions: but are the changes we've seen so far really revolutionary? Do they undergo an unusual intensity or revolutionary period of semantic change? Which words undergo the sharpest and most sudden forms of semantic change, and which the dullest? Now supplied with a computational measurement of semantic change and semantic novelty, we are once again prepared to ask these inductive, bottom-up questions of words' semantic histories. Though we will return to a more detailed accounting of these words, and of the specific kinds of change they undergo across their periods of pivot and accelerated change, the words in Figure 12.5 – chosen because statistically significant, historically distributed and interesting to the intellectual

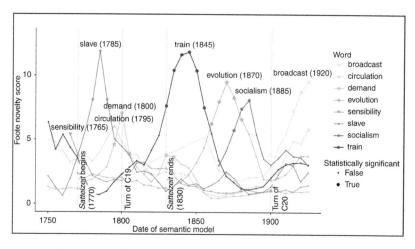

Figure 12.5 Novelty scores for keywords, 1750–1940. Source: BPO.

historian – give a sense of the range of semantic pivots in the underlying data.

The word slave, for instance, pivots sharply in meaning in the 1780s: before this point, its most similar words had been tyrant, wretch, victim, traitor and coward – generic terms for suffering and dependence. But afterward, its closest semantic neighbours in the data are instead negro, slavery, planter, trader and contraband – a semantic shift which reflects the growing abolitionist movements of the 1780s and '90s and the new discursive pressure they placed on the economic and political reality of slave trade and slave labour.

In fact, a number of words' pivot-points appear on this graph for a number of reasons: technological, ideological, economic, conceptual. Train, for instance, like station, pivots in the 1840s, shifting from a poetic term for a throng or procession into a locomotive; similarly, the word broadcast transforms in the early twentieth century from the broadcasting of seeds to radio waves. Words pivoting as a direct result of new intellectual and political currents also appear, such as evolution or socialism in the nineteenth century, or arguably the cult of sensibility in the eighteenth. Other, subtler changes also manifest, as when a number of terms slide into quantitative and economic meanings: circulation passes from primarily the circulation of fluids (in the data similar to digestion, perspiration, moisture) to more abstract, social and economic circulations (publication, currency, exportation); just as the word demand pivots in 1800, from interpersonal verbs of refuse and accept into abstract singular nouns of employment, profit and export. These data measuring and comparing the novelty of words, the shape and sharpness of their points of change, therefore end up making visible a wide range of words and their forms of semantic change over this period.

12.5   Semantic Revolutions

This chapter, through a methodological chain that increases in scale, robustness and sophistication as it proceeds – from semantic neighbourhoods, to the distances between these neighbourhoods, to a distance matrix among all neighbourhoods and a measurement of the statistical significance of these distances – hopes to have, in the first instance, demonstrated a variety of ways in which the history of semantic change can be apprehended in computational semantics. It also hopes to have shown that these methods can both re-examine existing hypotheses about semantic change as well as discover new words, clusters and processes for closer analysis, both digitally and through closer reading. Although we lack the space here to discuss and analyse these new words and changes in any considerable detail, their nature and placement raise questions about the aggregate shapes and curves of semantic change over this period. If the words in Figures 12.4 and 12.5 pivot when they do, when do the majority of words undergo their points of accelerated change – if ever?

The methodology constructed piecemeal in this chapter suggests a final, cumulative experiment, one which directly bears on Koselleck's historical-semantic project. Namely: *was* there a *Sattelzeit?* Was the period between 1770 and 1830 indeed the most turbulent and transformative semantic period of the modern era? Is Koselleck's hypothesis that 'the rate of change in social and political terminology has accelerated since 1750' corroborated or contested by these data? The distance and novelty measurements developed above help to respond to this difficult question for which, as Koselleck wrote, 'as yet no unambiguous answer can be given'. Figure 12.6 shows when words most commonly hit their pivot-point,[38] their peak novelty score, for a variety of significance thresholds: (a) all words; (b) words with significant novelty score in at least one period;[39] (c) those with a significant novelty score and

---

[38] A pivot-point is the period during which a word reaches its peak novelty score (see Section 4). These pivots are counted across four significance thresholds: (a) for all words; (b) all words with a statistically significant novelty score (p<.05); (c) all words in (b) with a significant magnitude of semantic change across pivot points (>75% percentile); and (d) for all words in (c) which lack the letters 'f' or 's' (frequent OCR error).

[39] A significant novelty score is defined as a Foote novelty measurement of p<=0.05 in a given half-decade semantic model, while using a moving historical window (Foote

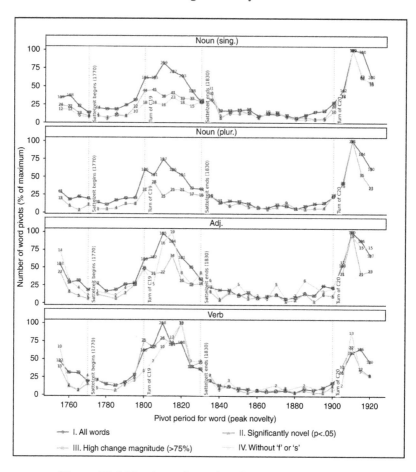

Figure 12.6 Number of words whose meanings pivot in a given historical period. Source: BPO.

a significant magnitude of change;[40] and (d) those words in (c) that also happen not to contain the OCR error-prone letters 'f' and 's' in order to

matrix size) of sixty years: six data points of half-decade models, for thirty years on either side. Similar results are obtained with windows of forty to sixty years.

[40] A significant magnitude of change is defined as one in the 75th percentile or above along two local neighbourhood measurements of semantic change. Both are calculated from a word's semantic-historical distance matrix: (a) the average distance between a word's pre- and post-pivot historical periods; (b) the average distance among all a word's periods.

confirm that transcription issues are not responsible for the historical timing of the results.[41]

As can be seen, across parts of speech and significance thresholds, two historical periods stand out as particularly charged with semantic pivots. In the first of these, from roughly 1790 to 1830, hundreds of nouns, adjectives and verbs significantly pivot in meaning. By contrast, in the forty years preceding or following this period, only dozens, not hundreds, of words meet the same statistical threshold. Not until the early twentieth century does the rate of semantic change accelerate again, suddenly bursting with pivot-points in roughly the shorter period of 1905–25.[42]

Two periods, then, of accelerated semantic change, at the turn of the nineteenth and twentieth centuries. Why? For statistical reasons and quirks of the data, or as driven by real historical-semantic forces – or both? Indeed, in the former case, although both the earliest and last of the periods along the timeline show a greater likelihood to rise in their number of significant pivot-points, these are also the periods for which the underlying textual data is sparsest, and so the semantic models produced most idiosyncratic and unreliable – especially in the earliest periods for which these issues are compounded with OCR errors. At the same time, many of these changes bookending the period seem real enough: broadcast, as we saw, shifts from the broadcasting of seeds to radio waves, along with a number of other technologically rooted semantic changes; and words like sensibility, well known to undergo a revolution of meaning in the mid-eighteenth century, are among those whose peak novelty score occurs on the earliest dates on this graph.

Although we will consider seriously the historical content of these earliest and latest periods of semantic change, the sustained rise of semantic pivot-points nearer the middle of the timeline ought to attract our especial attention. No statistical anomaly can so easily explain their historical position in the last decade of the eighteenth century and first three of the nineteenth. I need not remind the reader that these years of accelerated semantic change coincide almost perfectly with the periodisation of 1770–1830 given in Koselleck's usual accounting of the Sattelzeit. At the same time, fewer words reach their pivot-point in the later decades of the eighteenth century than one would expect from many of Koselleck's and Williams's historical accounts; and indeed these data

---

[41] These letters are frequently confused for one another by OCR algorithms on account of the 'long S' printing practices in the earlier parts of our period.

[42] Because the Foote novelty metric parameters used here cast a sixty-year moving window over the historical data, or a thirty-year window to either side of any year, the x-axis must end in 1930, despite the underlying data extending to 1960.

suggest that the most semantically turbulent period followed in the wake of the Jacobin revolutions, not in their anticipation.

Collectively, however, do these data begin to show, or at the very least outline, a great mass of pivot-points in modern conceptual language – a great 'saddle' or hinge in semantic history worthy of the strong periodising concept of a *Sattelzeit*? Or do they perhaps generalise this phenomenon of semantic turbulence, dislocating it from its singular position at the cusp of the nineteenth century and allowing it to re-emerge among other historical periods and contexts? Certainly, as in Figure A12.4, provocatively *plural* outlines of historical-semantic change seem to glow through the data. This figure superimposes onto one image the historical-semantic distance matrix for every word with a statistically significant pivot-point anywhere from 1720 to 1960.[43] Even with each of these distance matrices averaged and merged onto one another, historical contours of accelerated and decelerated change do not wash out but remain distinctly visible. If the historical-semantic distance matrices we've seen so far for specific words act like an 'ultrasound' for their changing boundaries and shapes, then what developing forms of semantic history does this aggregated distance matrix reveal?

12.5.1 Annotating Semantic Change

More work must be done to investigate and bring out the meaning of these strange historical shapes, which become visible only under the 'macroscope' of these computational-semantic sensors.[44] What kinds of 'saddle', hinge or turn do these data reveal, generalise and problematise? Are the pivot-points of the early twentieth century like those of the early nineteenth? Work is ongoing in this project in order to address these questions in more detail.

Still, for now, I offer a preliminary conclusion, based on my manual annotation of more than 500 significantly changing words. I have found that sifting through the results for words' novelty and magnitude of change is the most effective means by which to apprehend their signifi-cance and representativeness in their larger context of words' semantic shifts. Aggregating these (non-exclusive, 'tag'-like) annotations offers a usefully intermediate position between the epistemological distance of quantitative data and closeness of extended histories of specific words.

---

[43] In this case, significance is defined as having a Foote novelty score with $p<0.05$ in two consecutive periods.

[44] For a now classic account of the unique macro-analytic perspective of digital analysis of literary and cultural history, see Matthew Jockers, *Macroanalysis: Digital Methods and Literary History* (Champaign: University of Illinois Press, 2013).

Annotations offer a mode of 'anecdata', as it has been pejoratively, and I think unfairly, called. Even if provisional in structure and inaccurate in some of its details, these annotative schema often reveal both large as well as subtle differences between and among their objects of comparison. In Tables A12.6 and A12.7, for instance, I show samples of the most statistically significant pivot-points across the two forty-year periods of accelerated change we've seen, in 1790–1830 and 1910–50. I have annotated these words for what appear to be the major technological, social, political or other historical processes driving their semantic turn. I then arrange them according to the most common of their assigned changes.[45] In Table A12.6 are the annotated pivot-points for the semantically turbulent period of 1790–1830.

These annotations are provisional and ongoing; I do not wish to place undue evidentiary weight on their structure or frequency. Nevertheless, as they proceed, they continue to confirm a few elementary differences in the logic of semantic change between these separate historical periods. Here, in this period of the 'classic' *Sattelzeit* at the turn of the nineteenth century, words often – as predicted by Williams and Koselleck – further abstract and often nominalise. Issues, for instance, nominalises into an abstract object (neighbours: considerations) from the concrete verb of issuing or pouring forth; biologically rooted words like circulation and vita take on new, more abstract, economic or characterological meanings; and words like agricultural and rural trade concrete associations with their landscape and trade (fisheries, groves, gardens) for more abstract conceptualisations of their social and economic function (industrial, commerce, districts). Or, also as described by Koselleck, words re-spatialise and temporalise in the period: prospects, for instance, shifts from primarily a spatial perspective of distance, order and admiration (scenery, mountainous) to a temporal one of hope, expectation and uncertainty (prosperity, anticipations). However, these are only some of the many semantic changes undergone by these words; readers are invited to peruse the table for closer details.

For now, I would like only to contrast broadly these processes (in Table A12.6) driving the first period of accelerated semantic change of 1790–1830, with those driving the period in the early twentieth century (Table A12.7). Here, the most commonly annotated changes within words pivoting in this period are concretisation, commodification and

---

[45] Invalid words (OCR error and so on) were removed from the sample used. Words were chosen and annotated randomly from among those which showed both a statistically significant novelty score as well as a magnitude of semantic change above the 75th percentile: in other words, the significance level 'III' in Figure 12.6 (see the note to that figure for more details).

professionalisation. Blemishes and cleanse, for example, lose their more abstract, moral senses of forgiveness (purified, failings) in their new commercial and advertising frenzy of skincare (wrinkles, pores, lotion). Words like elastic and contrasting, once abstract properties of elasticity (transparent, fluid) and comparison (interspersed, mingled, combining), likewise lose themselves in commodification: with elastic now tied to words like waist and buttons, and contrasting to bodice, satin and embroidery. A range of words further specialise in meaning, as in the many words for the academic disciplines and professions (chemistry, physiology, even sports like racing), or further scale upward through industrialisation and automation (machines, brake, even metal transforms in its wake). Again, however, the many vectors of semantic change among these words are more complex than can be accounted for here; the reader is invited to peruse Tables A12.6 and A12.7 for more examples.

For our purposes here, a clear enough difference emerges between the kinds of semantic change driving these first and second periods of semantic 'revolution'. The predominant forces behind the semantic pivots of the early twentieth century seem to be those reifying words into concrete commodities, products or advertised consumer goods; but the forces driving words to their pivot-point in the early nineteenth century are more likely to involve complex abductions of existing concrete terminology into the abstract, rarefied and often nominalised status of a social, political or economic concept.

However preliminary and rudimentary, the apparently inverse picture of these two historical formations of historical-semantic change suggests important further consequences for this study. Besides the original *Sattelzeit* period of the late eighteenth and early nineteenth centuries, the only other historical period to emerge from these data as one of significantly accelerated semantic change is the early twentieth century. That this latter period should contrast with the former along specifically the general semantic lines of abstraction versus concretion, of broad social and economic concepts versus the specific qualities of commodities and machines, seems, on the one hand, to support the *Sattelzeit* hypothesis – namely that a revolutionary period of conceptual change specifically characterised by new semantic conditions of nominalisation and abstraction took shape over the late eighteenth and early nineteenth centuries. On this view, these data do indeed locate and vindicate this *Sattelzeit* at more or less exactly where one would expect it to be, and whatever semantic changes taking place in the early twentieth century must belong to a different order of semantic history – an order which, perhaps, given its greater proximity to terms for skincare products, for example, over sociopolitical concepts, may weaken or even sever the link between semantic and intellectual histories, between the histories of words and the histories of ideas.[46]

On the other hand, this latter, twentieth-century exception to the traditional notion of *Sattelzeit* also suggests ways in which that historical framework might be updated, extended, generalised and refined. Seen in Figure 12.6, in other words, may be not one but two *Sattelzeiten*. On this view, the historical phenomenon which the thesis of *Sattelzeit* describes – a collective turning-point in the conceptual organisation of modern society – occurs not once at the onset of this imagined modern condition but multiple times across its modern history, periodically renewed and reshaped along different axes and logics of semantic change. Further work is ongoing in order to examine this updated hypothesis of a plural, multidimensional *Sattelzeiten* – work for which a digital history of ideas offers a unique means by which, as Niklas Olsen wrote of the ideal of Koselleck's work, one might write 'history in the plural'.[47]

---

[46] This commercialisation of certain words (blemish, cleanse) in the earlier twentieth century no doubt arises for a variety of reasons, including genre shifts and re-orientations in the periodical corpus within and among advertisements and discourse types. These issues warrant further investigation.

[47] Olsen, *History in the Plural*, 303.

Index